Socially Mixed Economies

Socially Mixed Economies

How Social Gains Develop in Opposed Systems

John Weber

LEXINGTON BOOKS
Lanham • Boulder • New York • Oxford

LEXINGTON BOOKS

Published in the United States of America
by Lexington Books
4720 Boston Way, Lanham, Maryland 20706

12 Hid's Copse Road
Cumnor Hill, Oxford OX2 9JJ, England

British Library Cataloguing in Publication Information Available

Library of Congress Cataloging-in-Publication Data

Weber, John, 1910–2001
Socially mixed economies : how social gains develop in opposed systems / John Weber.
p. cm.
Includes index.
ISBN 978-0-7391-0270-1
1. Comparative economics. 2. Mixed economy. 3. Welfare economics. I. Title.

HB909 .W43 2001
330—dc21

2001029670

*For my fine daughters Linda and Jo,
acknowledging their wise care for
the good sense of the book*

Acknowledgements

In Memory of John Weber
1910–2001

John Weber was a visionary of tremendous strength and integrity, with an unwavering belief in the supreme value of labor—in any economic system. He passed away shortly after completing the final draft of this book but shortly before publication. Editing and typesetting his work was an honor and a privilege. It was also an extraordinary opportunity to witness at close hand the author's sharp intelligence, the precision with which he approached every word, his passion for the ideas he sought to convey, and his enormous capacity for hard work. Having worked closely with the author from its inception, this book is presented with confidence that the few posthumous editorial changes made accurately reflect the author's meaning and intent.

I am grateful to many people for bringing this book to completion so that the ideas contained herein could be shared with the world. For each of the previous and current iterations of this book my sister, Linda Weber, offered insightful and invaluable counsel to both the author and myself. She also supported me at every turn during its final preparation. Just prior to publication, when I could no longer obtain the author's input, several individuals stepped in to assist. I am grateful to Dr. Marsha Epstein, David Gorin, Noah Gorin, Kathryn Popper, Bob Kimmel, Carl Shames and Becca Wilson.

The author was deeply grateful to everyone in the academic community who commented on the manuscript. Paul Buhle generously provided wise counsel throughout the development of the book. James Lawler recognized early on the value of the author's ideas, and enthusiastically embraced the usefulness of the text for the college classroom. The author enjoyed and was inspired by stimulating exchanges with Robert Hethmon. I also thank these individuals for assisting me in the final production stages.

Members of the Committees of Correspondence for Democracy and Socialism championed the author's ideas, engaged in lively debate and inspired him to publish his work. Muriel Shapiro opened her home to host a forum for the dissemination of the ideas in the book. I am grateful for her ever-present friendship.

In a letter to Steven Wrinn of Lexington Books, the author wrote, "I am grateful to Dean Birkencamp [of Rowman & Littlefield] for his thoughtful suggestions and for recommending your consideration of the manuscript." Without the foresight of these two individuals and the efforts of Emily Garlin and Lloyd Brown, it is doubtful that this work would have ever reached a public readership. And to the publication staff—Jason Hallman, Martin Hayward, and Melaina Balbo and many others working behind the scenes—your skill, care, and kindness will always be remembered.

In loving memory of my father, I entrust these pages to you, the reader. Throughout his ninety-one years, Mr. Weber was passionately committed to a just and peaceful world. May you be inspired to cultivate an open mind and to carry his mission forward.

Jo Weber Kimmel
June 2001

Contents

Acknowledgements—In Memory of John Weber		vii
Foreword by James Lawler		xi
Preface		xvii
1	Subverted at Birth	1
2	The Socialistic Shorter Work Day	11
3	The Grandest Concession	15
4	What If They Have No Boots?	21
5	Two Centuries: Two Concessions	25
6	Double Trouble for Women	31
7	The Movement toward an Economic Bill of Rights	45
8	The Second Reconstruction	53
9	Health Care as Socialist Intruder	57
10	The Forty-Four Main Concessions and Some Patterns Observed	65
11	Two Worlds or One?	69

12 The German Model 75

13 French and Italian Statism 81

14 The Wayward Six in Eastern Europe 89

15 The Vietnamese and Cuban Models 101

16 India's Special Ways toward the Mix 117

17 The Portent of "Chinese Characteristics" 131

18 Four Mixtures Made in Russia 147

19 The Arena of Future Third Ways 185

Index 189

About the Author 195

Foreword

In his preface to the *Philosophy of Right*, Hegel wrote that no one who studies the natural world ever supposes that the task of scientific thought is to understand how nature ought to be. It is enough for scientists to understand how in fact nature is, and by what laws it comes to be what it is. In the study of human relations, however, it is commonplace for social thinkers to be unhappy with the existing world and to look outside it for some remedy based on an author's ideal portrayal of how society ought to be. For the affairs of social and political life to be put aright, then, it is on the conscience of society to recognize the truth that the thinker is supposed to have discovered and on this basis to make the desirable changes.

But the real task of a philosophically grounded social science, Hegel counters, is "to recognize reason as the rose in the cross of the present and thereby to delight in the present . . ."[1] Hegel cryptically rejects looking for roses or ideal societies in the future only or in the afterlife, rather than in the tribulations of the present. (The Prussian monarch of the time was a member of the otherworldly sect of Rosicrucians.)

The Left in the United States is too often discouraged by what seems to be the endless postponement of hopes and dreams, and by a conception that the tide of history is all in the opposite direction. John Weber's book is an encouragement to look again at the cross of the present reality and to see some roses there, in fact a sizable garden of them. The objective of Weber's book might well be described by this Hegelian mixed metaphor: to discern the rose that is coming into bloom in the thorny tangle of events; to recognize the emergence of new life in the crucifixion of the times.

The effect on the reader may be to achieve in some part the famous Hegelian "reconciliation" of consciousness with reality. Where humanistic moral criticism seems powerless and empty in the face of the brutalities of empirical powers, reconciliation of thought and reality is attained by discovering a rationality in events that accords with the best aspirations, but that is achieved in ways that are not as straightforward as abstract social criticism would have it. As Hegel would put it, reason operates in history with cunning rather than with purity of intention.

What else can one say of Weber's exploration of U.S. history and then of contemporary trends in major parts of today's world? Frequently, he discovers a progressive realization of the highest aspirations of a humanistic morality through concessions granted most unwillingly by a capitalist class intent on maximizing private profits. It then turns out, retrospectively, that the goals of capitalism had thereby been achieved despite itself. Sometimes Weber finds, on the other hand, that anticapitalist socialist states have overestimated their abilities and are making concessions to capitalism. Between these two developments, some middle state is being realized that is different from what the proponents of opposite systems had intended.

The property-owning elites, who gathered in Philadelphia to write a U.S. Constitution were not, as Charles and Mary Beard's classic history demonstrates, staunch advocates of democracy. But they knew that, in order for their revolution against English colonial despotism to survive, their proposals had to be acceptable to an armed citizenry on the brink of revolt. The Bill of Rights was the outcome of a crossfire of conflicting tendencies, the diagonal of a kind of parallelogram of forces moving in different directions but capable of finding a medium to hold things together.

The Civil War Amendments to the Constitution advanced the cause of democracy once more. In the North as well as the South, the abolition of slavery after a brutal war forcibly imposed changes on U.S. ruling groups consistent with the original declarations of the American Revolution. This concession to crucified humanity—which Lincoln at the start of the Civil War firmly opposed—proved eventually to be a boon to industrializing America.

The simple demand of exhausted labor for a limitation of the workweek seemed to U.S. economic elites to be the death of the free enterprise system. Hence their repeated resistance for a period of over a hundred years to incursions on what they believed to be inherent property rights. But in the upheavals of the thirties, enhanced by the specter of communist revolution from Soviet Russia, the outcome of a century of conflicting class orientations was the forty hour week. Far from diminishing the viability of capitalism, this "concession" to what many regarded as nothing less than socialism, inaugurated an unparalleled period of capitalist development and general prosperity in the "Golden Era" following the Second World War. The list of such humanistic achievements of American history obtained by the devious method of compelled reconciliation of differences—Hegel's cunning of reason which Marx revised as class struggle—can be extended to women's suffrage, pension guarantees, recognition of native sovereignty, enhanced civil rights, Medicare and Medicaid, abortion rights. Weber's list of "44 concessions" is a healthy reminder to a would-be alienated consciousness that reality is not as irrational or inhumane as might at first appear to be the case.

What are we to make, on the plane of the general philosophical conception, of this drift of our history in favor of humanity? Is this the process of maturation of capitalism, its natural evolution with a human face? Are we at the end of the century, with the death of "communism," witnessing the triumph of "liberal democracy" as the "end of history"? Fukuyama's famous thesis,[2] appealing as it does to Hegel's authority, might seem warranted by what has been said here. Weber's book, on the other hand, casts doubt on this capitalist triumphalism. His history is not about the forward march of enlightened capitalism but about "concessions" that repeatedly went against the grain of the capitalists themselves.

The idea of "concessions" suggests a different interpretation: that it is not a humanistic capitalism that is being constructed, but some other reality, budding and flowering in the thorny tangle of the private profit system. Give free rein to the acquisitive spirit of capitalism (as we see with the post-USSR development of capitalist globalism) and the humanist institutions of health care, pensions, unemployment insurance, etc.—the flowers that apologists sometimes credit capitalism for assiduously cultivating—are pruned away in the name of deficit reduction and international competitiveness. If history provides any lessons, we should expect, as a result of this reversion of capitalism to pure type, some new, worldwide crucifixion.

What name should we give this reality of a capitalism that alternately prohibits and permits something uncapitalistic, a name that includes those "best things" that capitalism has conceded in the give-and-take of modern world history? Weber argues that what has come into existence is not mature capitalism but "The Socially Mixed Economy." It is capitalism mixed with socialism.

This description implies two pure systems, two opposite extremes—the purely capitalist extreme of a society totally subordinated to the pursuit of private wealth, on the one hand, and the purely socialistic extreme, where the socially organized pursuit of social wealth dominates, on the other. In the Socially Mixed Economy what exists is neither the one nor the other, but a mixture of the two. It is the paradox of a capitalism that can only survive as capitalism by becoming less capitalistic as it goes along, by incorporating elements of an alternative, socialist society.

The concept of the Socially Mixed Society might be challenged by questioning whether we can really speak knowledgeably about a mixture of things that by themselves exist only through mental abstraction. If what exists is a mixture, this implies that we can know something about its two main ingredients. But where do we look to see the pure systems themselves? With an eye to horrors of the nineteenth century factory system with child labor, company towns, and endless hours of work, we can speak knowledgeably enough of a pure capitalism.

But what about the other ingredient of the mixture: the socialist or communist society? What do we know about this so as to be able to describe the Socially Mixed Economy as involving some of its elements? Do we have to construct a conceptual model of an ideal society, and on the basis of this model, identify certain elements of the existing world as components of this ideal? Such a procedure would violate Hegel's strictures against constructing ideal worlds in order to evaluate and reform the existing one. There is no ideal rose garden in the sky or in the mind that enables us to identify the existential roses. On the contrary, we build our ideal heavens, our mental gardens out of real experiences, out of aspects or fragments of the existing reality. In constructing our ideal heaven we implicitly say: if only this particular rose and more like it could exist without the forbidding tangle of thorns that covers it in actuality.

To understand the socialist component of the mixture it is not necessary to concoct artificial heavens. Just as the nineteenth century has shown us what pure capitalism is like, so the twentieth century has given us examples of "real socialism." This term was used by apologists for socialism who wanted to avoid criticism from democrats by invoking the spirit of Hegel: our socialist society may not conform to your ideals, they said, but it is a reality that has solved many of the basic problems of capitalism. But this so-called real socialism, in which all productive property was owned and organized by the state, has almost everywhere been abandoned by the socialists themselves.

This amazing event in our recent history has given credence to the idea that capitalism has proved itself to be "the end of history." But here too, John Weber, in his detailed and highly readable examinations of Vietnam and Cuba, China, and Russia, has something important to say to the apologists of capitalism. In the historic struggle of humanity against the depredations of "pure capitalism" as it really exists, there has emerged, in the noncapitalist world of poor peasant societies, the supposed alternative of "pure socialism." Weber argues that we should rather speak of premature socialist societies. Faced with the alternative of third world dependence on imperialist Western nations, great states of the non-Western world, primarily Russia and China, attempted to bypass capitalism altogether. Today, where socialist states still survive, this premature "pure socialism" has been abandoned, but not in the name of "pure capitalism." The demise of traditional socialist states has not meant the triumph of capitalism in its pure form, but rather a solidification of the Socially Mixed Economy.

Of particular interest is Weber's argument that since the time when the Yeltsin government abandoned the pure capitalist methods of "shock therapy," Russia entered upon its fourth attempt in this century to create a Socially Mixed Economy.[3] The first was in the immediate aftermath of the Russian Revolution, when the Bolshevik government embarked on the creation of what Lenin called "state capitalism." The armed intervention of Western capitalist states in the

Russian Civil War led to the abandonment of this Socially Mixed Economy model of development involving state-regulated capitalist industries, and the creation of the "pure socialism" of what was known as "war communism." Paradoxically, the interventions and pressures of pure capitalism led to the creation of "pure socialism" as its antithesis.

Soon recognizing that omnipresent state control of production was a failure, and threatened with massive revolt on the part of alienated peasants and hungry workers, the Bolsheviks under Lenin returned in 1921 to the spirit of the Socially Mixed Economy with the New Economic Policy. Partly because of continued pressures and threats from the West and partly for internal ideological and political reasons, Stalin in 1929 abandoned the Socially Mixed Economy for what has come to be called the communist system, sometimes described as command or state socialism. The intervening sixty-five years has provided history with the model of society that people today identify with socialism.

In 1985, Mikhail Gorbachev led the Soviet Union once more on the path of the Socially Mixed Economy—anticipated by Deng Xiaoping's "Market Socialism," which was launched shortly after the death of Mao Zedong in 1976. Characteristic of this market society in both the Gorbachev and Deng reforms is a variety of forms of property, including state property and private capitalist property, but also a significant degree of cooperative property—of worker-owned enterprises which fail to fit neatly in the column of pure capitalism or pure socialism.

The attempt to produce pure capitalism in Russia, beginning in January of 1992, accelerated the creation of capitalist enterprises in Russia but it also accelerated the creation of worker-owned cooperatives, while state-owned enterprises continued to compose a substantial part of the Russian economy. In recognition that the pure capitalist model of development has been a failure, Russia is now settling into a middle course.

Contrary to intentions, then, what has emerged is not capitalism but the Socially Mixed Economy. It may be one of those Hegelian ironies of history that, after his eight year ruinous regime, the pro-capitalist Boris Yeltsin should find himself alongside the communist Vladimir Lenin having had to lead a predestined Socially Mixed Economy. Of course a distinction must be made between one in which capitalists make concessions to socialism and one in which socialists make concessions to capitalism.

In connection with the debate over medical reform in the United States, Weber's chapter on Germany reminds us that the alternatives to the mostly private medical system in the United States are not limited to choosing between some form of state-regulated capitalist management of medicine, as in the defeated Clinton plan, and the "socialist" state management of medical finances of the Canadian government. The German medical system is neither primarily state-run nor privately managed under state regulation, but a cooperative nonprofit system administered independently of the state. A true mixture of capitalism and socialism should contain not only a combination of private enterprises and public ones, but also more genuinely intermediate forms that are neither the one nor the other.

The idea of the Socially Mixed Economy implies that we find ourselves now in a transitional state of affairs, with the direction of evolution going from capitalism to socialism. From the roses gathered along the way we begin to get a glimpse of the rose garden of our future. The mistake of idealistic social reform is to believe that it is possible to go from one extreme to another without passing through the midpoints. The methodology of such abstract reformism inevitably results in a simplified picture of the goal itself, as was the case in both Stalinist and Maoist conceptions of socialism where one man's ideas were substituted for the multiplicity of initiatives necessary to a vital social life.

Against abstract reformism, concrete reformism must take its cue from processes occurring in the actual world. It is over 150 years since Marx wrote the *Communist Manifesto,* whose communist program called for such reforms as the progressive income tax, inheritance taxes, the creation of a national bank, state ownership of communications and transportation, as well as "Free education for all children in public schools."[4] The eventual implementation of major planks of the revolutionary program was due to the fact that they reflected midpoints in a process rather than end points. Marx, this intrepid Hegelian, is often accused of greatly underestimating the survival power of capitalism. But capitalism has only survived by achieving many of the goals proposed by the most famous of all the communists. Has capitalism in this way succeeded in outwitting communism, or is it the other way round?

James Lawler
Philosophy Department
State University of New York at Buffalo

Notes

1. G. W. F. Hegel, *Elements of the Philosophy of Right* (Cambridge: Cambridge University Press, 1991), 22.

2. Francis Fukuyama, "The End of History?" *The National Interest* 16 (Summer 1989): 3-18; *The End of History and the Last Man* (New York: Avon Books, 1992).

3. James Lawler, "Lenin and the Socialist Transition in Russia," in *Research in Political Economy* 15 (Bloomington, IN: JAI Press, 1996).

4. Karl Marx and Frederick Engels, *Collected Works*, vol. 6 (Moscow: Progress, 1976), 505.

Preface

World politics, throughout and beyond the twentieth century, has been signally marked by the juxtaposition of social systems. Whether in ebb or flow, this circumstance has persisted through times of deadly contention and times of peaceful coexistence.

This study is concerned with one aspect of that historical process: the trend toward the development of socially mixed economies within given countries, especially contrasting the ways in which social gains are made within opposed systems.

To form an all-sided view, the study contrasts four leading capitalist countries (United States, Germany, France, and Italy) with the four that made socialist revolutions (Russia in 1917, China in 1949, Cuba in 1959, and Vietnam in 1975). It also deals with eight "middling" or variable countries (Sweden, India, and the six in eastern Europe). The study is limited to these sixteen because they are sufficiently diverse and influential to indicate a general trend.

Except for a chapter in which two world-class economists, friends from opposite economies, discuss the interesting possibilities for future convergence, the study rigorously avoids theoretical or speculative conclusions. It makes no predictions, presenting its view of the trend solely on the facts. It goes back as far as needed to dig out its roots and the nature of its development.

It should be noted that the conventional academic use of the term *mixed economy* refers only to the varying mixtures of public and private funds employed in democratic capitalist countries. While the present study also deals with the related issues of statism, it moves beyond, being concerned with the play of capitalist and socialist structures within an economy. To make clear the difference in concept, the term *socially mixed economy* became necessary.

Obviously, the prime interest in the subject of the study derives from the possibility that, if socially mixed economies continue to develop more broadly, this can have important, unprecedented consequences in world politics. Consider that outstanding thinkers in both political persuasions have been known to transcend the thrust of their own class ideologies. Two examples suffice.

It was the mastermind of world socialism, Karl Marx, in the 1848 *Communist Manifesto* (coauthored with Frederick Engels), who emphasized the positive contributions of capitalism to social progress. And it was the leader of world capitalism through the crises of the Great Depression and World War II, Franklin Roosevelt in his 1944 speech to Congress, who proposed the daringly leftist Economic Bill of Rights, denounced at the time as socialistic.

Accounts of the succession of social systems have sometimes been oversimplified to appear to have occurred universally in linear fashion, say beginning with primitive communal or tribal life, going to ancient, classical societies based on slavery, followed by feudalism, then capitalism and finally, occasioned by revolutions, attempts at socialism. However, while history does show instances of countries or areas where a new system developed out of its predecessor in the list, there are others that did not follow this mode of operation.

One of the most anomalous in this respect is the part of the North American continent that became the United States. There was no growth of colonial capitalism or its component slavocracy out of the primitive communism of the Indian tribes other than by genocidal conquest, which can hardly be considered economic development from within a predecessor. Nor was there any feudalism at all from which to grow. U.S. capitalism grew from within itself, as a colonial backwater of British mercantilist capitalism, born out of what has been credited as a revolution but was actually a war of independence. Its socialist and labor movements, often vigorous, have been active in scattered fashion throughout its history, held down to minor status with its political strength never rising above a million votes.

People's histories, looking from the bottom up rather than from the top down, have made it very clear that social progress has not been as benignly achieved as establishment ideologues usually make it appear. Almost always it is rather the end result of long-lasting, bitterly hard-fought, sometimes bloody struggles between the few who own the means of production, which enables them to exercise political power, and the many who do not.

A sense of alienation develops among people who have been put down which, when it takes on forceful expression, becomes a matter of rising concern for those in power. Thus, social gains for people in the various under classes take the form of concessions when force fails. The people's demands, reluctantly granted in part or in full, are usually won at the times when one power or another in the rulership comes to realize that the damage the struggle is doing to its interests is becoming intolerable or even threatening its survival.

Moreover, the concessions fill no systemic need in the capitalist process but only comprise ways and means for a better life. This is said to exemplify socialist aims and this is the way they come to be characterized. A paradox develops here. When a concession called socialistic works to bring an increase in the purchasing power of a mass population this creates a broader social base. Subject to competition and other possible constraints, the concession then turns out to have resulted in more profits for the concerned capitalists.

Notwithstanding efforts to roll back some of the economic, social, and political concessions, most of them have become so durable that the leading countries cannot be deemed to have purely capitalist economies. They can be seen, although not so labeled, to have socially mixed economies in fact, dominantly capitalist but making significant use of socialistic practices.

As to the twentieth century's four socialist revolutions, history played a tragic trick on socialist doctrine. Not one of these occurred where it was logically to be expected: in a highly advanced country, one with plentiful productive forces, and enough capital to build the economy of abundance necessary for socialism. All four took place in hopelessly backward economies. In every case their survival required foreign capital. Right from the start, for example, it was Lenin who had to decide for a socially mixed economy, calling for an open state capitalist system under socialist control, inviting domestic and foreign capital.

It may come as a surprise that the United States, the citadel of world capitalist power, has made so many concessions of a socialist inclination. This state of affairs, its extraordinary history, and its unique role in the world made it necessary to give it much more space than any other country.

The Cold War which the United States sedulously promoted for more than forty years is now long gone, a degree of nuclear disarmament is under way, international trade has been shedding hostile political inhibitions, and the world is becoming decidedly multipolar. The atmosphere appears now to be much more hospitable to the ways in which social gains can be made in both opposed systems.

Chapter 1

Subverted at Birth

The Great American Precursors

History reveals that some of the basic features of a new social system—one that may be coming to transcend its predecessor—can arise in embryonic form within the old system. These features may even at times exist in early stages of the old system. It is as if social changes taking a revolutionary form exhibit also an evolutionary aspect.

So it was with capitalism transcending feudalism. So it has also been in the instances of socialism making revolutionary efforts to transcend capitalism. It is evident to any unprejudiced observer that some of the best things in modern capitalist societies are of a socialistic nature, even if not consciously so identified.

There is a parallel significance in the fact that consciousness itself, deriving as it does from material foundations, also displays embryonic features of the new within the old. In fact, the evolutionary aspect of revolutionary ideas aids us in gaining a deeper understanding of the ways and means of such transcendence. Socialists envisioning revolution aimed at eventually achieving a classless communist society have always recognized that one must begin by understanding the class nature of existing society. It is instructive to compare the developed form in which Karl Marx and Frederick Engels stated this in 1848 and the more elementary form in which James Madison expressed it sixty-one years earlier in 1787.

The main text of the *Communist Manifesto* opens with the classic statement:

> The history of all hitherto existing society is the history of class struggles. Freeman and slave, patrician and plebeian, lord and serf, guild master and journeyman, in a word, oppressor and oppressed, stood in constant opposition to one another, carried on an uninterrupted, now hidden, now open fight, a fight that each time ended, either in a revolutionary reconstitution of society at large, or in the common ruin of the contending classes.[1]

And here is Madison's prior view:

> The most common and durable source of factions has been the various and unequal distribution of property. Those who hold and those who are without property have ever formed distinct interests in society. Those who are creditors, and those who are debtors, fall under a like discrimination. A landed interest, a manufacturing interest, a mercantile interest, a moneyed interest, with many lesser interests, grow up of necessity in civilized nations, and divide them into different classes, actuated by different sentiments and views. The regulation of these various and interfering interests forms the principal task of modern legislation and involves the spirit of party and faction in the necessary and ordinary operations of government.[2]

Another American precursor of a basic principle of socialist thought, the Marxian labor theory of value, is usually attributed to Adam Smith's statement of it in 1776 in *The Wealth of Nations;* but it was anticipated almost half a century earlier by Benjamin Franklin. His 1729 argument for a paper currency was fortified by a detailed explanation of why labor, rather than gold or silver, is the basis of value; Franklin summarized it in a simple statement. "Trade in general being nothing else but the exchange of labor for labor, the value of all things is, as I have said before, most justly measured by labor." Marx credits this "first essay" by Franklin, saying that "he, one of the first, hit upon the true nature of value."[3]

It is noteworthy that democratic capitalists and democratic socialists have both made use, though for unlike purposes, of the same insights to basic social forces and that Americans were the first to do so.

Class Consciousness in the Founding of the United States

The two primary aims of the Committees of Correspondence and the Sons of Liberty, led by Samuel Adams, the American Revolution's chief propagandist, were clearly expressed in the frequent slogan "Liberty and Property." It may be surmised that the tactful statesman, Thomas Jefferson, understood this would not suffice to inspire propertyless workers to shoulder muskets, whereupon he substituted the all-embracing slogan "Life, liberty, and the pursuit of happiness." This did "give backbone" to the underprivileged. Significant also is the fact that many indentured laborers were induced to enlist in the army by having their indentures lifted, for which their masters were compensated.[4]

Many years were to pass before most of the democratic rights attributed to the revolution, including the right to vote, would be extended—and only after many hard and bitter struggles—to women, propertyless workers, indentured servants, Indians, and enslaved black Americans. Only a minority benefited from the new government and only the wealthy were in a position to present themselves for service in the government. Out of an estimated population of three to four million, historians agree that only 160,000 men elected the delegates to the Constitutional Convention, of whom about 100,000 favored it.

Of the fifty-five men who gathered in Philadelphia in 1787 to draw up the Constitution, a majority were lawyers by profession. Most were men of wealth in land, slaves, manufacturing, or shipping. Half of them had money loaned out at interest. Forty held government bonds, according to the records of the Treasury Department.

They had every reason to want a strong federal government. The manufacturers needed protective tariffs, the moneylenders wanted to stop the use of paper money to pay off debts, land speculators wanted protection as they invaded Indian lands, slave owners needed federal security against slave revolts and runaways, and bondholders wanted a government able to raise money through nationwide taxation to pay off their bonds.[5]

Other than for a bit of rhetoric in the Constitution's Preamble about establishing justice and promoting the general welfare, these men saw no need for what were later to be known as socialist notions, which could have made the basic laws of their newly born capitalist nation more palatable to the underprivileged, the poorly propertied, and the propertyless. There was a durable lesson to be learned, however, when these numerous and economically essential people put up a stormy struggle for a bill of rights. Success came rapidly. Within a year from the time that a sufficient number of states had ratified the Constitution, the first Congress felt compelled to adopt ten amendments reflecting the Bills of Rights already adopted by a number of other states. The Congress sent the Bill of Rights to the states for approval, which they quickly granted, a number having made this a condition for ratification of the Constitution.

The entire future development of the U.S. economy was to be influenced fundamentally by this political change in the Constitution. Its long-term effects were so far-reaching that it can be said that, with the adoption of the Bill of Rights, pure capitalism was being subverted at its birth. At the very outset of its independent burgeoning, the new ruling class had found it necessary to make basic concessions to its underclasses.

The Great Ideological Divide

As a thought experiment, consider that if one sought to transplant some existing capitalist democratic institutions to an American socialist society one would have to discard the unamended Constitution as originally ratified, because of its deprivations of liberty, but one would find the Bill of Rights almost entirely compatible with socialist principles.

This is true whether one views it as the first ten amendments or, in Judge Learned Hand's thoughtful preference, as the first eight and the fourteenth amendments. (The reservation implied in the word *almost* has to do with the wording of eminent domain at the end of the fifth amendment, where it calls for "just compensation" when taking private property for public use. A socialist government could easily honor this in the case of personal private property but would find it next to impossible where very large means of production were involved.)

The seeds of what may be called premature socialism, as reflected in the Bill of Rights, lay in the common people's insistence on protection from deprivations caused by the arbitrary rule of the well-born: those who deeply believed that the privileges of property were a matter of natural right. The logic of it was that the more property one had the more privilege one could require whereas a lack of property quite naturally would and did mean a lack of rights, so much so that propertyless people were almost always denied even suffrage. An exception was in the Pennsylvania Constitution, where two leaders with the common touch born of personal experience, Tom Paine and Benjamin Franklin, pushed through a provision for universal suffrage (for free males, that is).

When Alexander Hamilton, John Adams, and John Jay fought strenuously against inclusion of a bill of rights in the constitution, they did so deceptively. They unblushingly used the sophistry that it was unnecessary because the constitution did not specify any ways of violating such rights. Their true view was expressed by John Jay when he said that those who own the country should govern it.[6]

When Thomas Jefferson, James Madison, and Benjamin Franklin fought just as strenuously for inclusion of a bill of rights, it was not to be thought they were opposing property rights as such. So deeply ingrained was the status role of property that Jefferson, wishing to extend suffrage to all free men, could only think of doing so by proposing that fifty acres of land be given to each man lacking property, thereby gaining something of a "natural" stake in the affairs of the nation!

They all, conservatives and liberals alike, had a mentor in this respect—the English philosopher John Locke—who was held in high regard throughout their times. He wrote: "The great and chief end, therefore, of men's uniting into commonwealths and putting themselves under government is the preservation of their property."[7]

Both wings of the new and ambitious ruling class were in favor of property, both were for a controlled democracy, and both supported territorial and economic expansion. What then was the great ideological divide in ruling circles? Policy differences can arise in many unpredictable ways but, from the beginning and recurring all through U.S. history, the prime conflict among capitalist movers and shakers has been between those willing to risk operating the system on a broad social base and those unwilling to face the risks, preferring to operate it on a narrower social base. The former approach tended to be less repressive, the latter more repressive.

The conflict has never been resolved and has moved like a shifting tug of war, with those favoring a broad social base prevailing more often than the other side. An early example came barely seven years after ratification of the Bill of Rights when, with John Adams as president, Congress violated the first amendment by passing the Alien and Sedition Acts of 1798. The political high-handedness of such partisan repression is said to have ruined the Federalist Party, notwithstanding immediate approval of the Acts by judges of the Supreme Court. Two years later Jefferson became president and the abomination was brought to an end by being allowed to lapse.

Even when limited and controlled, as it has been throughout U.S. history, democracy has greatly enhanced the development of the extraordinary depth and breadth of American capitalism. That it would work this way was recognized by a great socialist thinker, Frederick Engels, who wrote that "the logical form of bourgeois domination is precisely the democratic republic."[8]

The essence of the matter is that democracy allows the system to operate on a broad social base. This involves a rising standard of living, which expands the market for capitalist goods, with all sorts of smallholders also benefiting when workers or farmers make gains. Employers, however, do not volunteer to raise wages and improve working conditions and so, when there is a rise in the standard of living, it is almost always brought about by embattled employees or other lower class contenders. This involves risks for the ruling class that became evident in the earliest days.

Rebellious economic and political activities by workers and farmers took place in the 1780s and 1790s, and in a few instances even before the Revolution. Organizations sprang up acting in the same way as unions, involving mechanics, artisans, bakers, bricklayers, carpenters, tailors, seamen, printers, shoemakers, cabinet makers, and others, some even engaging in strikes demanding higher pay and improvements in working conditions. Some also demanded a voice in politics, which they felt the rich had arrogated to themselves.[9]

Early Socialist Ideas

The economic depression that followed the Revolutionary War also threatened many farmers with ruin, causing armed resistance to some of the many foreclosures as well as to what had become heavy taxation. Most notable among these violent protests was Shays' Rebellion, put down like the others by force. An interesting expression of the ruling class view came in General Henry Knox's 1786 letter to George Washington informing him that these rebellious farmers held dangerous and pernicious views. The rebels' creed, Knox wrote, "is that the property of the United States has been protected from the confiscations of Britain by the joint exertions of all, and therefore ought to be the common property of all."[10]

The common property of all? A socialist idea! A communist idea! A truly dangerous idea for those who held that private property was a natural right. No awareness existed as yet of the nature and the juxtaposition of capitalist and socialist systems as such. Generations would have to pass before they could even be called premature socialists—but subversive they already were—and they bred chaotic fears among the powers that be.

Even Irishmen and Frenchmen in the United States were looked on as dangerous subversives, after the French Revolution and the Irish rebellions. The Sedition Act made it a crime to say or write anything "false, scandalous, and malicious" against the government, Congress, or the President, with intent to defame them, bring them into disrepute or excite popular hatreds against them. Ten Americans were put in prison for utterances against the government.

The economic basis of these fears was quite clear. John Adams' views concerning the exercise of political power were the same as those of Alexander Hamilton, who had led troops to put down the rebellion in western Pennsylvania. Impoverished farmers had been trying to make ends meet by turning grain into whiskey and selling it, a perfectly legitimate practice. When the Whiskey Tax was enacted it had such ruinous effects that whiskey makers refused to pay it, especially when considering the reason for the tax. Hamilton had instituted it for the express purpose of paying the government's debt to bondholders—who were mostly wealthy—for bonds that had been issued to finance the Revolutionary War. For the likes of Hamilton, squeezing the poor to pay the rich was a normal democratic process.

Confrontations like Shay's Rebellion and the Whiskey Tax resistance stimulate popularity for socialist ideas even before they come to be known as such. As for common property, its use both as a concept and as a practice had been known through the ages and in many countries, especially among farmers sharing pastureland. In fact, it was in this way that areas came to be known as "commons" in American towns both before and after the Revolution. Only the rampant development of capitalism did away with their communal productive use.

On this score, justice for Benjamin Franklin required a sort of socially mixed economy. He judged that an individual's private property should be severely circumscribed in quantity. In his view as expressed in 1783, "Only that property necessary to a man, in terms of his conservation and the propagation of children is his natural right, of which none can justly deprive him, but all property superfluous to such purposes is the property of the public."[11]

The Bill of Rights

The extraordinary good fortune attending the rise of U.S. capitalism made possible a wide alternation of policies. Whenever the developing ruling class found itself under great social pressure, potentially endangering its tenure, it would rely on brutal repression, if it could safely carry it off, or on the granting, when necessary, of socially progressive concessions to its underclasses. The newborn government put down some rebellions by force but also granted such clamorously demanded democratic rights as it could not resist, hoping such action would assist the expansion of its domain—which it did. The Bill of Rights comprises twenty-three such concessions, as numbered below.

In the First: Congress shall make no law (1) respecting an establishment of religion, or prohibiting the free exercise thereof, or abridging (2) the freedom of speech or (3) the freedom of the press, or the right of the people to (4) peacefully assemble, and to (5) petition the government for a redress of grievances.

In the Fourth: (6) The right of the people to be secure in their persons, houses, papers and effects, against unreasonable searches and seizures shall not be violated, and (7) no warrants shall issue but upon probable cause, supported by oath or affirmation, and particularly describing the place to be searched, and the persons or things to be seized.

In the Fifth: (8) No person shall be held to answer for a capital or otherwise infamous crime, unless on a presentment or indictment of a grand jury, except in cases arising in the land or naval forces, or in the militia, when in actual service in time of war or public danger; nor shall any person (9) be subject for the same offense to be twice put in jeopardy of life or limb; nor (10) be compelled, in any criminal case, to be a witness against himself; nor (11) be deprived of life, liberty, or property, without due process of law; nor (12) shall private property be taken for public use without just compensation.

In the Sixth: In all criminal prosecutions the accused shall have the right to (13) a speedy and public trial, by (14) an impartial jury of the State and district wherein the crime shall have been committed, which district shall have been previously ascertained by law; and to (15) be informed of the nature and cause of the accusation; to (16) be confronted with the witnesses against him; to (17) have compulsory process for obtaining witnesses in his favor, and to (18) have the assistance of counsel for his defense.

In the Seventh: In suits at common law, where the value in controversy shall exceed twenty dollars, (19) the right of trial by jury shall be preserved; and (20) no fact tried by a jury shall be otherwise reexamined in any court in the United States, than according to the rules of the common law.

In the Eighth: (21) Excessive bail shall not be required, nor (22) excessive fines imposed, nor (23) cruel and unusual punishment inflicted.

(Four amendments have come by now to have so little significance that they can be left out of enumeration. They are the Second: the right to bear arms in support of a militia; the Third: no quartering of troops in civilian homes except in wartime by legal arrangement; the Ninth: the enumeration of rights in the Constitution shall not deny or disparage others retained by the people; and the Tenth: the powers not delegated to the federal government by the Constitution, nor prohibited by it to the people are reserved to the states respectively or to the people.)

With the sole exception of the item listed as twelfth, requiring just compensation for private property taken by public domain, none of the twenty-three rights or requirements could be considered inherently essential to the economic operation of a capitalist system. Indeed, these rights could only benefit the individual capitalist when charged as a lawbreaker of some sort. In their ruling class situations, Alexander Hamilton, John Adams, John Jay, and reactionaries like Gouverneur Morris were perfectly right: they could get along very well without the entire Bill of Rights!

After all the centuries in which the dominance of pelf and privilege had been asserted as a matter of right, here for the first time was a document of basic law enacted by a new and exploitative ruling class which granted detailed rights and privileges to all who had by then been allowed citizenship, including the less privileged common people.

In this way, the birth of this newly independent capitalist system unwittingly brought with it some basic elements of a system that could be anticipated to succeed it, such as socialism. Awareness of the social revolutionary potential in such concessions would develop with the growth of capitalism and the class conflicts that arise within it, resulting in attacks on the Bill of Rights. Capitalism cannot endure without limiting and controlling democratic rights whereas a truly socialist system requires the fullest extension of democracy, and is for all practical purposes synonymous with it. Socialists can well consider the Bill of Rights a great precursor.

The Basic Problem of Rulership

In order to win independence from the stultifying controls of British mercantilism, the leading colonials had to present the cause of the Revolution on a classless basis. They had to win over a substantial number of the very people they were variously exploiting to the conviction that the main source of their difficulties, the true oppressor of all American colonials of any class, was King George III. And this was no easy task, considering the wretched history of colonial capitalist development for the century and a half preceding independence.

Consider that 1619 was both the year the first representative assembly was formed, the Virginia House of Burgesses, and the year that the first twenty Negro slaves arrived. Surely these wretched souls, as their numbers grew, could not be looked to for support in the cause against the King. A great number of the settlers kept arriving through the years as indentured workers, deceptively forced into such miserable conditions of life as to become rebellious. Surely these could not be looked to for support. Risking savage punishment, many in fact ran off, some in the company of runaway slaves, male and female. Those who made their way to the Indians were known to have found a much superior life there and, when later offered "rescue" and "freedom," declined to leave.

Conditions for others also, so-called freemen, were none too good and they were the main voices of social protest. It is known that in the eighty-four years between Bacon's Rebellion in Virginia in 1676 and the year 1760 there had been eighteen uprisings aimed at overthrowing colonial governments. There had also been six black rebellions, from South Carolina to New York, and forty various riots.[12] Upon whom, then, could colonial leaders rely in a war for the economic and political power that required independence in order to prosper?

Colonial America was a land extraordinarily favored for the development of reproductive forces. It was therefore possible, notwithstanding all the toil and trouble, repression and brutishness, for an extraordinary amount of upward mobility to make its way. The number of such personally enterprising people grew constantly so that it was possible for the *Pennsylvania Journal* to write in 1756:

> The people of this province are generally of the middling sort, and at present pretty much upon a level. They are chiefly industrious farmers, artificers or men in trade; they enjoy and are fond of freedom, and the meanest among them thinks he has a right to civility from the greatest.[13]

It was this section of the population, a sort of middle class, whose loyalty the ruling class was buying with concessions. To call them "the people" was, of course, to omit black slaves, white servants, displaced Indians and, as economic and political movers, virtually all women. In those times, however, such exclusions from effective citizenship were generally not considered abnormal.

A major lesson learned by ruling class Americans from the Revolutionary War and the experience of the struggle over the Bill of Rights, and one to be applied in later social conflicts, was that in certain situations the sharpness of class struggle could be blunted by means of concessions, even protosocialistic ones, without significant damage to their own wealth or power. Overreliance on concessions could be problematic in the long run, yet allowing the class struggle to come to the breaking point would prove even more problematic. Besides, one could ask, when has it ever been possible to predict the future?

They could not know it then but in that misty long run a sizable succession of concessions would come to be born, almost always after great labor pains, and would bring to attention the intriguing concept of the socially mixed economy.

Notes

1. Karl Marx and Frederick Engels, "Manifesto of the Communist Party (1848)," in *Karl Marx and Frederick Engels, Selected Works* (New York: International Publishers, 1986), 35-36.
2. James Madison, "Federalist Paper No. 10," in *The Federalist Papers*, ed. Clinton Rossiter (New York: The New American Library, 1964), 79.
3. Marx, "Wages, Price and Profit," in *Selected Works*, 204.
4. Philip S. Foner, *History of the Labor Movement in the United States*, vol. 1, *From Colonial Times to the Founding of the American Federation of Labor* (New York: International Publishers, 1982), 33, 43, 47.
5. Charles Beard, "An Economic Interpretation of the Constitution," as summarized by Howard Zinn, *A People's History of the United States* (New York: Harper & Row, 1980), 89-90.
6. Herbert Aptheker, *Early Years of the Republic* (New York: International Publishers, 1990), 61-62.
7. John Locke, "Of the Ends of Political Society and Government," Ch. IX §124 in *The Second Treatise of Government* (New York: Cambridge University Press, 1963), 395.
8. Frederick Engels, letter dated March 24, 1884, quoted by Aptheker, *Early Years*, 57.
9. Aptheker, *Early Years*, 139-48 passim.
10. Howard Zinn, *A People's History of the United States* (New York: Harper & Row, 1980), 95.
11. Herbert Aptheker, *The American Revolution 1763-1783* (New York: International Publishers, 1985), 269.
12. Zinn, *A People's History*, 59.
13. ———, *A People's History*, 57-58.

Chapter 2

The Socialistic Shorter Work Day

The Beginnings

The next great concession after those in the Bill of Rights came in the shortening of the work day, the result of the turbulent Ten-Hour Movement which extended throughout the first half-century of the new nation. It was paralleled in England where the Ten-Hour Bill, for which the workers there had been fighting for thirty years, was made a law in 1847. Here, however, success did not come in those years in the form of national legislation, but rather as a gradual general acceptance that was forced in workplace after workplace on very reluctant employers.

It is known that in 1791, even before the first permanent unions were formed, the Philadelphia carpenters went on strike for a ten-hour day and additional pay for overtime—but the outcome is not known. It was the first step taken by American labor for a shorter work day.[1]

So utterly wretched were the customary conditions of labor, that both spontaneously and through trade union organization, a great many strikes took place—more often than not roughly put down—for wage increases, and against wage cuts, delayed payment, inhuman treatment, and other abuses. Not the least of these abuses was being worked to exhaustion from sunup to sundown, usually thirteen to fourteen hours a day.

A climax was reached in 1835. The great Philadelphia general strike had taken place early that year and great enthusiasm arose as word of it spread

—with help from the labor press—to cities in New Jersey, New York, Connecticut, Massachusetts, Maryland, and even South Carolina. A wave of strikes swept the country, most of which were successful. By the end of 1835, with the exception of Boston, the standard day's work for skilled mechanics was ten hours (118).

Indigenous Socialist Ideas

Socialist ideas were being expressed in those years without awareness of socialist doctrine. The influential Seth Luther, a leader of the New England Association of Farmers, Mechanics, and Workingmen, included the following in his widely read "Address to Workingmen of New England," among other stirring calls to action:

> Let us be determined no longer to be deceived by the cry of those who produce nothing and enjoy all, and insultingly term us—the farmers, the mechanics and the laborers—the lower orders, and exultingly claim our homage for themselves, as the higher orders—while the Declaration of Independence asserts that 'All men are created equal.' (107)

The *Working Man's Advocate* of October 1, 1830, declared that the Revolution of 1830 in France, limited though it was, convinced Americans that the workers were 'the masters of their own liberties, that they have but to will it, and cooperate one with another, and they must be free' (107).

The historic significance of the movement for the shorter workday, aside from demonstrating to workers the possibility of reducing the domination of employers over their daily life, rests primarily in wresting a bit of time for self-cultivation. More precisely, time for gaining some knowledge of the nature of the society in which, from time immemorial, they had been born to be, and to remain, beasts of burden. It would mean learning how to bring about a better life. Many reflections of this came to the fore.

In 1835, the National Trades' Union urged all affiliated bodies to agitate for the establishment of libraries in cities, towns, and villages "for the use and benefits of mechanics and workingmen." In Philadelphia, a Society for the Diffusion of Knowledge Among the Working Classes was established in 1835 "not only to enlighten the mind upon general subjects, but to teach that class, who supply the fountain of existence, whence their evils spring and how to remedy them."

In Rochester, New York, a Mechanics' Literary Association was formed in 1836 by the trade unions and the circular announcing it said:

> We know that the laboring class has for ages been in the habit of looking up to the learned professions for all the knowledge that is necessary in guiding the

> affairs of State, or in ruling the affairs of men, and it requires no very discerning eye, to see that all rulers rule for their own benefit, rather than for the benefit of the many (115 fn).

It may be thought that the socialist flavor of these activities and statements could have been influenced by the Utopian Socialists Count St. Simon and Charles Fourier in France, and Robert Owen in England (also in America) for they became prominent in the early 1800s; but there is no evidence of this. Counting as the Utopians did on upper class good will for their schemes, they influenced mainly detached intellectuals. They made a stir in Europe, especially Owen and his extraordinary project in England at New Lanark. High-minded inclinations notwithstanding, Robert Owen, for example, disdained workers as lacking in intelligence and other qualifications to have any say in management of his projects. And none of those enterprises ever lasted long enough to be of any continuing significance, numerous though they were.

The indications are that the proto-socialist flavor of early American labor viewpoints was derived from the radicalism of the Revolution, in particular the abstractly egalitarian principles of the Declaration of Independence, the Bill of Rights, and the leading proponents of human rights. The United States was favorably disposed in the late 1820s to become the place where the first Workingmen's Parties would arise.

Socialist parties and their revolutionary programs did not yet exist. However, if socialism was ever to arise out of conscious popular action, it would be wise to begin the process with reforms that would alter the relations between capital and labor. As it happened, practice preceded theory and found expression in various ways.

Early labor organizations of all sorts played a great part in bringing about mechanics' lien laws, the abolition of imprisonment for debt, the abolition of compulsory militia service, development of the public school system, and other social gains that took years and years of political struggle. An awareness of the importance to them of available democratic rights no doubt accounts for the fact that labor organizations tended to celebrate the Fourth of July more actively than their employers, frequently referring to the blood shed by their peers in the Revolution.

The Growing Recognition of Labor

It was not only great statesmen like Jefferson, Franklin and, later, Lincoln and Franklin Roosevelt who saw the importance of expressing respect for the role of the working class in society. Even lesser lights like Andrew Jackson and Martin Van Buren spoke up for labor, having been backed by workers' organizations in their fight as Presidents against monopoly banking practices.

Jackson said: "Without labor prospers, commerce and manufacturers must languish and the country be distressed. This is a government of the people, for their happiness and prosperity, and not for that of the few at the expense of the many." And Van Buren said, after issuing an executive order establishing the ten-hour day for federal employees on public works without a reduction in pay:

> The labor of an industrious man is in my judgment only adequately rewarded, when his wages, together with the assistance of those members of his family, from whom assistance may reasonably be required, will enable him to provide comfortably for himself and them, to educate his children and lay up sufficient for the casualties of life; and all attempts to depress them below this equitable standard, are in my opinion at war as well with the dictates of humanity as with a sound and national policy. (163, 166)

Employers, however, had to be forced to respect the value of labor. They fought any shortening of the workday with every brutal weapon they could use. When circumstances permitted, they were able to eliminate some of the gains made by the workers. However, even when the severe depression known as the Panic of 1837 laid waste most of the existing trade unions, the workers courageously picked themselves up off the ground and rebuilt their unions. They also tried legislation.

Between 1847 and 1851, they forced the enactment of Ten-Hour Laws in a number of states but a typical weakness was that they could be evaded by agreement between employer and employee. So many workers refused such contracts that the loophole proved useless—but the laws also proved useless, not being enforced.

Relying on themselves, and on their unions, the workers fought their way back to the point where, by 1860, skilled mechanics and some others had regained the ten-hour day. Factory workers may have been working as much as eleven hours, but the twelve and a half-hour work day, which had been the average thirty years before, had been knocked out. The way was now paved for the eventual achievement of the eight-hour day—but other great social struggles would first have to take place.

Note

1. Philip S. Foner, *History of the Labor Movement in the United States*, vol. 1, *From Colonial Times to the Founding of the American Federation of Labor* (New York: International Publishers, 1982), 102.

Chapter 3

The Grandest Concession

Abolition as Social Progress

Aside from the limitations and the timely military purpose of the Emancipation Proclamation of January 1, 1863, the measures taken for the full abolition of slavery comprise the grandest concession made by the American ruling class to a specific underclass. Its relative grandeur rests mainly on four features.

First, its human value: the freeing of four million people from the abominable oppression which had been the law of the land for them for 244 years and against which many of them had fought to the death in more than 250 significant revolts. While there were instances in which some poor whites took risks to help them—and others in which runaways were helped by white abolitionists—the slaves knew they had to depend mainly on their own valor. This was clearly shown by the 186,000 black volunteers who fought bravely in the Union army, disregarding the discrimination faced even there, including lower pay than white soldiers. Acts of heroism were recorded, with 68,000 giving their lives. Some served with such distinction as to gain promotions as high as major and lieutenant colonel.

Second, its progressive capitalist value: destroying the economic power and with it the political ability of the plantation South to hinder the territorial spread and general development of industrial capitalism and its most productive force: wage-labor. Had the North been able to gain the upper hand and end the war without abolition, as some in the North had proposed, it would not be long before the war would have had to be fought all over again. Such was the urgent need of the wasteful plantation economy for more land and the spread of more slave labor. Without the abolition of slavery, the Civil War could not be considered what the historian Charles Beard rightly called it, the Second American Revolution.

Third, its labor value: eliminating the downward pressure on wage levels resulting from the growing use of slave labor in factories. Southern arrogance against the labor movement had been even more vicious than the worst attitudes of Northern employers. Instances had been increasing where Southern publicists had been seriously preaching the naturalness of what they called their "peculiar institution," advising the North to subject all workers to the master-slave relation—an association which they likened to the parent-child relation. Preposterous as this might sound, it found hospitality among some Northern capitalists, especially those that were directly profiting from trade with the South and were the core of the Copperhead opposition to Lincoln.

Fourth, its socialist value: expropriating the expropriators in exactly the same manner as in a socialist revolution. In one grand stroke, the Proclamation in effect confiscated three billion dollars worth of property in slaves without one cent of compensation.[1]

The fact that this technically violated the Fifth Amendment was treated as nothing more than one of life's little ironies. It served the interests of capitalism. It served the outlook for socialism. Notwithstanding the long struggle yet to come against the burden of racist handicaps, millions upon millions of African-Americans would now be in a position to join their white sisters and brothers in the march of social progress.

The Socialist View of the Civil War

Among other considerations, the Civil War and abolition held a special significance for Karl Marx:

> In the United States of America, every independent workers' movement was paralysed as long as slavery disfigured a part of the republic. Labor in a white skin cannot emancipate itself where in a black skin it is branded. However, a new life immediately arose from the death of slavery. The first fruit of the American Civil War was the eight hours' agitation, which ran from the Atlantic to the Pacific, from New England to California, with the seven-league boots of the locomotive. The General Congress of Labor held at Baltimore in August 1866 declared: 'The first and great necessity of the present, to free the labor of this country from capitalistic slavery, is the passing of a law by which eight

> hours shall be the normal working day in all states of the American Union. We are resolved to put forth all our strength until this glorious result is obtained.[2]

He also took note of supportive resolutions, one passed by the Working Men of Dunkirk in New York State and another, which he wrote in September, 1866, passed by the Congress of the International Workingmen's Association held in Geneva and which had been proposed by the London General Council.

To a socialist, typically with faith in the future, the durable, structural concessions made by a capitalist ruling class to its underclasses, regardless how reluctantly, regardless how much resisted before and after, operate to one extent or another as precursors of socialism. Such, no doubt, was the spirit of the First International, known then as the International Workingmen's Association, when on January 7, 1865 it sent to President Lincoln a stately Address which congratulated him on his reelection. Written by Marx, it eloquently analyzed the world-historic importance of the success of the Northern cause and ended with this statement:

> The workingmen of Europe feel sure that, as the American War of Independence initiated a new era of ascendancy for the middle class, so the American anti-slavery war will do for the working classes. They consider it an earnest of the epoch to come that it fell to Abraham Lincoln, the single-minded son of the working class, to lead the country through the matchless struggle for the rescue of an enchained race and reconstruction of a social world.

The statement was signed by fifty-eight members of the Central Council.

Following protocol, Lincoln responded cordially in a letter from his Minister to England, Charles Francis Adams, to A.W. Cremer, the General Secretary of the I.W.A. in London, ending with this statement:

> Nations do not exist for themselves alone, but to promote the welfare and happiness of mankind by benevolent intercourse and example. It is in this relation that the United States regard their cause in the present conflict with slavery-maintaining insurgents as the cause of human nature, and they derive new encouragement to persevere from the testimony of the workingmen of Europe that the national attitude is favored with their enlightened approval and earnest sympathies.[3]

The importance of the exchange was clear. Marx wrote from London to Engels February 6, 1865, to say: "Lincoln's answer to us is in today's Times."[4]

Lincoln's Views on Labor

The "single-minded son of the working class" made some memorable pro-labor speeches consistently through the years. In September 1859, at a State Fair sponsored by the Wisconsin Agricultural Society, he attacked the mudsill theory of labor which claimed that "a blind horse upon a treadmill is a perfect illustration of what a laborer should be" and that "the education of laborers is not only useless but pernicious and dangerous."

Free labor, said Lincoln, was the chief bulwark of America's freedom, and it was labor, not capital, which was "the source from which human wants are mainly supplied." The mudsill advocates put capital first and labor last. Lincoln said he stood for the opposite point of view:

> that labor is prior to, and independent of capital; that, in fact, capital is the fruit of labor, and could never have existed if labor had not first existed; that labor can exist without capital, but that capital could never have existed without labor. Hence . . . labor is the superior . . . greatly the superior of capital.

In his New Haven speech of March 6, 1860, in reference to the great shoe strike then in progress, Lincoln said:

> I am glad to see that a system of labor prevails in New England under which laborers can strike when they want to, where they are not obliged to labor whether you pay them or not. I like the system which lets a man quit when he wants to, and wish it might prevail everywhere. One of the reasons why I am opposed to slavery is just here.

Also in March 1860, he said: "If you give up your convictions and call slavery right, you let slavery in upon you. Instead of white workers who can strike, you'll soon have black laborers who can't."[5]

Four years later, The Iron Platform, put out by members of the New York Typographical Union, included this classic remark by Lincoln in their March-April report of a meeting with him: "The strongest bond of human sympathy, outside of the family relation, should be one uniting all working people of all nations and tongues and kindreds."[6]

One becomes ideologically prepared for a study of possible trends toward socially mixed economies when one realizes that it may have required a Karl Marx to analyze and establish the historic relation between different forms of social progress, but as U.S. history shows, it required an Abraham Lincoln to personify it.

Notes

1. W. E. B. Du Bois, *Black Reconstruction 1860-1880* (New York: Atheneum, 1975), 37.

2. Karl Marx, *Capital,* vol. 1 (London: Penguin Books, 1990), 414-15.

3. Karl Marx and Frederick Engels, *The Civil War in the United States* (New York: International Publishers, 1937), Appendix 279-281.

4. ———, *The Civil War,* 273.

5. Philip S. Foner, *History of the Labor Movement in the United States,* vol. 1, *From Colonial Times to the Founding of the American Federation of Labor* (New York: International Publishers, 1982), 292.

6. ———, *Labor Movement,* vol. 1, 335.

Chapter 4

What If They Have No Boots?

The Great American Precursors

The consequences of abolition were profound, especially as reflected in the period of Black Reconstruction, and its ramifications far-flung. The historic concessions made by those in power were codified in the Thirteenth, Fourteenth and Fifteenth Amendments to the Constitution, effective in 1865, 1868 and 1870. So shaken, apparently, were they by the realization that these concessions were not mere promises easily broken, but the law of the land, that they allowed a wide-ranging reign of terror to develop against their application in practice.

It was a volcanic expression of racism, "that bizarre doctrine of race that makes most men inferior to the few," in the telling phrase of W. E. B. Du Bois.[1] Underlying and threatening to disrupt every aspect of the development of American civilization, racism has run like a geologic fault-line from colonial days to the present, always ready to erupt.

It is difficult to explain the state of mind attending the savagery of the Southern backlash against abolition, the five thousand lynchings, and innumerable other small and large acts of barbarism over many years following defeat in the Civil War. Some light is provided by a memorable report Carl Schurz made of his visit to the South after the war:

> Wherever I go—the street, the shop, the house, the hotel, or the steamboat—I hear the people talk in such a way as to indicate they are yet unable to conceive

> of the Negro as possessing any rights at all. Men who are honorable in their dealings with their white neighbors, will cheat a Negro without feeling a single twinge of their honor. To kill a Negro, they do not deem murder; to debauch a Negro woman, they do not think fornication; to take the property away from a Negro, they do not consider robbery. The people boast that when they get freedmen's affairs in their own hands, to use their own expression, 'the niggers will catch hell.' (136)

A master race, long before and even more primitive than Hitlerism! They had no comprehension of what the North expected them to come to realize: that the exploitation of intelligent wage labor would prove superior to repressed slave labor as a secure source of profit and capital accumulation, and lead to a much more productive economy which could expand without laying waste the land.

It was more than having to face expropriation of their enormous property in slaves, defeat in bloody battles in which the tide was often turned by the despised freedmen, the war's ruination of their economy, and great loss of kith and kin. The Southern master race felt declassed, deeply degraded, and betrayed by their former capitalist partners who now, incredibly, required them to regard former slaves as equals before the law. Their fury was lasting and intense, and in the classically cowardly fashion of those born to bully others, they sought to bludgeon the black freedmen into the acceptance of abject submission.

Black Reconstruction

For one brief, shining, historical moment, the decade of Black Reconstruction, the government took action to put some flesh on the bones of the great concession of emancipation. After much dispute, the Freedmen's Bureau Bill was enacted in 1865. Lincoln signed it immediately and appointed the dedicated General Oliver O. Howard, who worked tirelessly as its Head Commissioner to make it succeed:

> The conditions facing the Bureau were chaotic. . . . In four years the Bureau issued over twenty-one million rations to the hungry and unemployed—fifteen and a half million to blacks and five and a half million to whites . . . the total cost of food and clothing, 1865-1871 was set down at $3,168,325 . . .
>
> The insistent demand of the Negro, aided by Army officers and Northern churches and philanthropic organizations, began the systematic teaching of Negroes and poor whites. . . . The Bureau furnished day and night schools, industrial schools, Sunday schools and colleges. Between June 1, 1865 and September 1, 1871, $5,262,511.26 was spent on schools from Bureau funds, and in 1870 there were in day and night schools 3,300 teachers and 149,581 pupils. Nearly all the present [1934] Negro universities and colleges, like Howard,

Fisk and Atlanta were founded or substantially aided in their earliest days by the Freedmen's Bureau. (226)

Martin Luther King, Jr. once remarked that you can ask a people to lift themselves by their own bootstraps but what if they have no boots? The Freedmen's Bureau provided some boots and a seemingly miraculous, unexpected surge in American civilization ensued. A brilliantly prophetic, spontaneous, and inspired effort moved a hopelessly downtrodden people onto the difficult but only road forward: Education! Booker T. Washington was fascinated by the upsurge:

> Few people who were not in the midst of the scenes can form any exact idea of the intense desire which the people of my race showed for education. It was a whole race trying to go to school. Few were too young, and none too old, to make the attempt to learn. As fast as any kind of teachers could be secured, not only were day schools filled, but night schools as well. The great ambition of the older people was to try to learn to read the Bible before they died. With this end in view, men and women who were fifty and seventy-five years old, would be found in the night schools. Sunday schools were formed soon after freedom, but the principal book studied in the Sunday school was the spelling-book. Day school, night school and Sunday school were always crowded, and often many had to be turned away for want of room.[2]

Winning Out Over Defeat

Du Bois's deep study of Black Reconstruction convinced him that

> Had it not been for the Negro school and college, the Negro would, to all intents and purposes, have been driven back to slavery. His economic foothold in land and capital was too slight in ten years of turmoil to effect any defense or stability. His reconstruction leadership had come from Negroes educated in the North, and white politicians, capitalists and philanthropic teachers. The counterrevolution of 1876 drove most of them, save the teachers, away. But already, through establishing public schools and private colleges, and by organizing the Negro church, the Negro had acquired enough leadership and knowledge to thwart the worst designs of the new slave drivers. They avoided the mistake of trying to meet force by force. They bent to the storm of beating, lynching and murder, and kept their souls in spite of public and private insult of every description; they built an inner culture which the world recognizes in spite of the fact that it is still half-strangled and inarticulate! (667)

It was in this stubbornly courageous and subtly civilizing way that African-Americans saw to it that they would remain emancipated and continue their advancement. Experience must have taught them to be wary, to suspect that the fortuitous marriage between Northern capital and abolition-democracy (Du

Bois's term) and its protection of the great concession could not be long relied upon. It could be expected that at some point Northern financial, industrial, and commercial interests would seek mutually profitable arrangements with Southern plantation interests, inevitably at the expense of both black and white labor. Here, in summary, is Du Bois' account of the betrayal:

> In 1876 came the bargain between Big Business and the South. . . . On the 26th of February there were three conferences. The outcome was an agreement. The Republicans guaranteed that Mr. Hayes, when he became President, would by non-interference and the withdrawal of troops allow the planter-capitalists, under the name of Democrats, to control South Carolina and Louisiana. They also agreed to induce president Grant to adopt the same policy before the end of his term. This meant that Southern landholders and capitalists would be put in complete control of disfranchised black labor. The Democrats promised to 'guarantee peace, good order, protection of the law to whites and blacks,' or, in other words, exploitation should be so quiet, orderly and legal, as to ensure regular profit to Southern owners and Northern investors. . . . Louisiana was told that Grant had promised action when the count should be completed, to rescind or modify all orders to enforce the laws in the South. . . . Federal troops were withdrawn under Hayes. The force behind the dictatorship of labor in the South disappeared. The last act was to appoint a Kentuckian and a Georgian to the Supreme Court. The deed was done. (691-92)

This setback would be followed by many years in which African-Americans would have to suffer foul abuse of many kinds and have to struggle against all manner of economic, social, and political handicaps—but the new basis for advancement could not be reversed. The blow struck by "abolition-democracy" was a body blow against racism, the most noxious form of class oppression, and education had opened the door to self-improvement.

The slow civilizing of the United States could now go forward—and the struggle did result in progress in civil rights, higher education, social and cultural status, unionism, the professions, sports, political activity, and a measure of economic improvement. Racism is far from being at an end but is facing determined black and white enemies. Related concessions won in more recent times are dealt with in chapter 8.

Notes

1. W. E. B. Du Bois, *Black Reconstruction in America 1860-1880* (New York: Atheneum, 1975), 725.
2. Sadler, *The Education of the Coloured Race*, 21, quoted by Du Bois in *Black Reconstruction in America 1860-1880* (New York: Atheneum, 1975), 641-42.

Chapter 5

Two Centuries: Two Concessions

The Nature of the Genocide

Unnecessary military pogroms rose in horror from early in the 1800s under Andrew Jackson in the southeast to what has been called the worst: the barbaric massacre of unarmed men, women, and children, savagely mutilated at Sand Creek in Colorado in 1864, right on up to "the last massacre" at Wounded Knee, South Dakota, in 1890. These and other inhuman forms of racist deprivation, together with imported and therefore lethal diseases, reduced the Native American population to three hundred thousand in 1900. It has recovered, especially from the 1970s on, to almost two million—but still bears many marks of the long traumatic experience.

That it constituted genocide cannot be disputed but there is some question as to its full numerical extent. For this, one must know the population before the white invasion began. An old and arbitrary estimate runs to about one million, but this has been strongly disputed by anthropologists, agrarian biologists, and many other scholars. They studied farmland acre by acre to calculate how many people it could have fed, and looked into ruins of Indian towns, irrigation canals, graveyards, and tax documents from the 1400s. They arrived at a population figure of ten million for the area of Canada and the United States and found, that far from an empty wilderness or a newly settled continent, it was a fairly densely populated land area with many large towns.[1]

Whatever their number—and it had to be a sizable number of millions—the natives were shocked not only by the mindless brutality but also by the enormous hypocrisy. Their pietistic conquerors had the strange habit of making lofty proclamations of human rights while behaving immorally and inhumanly toward them. For example, the first applicable law, the Northwest Ordinance of 1767 (ratified in 1789) stated:

> The utmost good faith shall always be observed toward the Indians; their lands and property shall never be taken from them without their consent; and in their property, rights, and liberty they never shall be invaded or disturbed unless by just and lawful wars authorized by Congress; but laws founded in justice and humanity, shall, from time to time, be made, for preventing wrongs being done to them and for preserving peace and friendship with them.[2]

Additional laws protecting the Indians were passed in the 1790s. All were simply never enforced.

Howard Zinn states that "The United States government had signed more than four hundred treaties with Indians and had violated every single one of them."[3] Chairman Bill Richardson of the House Subcommittee on Indian Affairs, cites a smaller, though large enough, number of treaties but fully agrees with the end result: "Of the 1.8 million Native Americans, 603,000 live below the poverty line. . . . The U.S. vowed that Indians would be housed, educated and provided with decent health care. We have failed on nearly every count, and every one of the more than three hundred treaties with tribes has been broken."[4]

There are 510 federally recognized tribes (also known, in groups, as "nations") and 310 reservations, 278 of which are administered as federal Indian reservations. The total area of all Indian reservations comes to about four percent of the area of the United States. What was stolen, then, was not all the land, only ninety-six percent! The government retains a trusteeship over even the four percent.

It can be said that the dispensation finally came: they are now allowed to live—but not to expect reparations. The cessation of the outright genocide in a number of generations has made it possible for gradual self-improvement for a growing, though not large, number of Native Americans—a tribute to their extraordinary endurance, perseverance, and insistence on maintaining tribal cultures. Their recent birth rate is about twice the national average. Americans of all origins would do well to learn about the ways of life of their native predecessors, doubly so when considering the possibilities in socially mixed economies.

Primitive Communism among the Original Native Americans

Professor Zinn informs us that

> From the Adirondacks to the Great Lakes, in what is now Pennsylvania and upper New York, lived the most powerful of the northeastern tribes, the

League of the Iroquois, which included the Mohawks, Oneidas, Onondagas, Cayugas and Senecas, thousands of people bound together by a common Iroquois language. . . .

In the village of the Iroquois, land was owned in common and worked in common. Hunting was done together, and the catch was divided among the members of the village. Houses were considered common property and were shared by several families. The concept of private ownership of lands and homes was foreign to the Iroquois.

A French Jesuit priest who encountered them in the 1650s wrote: 'No poorhouses are needed among them, because they are neither mendicants nor paupers . . . Their kindness, humanity and courtesy not only makes them liberal with what they have, but causes them to possess hardly anything except in common.'

Women were important and respected in Iroquois society. Families were matrilineal. That is, the family line went down through the female members, whose husbands joined the family, while sons who married joined their wives' families. Each extended family lived in a 'long house.' When a woman wanted a divorce, she set her husband's things outside the door.

Families were grouped in clans, and a dozen or more clans might make up a village. The senior women in the village named the men who represented the clans at the village and tribal councils. They also named the forty-nine chiefs who were the ruling council for the Five Nation confederacy of the Iroquois. The women attended clan meetings, stood behind the circle of men who spoke and voted, and removed the men from office if they strayed too far from the wishes of the women.

The women tended the crops and took general charge of village affairs while the men were always hunting or fishing. And since they supplied the moccasins and food for warring expeditions, they had some control over military matters. As Gary B. Nash notes in his fascinating study of early America, *Red, White, and Black:* 'Thus power was shared between the sexes and the European idea of male dominance and female subordination in all things was conspicuously absent in Iroquois society.'

Children in Iroquois society, while taught the cultural heritage of their people and solidarity with the tribe, were also taught to be independent, not to submit to overbearing authority. They were taught equality in status and the sharing of possessions. The Iroquois did not use harsh punishment on children; they did not insist on early weaning or early toilet training, but gradually allowed the child to learn self-care.

All of this was in sharp contrast to European values as brought over by the first colonists, a society of rich and poor, controlled by priests, by governors, by male heads of families . . .

Gary Nash described Iroquois culture: 'No laws and ordinances, sheriffs and constables, judges and juries, or courts or jails . . . Yet boundaries of acceptable behavior were firmly set. Though priding themselves on the autonomous individual, the Iroquois maintained a strict sense of right and wrong . . . He who stole another's food or acted invalorously in war was "shamed" by his

> people and ostracized from their company until he had atoned for his actions and demonstrated to their satisfaction that he had purified himself.'
>
> Not only the Iroquois but other Indian tribes behaved the same way . . . They were people without a written language, but with their own laws, their poetry, their history kept in memory and passed on, in an oral vocabulary more complex than Europe's, accompanied by song, dance, and ceremonial drama. They paid careful attention to the development of personality, intensity of will, independence and flexibility, passion and potency, to their partnership with one another and with nature.[5]

The Conflict of Values

Native Americans could have adjusted to foreign ways had they wished to and had the foreigners treated them with normal consideration. For example, they could have created a written language had they felt the need for it. Proof of this can be seen when Sequoyah, chief of the Cherokees, simply invented one when, in his special circumstances, he found it advisable." The tribe bought its own printing press, and on February 21, 1828, he began publishing a newspaper, the *Cherokee Phoenix,* which appeared both in the English and the Cherokee languages.[6]

Among many Native Americans, the moral suasion of the old values persists into modern times. A 1993 report tells us: "Among the Sioux, generosity is the holiest virtue, and stinginess and greed are reviled. People share their bounty with family and friends, rather than save to build a better house or start a business."[7] If this is noteworthy in recent times, it is easy to see how Indian social values flew in the face of the crude, burgeoning capitalism of the eighteenth and nineteenth centuries.

Can the old be subversive of the new? Such thinking may well have been in line with the passage of the catastrophic Allotment Act of 1887, also known as the Dawes Act. Private property was to be forcibly imposed! Senator Henry Dawes told the senators and the nation that the Indians' handicap was their "communism" and that they had to learn "selfishness, which is at the bottom of civilization."

Almost half a century passed before the Dawes Act was finally declared invalid in 1934. By then the Indian nations had only 48 million acres left out of the 138 million they had occupied in 1887. Of what remained, 20 million acres were on arid land where little could be grown.[8]

Among those common people, however, who had firsthand experience with the natives, there was admiration for Indian communal values from the beginning. Like others who told of this, Benjamin Franklin wrote:

> When an Indian child has been brought up among us, yet if he goes to see his relations . . . there is no persuading him ever to return. But when white persons of either sex have been taken prisoner by the Indians and lived a while among them, tho' ransomed by their friends, and treated with all imaginable tenderness . . . yet in a short time they become disgusted with our manner of life, and

take the first opportunity of escaping again into the woods, from hence there is no reclaiming them.[9]

The Course of the Concessions

The first concession was the grant of fully effective citizenship. Specifying this for Native Americans would appear unnecessary, as it was ostensibly provided for all by the fourteenth amendment in 1868—but their rights under it were simply ignored. Nor could it have provided true citizenship rights, for in their circumstance they needed dual citizenship: to be recognized as a member of a sovereign tribe as well as a citizen of the United States at large. This was finally enacted in 1924, effective both on and off the reservation.

The second concession, notwithstanding overall control by Congress, was tribal ethnic sovereignty even where based on the practice of common property. Putting this concession into effect involved a series of Congressional actions following clear presidential statements. In 1968, Lyndon Johnson said: "We must affirm the rights of the first Americans to remain Indians while exercising their rights as Americans. We must affirm their rights to freedom of choice and self-determination."

Richard Nixon, who had been vice president in the termination era of the 1950s when the attempt was made to end tribal existence, denounced that policy in his 1970 Message to Congress, in a lengthy statement that came to be known as "the Nixon Declaration." It stated "the goal of any new national policy toward the Indian people: to strengthen the Indian sense of autonomy without threatening his sense of community."

In 1968, Congress prohibited states from acquiring any authority over Indian reservations without the consent of the affected tribe. An Indian Business Development Fund was created. The Indian Financing Act and the Native American Programs Act provided for loans to develop Indian resources. The Indian Self-Determination and Education Assistance Act of 1975 was important because it allowed Indian tribes to administer the federal government's programs on the reservation and thereby rid themselves of unnecessary domination. The Indian Mineral Development Act of 1982 gave tribes the flexibility to enter into joint-venture agreements with mineral developers. That year, the Indian Tribal Government Tax Status Act gave tribes many of the tax advantages of states, such as issuing tax exempt bonds to finance government programs.

The Indian Gaming Regulatory Act of 1988 has had dramatic results bringing wealth to those reservations in which casinos were viable, but nothing to lift other reservations out of their misery or to help that half of the Indian population who live elsewhere—off the reservation.

Policy changes as such have been progressive, but Indian tribal sovereignty has by no means been made absolute. The Supreme Court has held that the Commerce Clause and the Treaty Clause in the Constitution provide Congress with all it requires for complete control over Indian affairs. The Supreme Court has also cited two other justifications. The first is a rule of international law that states, "Discovery and conquest [give] the conquerors sovereignty over the lands thus obtained." In other words, to the victor belong the spoils. Second, there is the doctrine of trust responsibility. The promise in most treaties to "protect" the tribe gives the government "the duty to regulate Indians for their protection." Such are the arbitrary notions called principles.[10]

Notes

1. Hans Koning, *The Conquest of America* (New York: Monthly Review Press, 1993), 11-12.
2. Herbert Aptheker, *Early Years of the Republic* (New York: International Publishers, 1990), 119.
3. Howard Zinn, *A People's History of the United States* (New York: Harper & Row, 1980), 515.
4. Bill Richardson, "More Power to the Tribes," *New York Times Op-Ed*, 7 July 1993.
5. Zinn, *People's History*, 19-22.
6. ———, *People's History*, 135-36.
7. Timothy Egan, "150 Years Later, Indians Cope with Bitter Results of Whites' Arrival," *New York Times*, 1 June 1993.
8. Koning, *Conquest of America*, 104.
9. ———, *Conquest of America*, 61.
10. Stephen L. Pevar, *ACLU Handbook: The Rights of Indians and Tribes*, 2nd ed. (Carbondale: Southern Illinois University Press, 1992), 8-9 with footnoted attributions.

Chapter 6

Double Trouble for Women

The Great American Precursors

Why did it have to take 130 years for American women (of any class!) to win their first major concession, the right to vote? Was it that, in addition to the same struggle as men against various oppressors, they had to struggle against male overlordship? Listen to Abigail Adams, writing in March of 1776 to her husband, the future second president:

> In the new code of laws which I suppose it will be necessary for you to make, I desire you would remember the ladies, and be more generous to them than your ancestors. Do not put such unlimited power in the hands of husbands. Remember, all men would be tyrants if they could. If particular care and attention are not paid to the ladies, we are determined to foment a rebellion, and will not hold ourselves bound to obey the laws in which we have no voice of representation.[1]

The great conservative, John Adams, responded by trying to laugh it off, trivializing his "saucy" wife's argument with a joke, but ended seriously by noting that her code of laws, if enacted, would lead to social disorder, and said: "Depend upon it, we know better than to repeal our Masculine systems."[2] And how did the greatest voice among the progressives of that day, Thomas Jefferson, treat such matters? He underscored his phrase "all men are created equal" by stating that American women would be "too wise to wrinkle their foreheads with politics."[3]

By the time the settlers invaded North America, the traditional ruling leaders had so thoroughly subordinated women that their degradation was close to that of slaves, with the added requirement of sexual services to be cheerfully and willingly performed.

Women simply had no rights; no legal redress against abuse, as husbands had the "right to chastise;" no property, as even inherited property went to the husband; no right to retain even earned income when such was allowed—and therefore, simply no means of any kind to live independently. Sexual activity outside of marriage led to "bastardy" for which the woman alone was held responsible and severely punished, the man being judged to have responded naturally to female attractions with normal urgency.

Was it always so? Not at all. If we look back to societal development in primitive times, all the evidence then, and for some time after, points to a natural division of labor, a mutually respectful, joint development of the means of survival.

With many pregnancies required for enough infants to survive for the propagation of the species, along with providing the extra hands needed to face the harsh challenges of their circumstances, women nursed children as long as necessary while gathering and preparing sixty percent of the food to sustain men faced with hunting for meat. Women even developed much of the arts and crafts. They, therefore, had no problem being regarded as equal partners. The mysteries of the mother-child relationship and its bonding effect caused the earliest expression of religion to involve references to Mother-Goddesses.

In primitive communist societies, whether practicing group marriage, the pairing marriage, or whatever, uninhibited by modern hypocrisy, the identity of a particular father was always uncertain, but the identity of the mother was obvious. It was therefore normal for familial descent and such heritage as mattered to be matrilineal (and matrilocal). Neither matriarchy nor patriarchy was known to exist. People learned from experience to avoid in-breeding and the practice developed of securing marital partners from neighboring gens (familial clans). Back then, and in such primitive communist societies as continued into modern times, surpluses for exchange and personal gain were not produced. Plant and animal products served only for immediate consumption or were stored for later use. Personal domination held no material benefit and could only disrupt the cooperation essential for survival.

In a brilliant and comprehensive historical study, Professor Gerda Lerner[4] explores how this changed through the ages with the development of patriarchy, the inter-tribal "exchange of women" in the Neolithic development of agriculture, and the ways in which women became a resource and were commodified—and all that followed in the complexities of societal development.

When trying to learn about their past, women faced an enormous handicap: their virtually complete exclusion from written history. The men who wrote it simply ignored them. The extraordinarily large number of outstanding women who left their marks on their times could not know their predecessors' accomplishments or how they had achieved them. This forced women to rebuild the struggle starting from scratch each time, until very recently, when women historians (and some men), with great difficulty, dug out the facts.

Winning the Vote

The struggle for women's rights was worldwide. It was not until the first sixty-three years of the twentieth century—and scattered throughout those years—that women's suffrage was enacted by 107 countries listed in the Handbook of International Data on Women. The United States became the fourteenth when it ratified the nineteenth amendment in 1920. Up until a few years before, the movement was limited to seeking suffrage state by state and had, in fact, won it in fifteen, beginning as far back as 1869, in Wyoming.

In the aggressive atmosphere of World War I, the association of the women's movement with pacifism tended to set it back, but under Carrie Chapman Catt's leadership, pacifism was de-emphasized and the country's need for women's active participation was brought to the fore. She began by exploiting Wilson's claim that the war was being fought for democracy, which she declared, begins at home. It was unwise to deprive women of the vote just when their war-work was needed. In fact, the country was relying on the efforts both of middle-class clubwomen who were selling war bonds, saving food and organizing benefits for the troops, as well as the efforts of working-class women who were taking on factory jobs left by enlisted men.

During the war, the membership of the National American Woman Suffrage Association doubled, reaching its peak of two million by 1919. It was pressing hard. At the same time, the pacifist National Woman's Party was picketing the White House. It was like a one-two punch, beating down President Wilson's resistance. On January 9, 1918, he called on House Democrats to support the federal amendment as "an act of right and justice" and the next day the House endorsed women's suffrage. Later that year, Wilson told the more reluctant Senate that the amendment was "vital to the winning of the war," but it was not until after the war, on June 4, 1919, that the Senate finally agreed. Fourteen months later the thirty-sixth state brought final ratification of the nineteenth amendment. Now no state could deny the vote "on account of sex."[5]

The Banning of Child Labor

The second great concession won by organized women was the ending of child labor. They had always, throughout their diversified history, been deeply dedicated to this cause. Early in the nineteenth century, the utopian socialist Frances Wright demanded that, instead of labor, education should be provided for children from the age of two on. In the abolitionist movement, and then in the Reconstruction period, and later as well, white women teachers made special efforts to work with black children.

Early in the twentieth century, there was action by labor leaders like "Mother" Mary Harris Jones, who led a parade of child workers from New Jersey and New York out to Oyster Bay on Long Island where President Theodore Roosevelt refused to see them. Women workers were acting in factory disputes to aid children who had gone on strike.

Just as they had turned President Wilson around on suffrage, women turned him around on child labor. He had opposed legislation against it on legalistic grounds, but along with Republicans, who had been brought around to stand against child labor, Wilson was finally persuaded, in his 1916 campaign, to come out strongly for the Keating-Owen Act and later signed it.[6] However, the Supreme Court declared it unconstitutional in 1918. Congress passed a constitutional amendment in 1924, but it was ratified by only six states.

Child labor was finally outlawed in interstate commerce as part of the Fair Labor Standards Act in 1938, and here again a woman was involved: Frances Perkins, Secretary of Labor in Franklin Roosevelt's administration. In the following years, all states passed laws regulating the employment of children.

The Winning of Equal Education

A third concession to women, granted very slowly over the whole course of American history and still not fully enforced equally with men, consists of the opportunities for advanced education and culture, especially for such learning as could lead to earned placement in leading positions in the vocations, in the professions, and in all levels of government.

The cost of free public education for underclass people—and almost all women were treated as if underclass—had traditionally been judged worthwhile only to prepare them for such vocational service as the times required. It had its tragi-comic aspects. A 1642 law in colonial Massachusetts specified that boys were to be taught reading and writing, but girls only reading! By 1771, this had progressed to the point where, among children apprenticed under the Poor Laws, boys were to be taught reading, writing, and "ciphering," which we can take to mean a bit of arithmetic, but girls were to be taught only reading and writing!

Until 1837, women could not enroll in any college or university. By 1870, they were 21 percent of all undergraduates, by 1880, 32 percent and by 1910 almost 40 percent. It was not until 1920, when women were 47 percent of college undergraduates, that women were beginning to reach equal access with men to college education. Yet in 1960, women were only 35 percent of all students with a B.A., or other first professional degree, and only 10 percent had doctorates.

The way women had to struggle for equal access to education in the United States is the same as it was in Europe: each level had to be separately and consecutively conquered. Resistance by individual men and by male-controlled establishments was relentless and unwavering. Women had to fight first for the right to learn, then for the right to teach, and finally for the right to affect the content of learning—a right still in the process of being won.[7]

Of special value in assuring durability of gains made and serious attention to further advances is the general institutionalization of women's studies programs, which rose most rapidly in the second half of the twentieth century. By the middle 1970s, some eighty institutions were already offering such programs and some two thousand courses were available on about five hundred other campuses. At the turn of the century, it was difficult to find a college anywhere in the country that was not offering courses in women's studies.

The High Hurdles of Property Rights

A fourth concession to women was the gaining over time of their right to independent ownership and control of property. Due to the general influence of independent property as a main aim of the Revolution, as well as differences in availability of land and other resources between the colonies and Britain, that right for women had its beginnings even before the Revolution.

Like all other rights for women, it was blighted by the heavy hand of male supremacy in the common law brought over from England. The classic eighteenth century British jurist, Sir William Blackstone, put it bluntly:

> By marriage the husband and wife are one person in law, that is, *the very being or existence of the woman is suspended during the marriage,* or at least is incorporated and consolidated into that of the husband, under whose wing, protection, and *cover* she performs everything; and is, therefore, called in our law-French a *feme-covert,* is said to be *covert-baron,* or under the protection and influence of her husband, her baron, or lord; and her condition during her marriage is called her *coverture.* Upon this principle, of a union of person in husband and wife, depend almost all the legal rights, duties, and disabilities that either of them acquire by the marriage.[8] *(Emphasis added)*

While such imported fantasies of legalism were at the outset deemed to be absolute law by force of custom, many departures cropped up in the uniquely American conditions of existence. There were many examples of women owning and managing farms, plantations, and other enterprises as inherited estates, which at their deaths, were to go to male heirs. This male preference would not last many years.[9]

Women had been eagerly awaited in the colonies, whether they came indentured to Virginia planters, in the hire of New Amsterdam merchants, or sheltered in New England families. Occasionally, a village or colony would allocate land to women. The town of Salem set out small maid-lots, and Pennsylvania offered seventy-five acres to all women over the age of fourteen.

In both New England and the South a colonial widow was assured of receiving at least one-third of her deceased husband's estate. The partial nature of women's freedom was reflected in the saying "The wife may be sovereign in her husband's absence but she must be subject in his presence." However, the fact that the household economy, at a time when the overwhelming mass of the population was engaged in agriculture, would have been crippled without the decisive labor of women, was bound to create growing respect for women's property rights.

Archaic remnants of British common law such as primogeniture and entail were out of existence in the United States within fifteen years after the Revolution.[10] About 1830, a widespread demand arose for the enactment of laws favoring married women's property. Between 1839 and 1850 most states passed legislation addressing this issue in some form. At least for future marriages, in such states, the husband would lose his traditional common-law estate in his wife's real property, as well as his right to her chattels, money, and "choses in action."

> Long before 1850 practically all vestiges of feudal land tenures had been abolished in the original states and one tenure had been substituted as basic, namely, freehold tenure in fee simple; and the principle of equal distribution among children, saving the widow's special share, had become the general rule applicable in cases where the owner died intestate. As feudal tenures were never introduced in the Western states, the rule of freehold tenure in fee simple and the principles of equal distribution were more easily established there as a matter of course.
>
> In this legal development the daughters of landowners became landowners in increasing numbers. Besides, owing to the amount and cheapness of land, unmarried women could acquire and did acquire, by various methods of purchase, inheritance, and devise, land holdings in all parts of the country, especially in the West. In this way their economic power was enlarged, and additional reasons were provided for modifying the common-law rules respecting the power of the husband over the wife's real and personal property.[11]

By 1890, state legislatures had removed the most objectionable legal bars to women's property rights. Little remained in the twentieth century to be fine-tuned in equalizing the property rights of men and women. However, an overshadowing problem that remained for women was how to earn sufficient income to acquire property.

The Unending Struggle for Equal Rights as Workers

A fifth concession to women may be said to consist of the 1963 so-called Equal Pay Law, which was strengthened, to some extent, by the 1964 and 1991 Civil Rights Acts and various executive orders. Unfortunately, these were all so narrowly drawn and bogged down by pettifogging interpretation that the concession cannot be said to have been an actual full winning of equal pay, but rather the establishment of equal pay as a legal principle. This facilitated the long-running battle of women's organizations and trade unionists, including male progressives, which did result in advances toward equality.

Lower wages for women, and its utility in lowering wages and working conditions for men, was a direct benefit to employers. This benefit has been the constant capitalist incentive to favor age-old practices of male domination and the promotion of false notions of "natural" female inferiority, and an alleged lack of financial need by women workers ostensibly supported by husbands, all the while avoiding acknowledgement of actual relative productivity. The latter statistic is always strangely missing from the plethora of business facts and figures.

Economic inferiority for women was imposed as customary at the birth of the nation. How employers did this is exemplified in the closing years of the eighteenth century by the Rhode Island textile firm of Samuel Slater, the first to utilize machinery on a scale that demanded a large, permanent labor force. Slater recruited entire families. Once transplanted from farm to factory, its inner hierarchy was translated into a wage scale.

A Massachusetts father contracted with Slater for the following pay: $5.00 a week for himself, but only $2.33 for his sister; $2.00 for his sixteen-year-old son; $1.50 for a son and a nephew, both thirteen years old; $1.25 for a twelve-year-old daughter; 83 cents and 75 cents for two girls, ten and eight years old respectively.

As the operation of factory equipment became simpler, it commanded lower wages and was increasingly delegated to women and children. An 1816 report on the U.S. cotton industry listed sixty-six thousand women operatives, twenty-four thousand boys and only ten thousand adult men. The piecework of a diligent seamstress in Philadelphia in 1829 would seldom bring her more than $1.25 in a six-day week. After paying her rent and fuel, she was left with 50 cents for food, clothing and medical expenses. In the 1830s in Lowell, Massachusettes, a day's pay for a typical male factory worker ranged from 85 cents to $2.00, but only 40 cents to 80 cents for women.

Inhumane conditions added to such exploitation often touched off defiant actions by women workers and many strikes were recorded—some marked by violence—from 1820 to 1850. There was a bit of a prospect for change when the Civil War took place. So many men were involved that many new employment opportunities were opened up for women—and a prospect for organized activity on a larger scale.[12]

In the situation in which women found themselves, trade unions appeared to be part of the solution—but were often part of the problem. Many male trade unionists were openly hostile, especially during unemployment situations resulting from the end of the Civil War. They felt women shouid be driven out of the trades and barred from joining their unions. Such a simple solution, however, was impossible. Economic necessity had brought thousands of women into industry, many of whose husbands had been killed or seriously wounded in that very bloody conflict.

The government had something to say on the subject also. Employers read with interest the report of General Travis Elias Spinner who had introduced fifteen hundred women into government offices during the war. Not only was the experiment a success but he reported that women were "doing more and better work for $900 per annum than many male clerks who were paid double that amount."

Some unions followed an enlightened policy. For example, a resolution adopted in June 1865 by the New York Journeyman Tailors' Union urged its members to "make every effort necessary to induce the female operatives of the trade to join this association, inasmuch as thereby the best protection is secured for ourselves as well as for the female operatives." However, since many unions were not prepared to accept women, they were often forced to form their own organizations.

During the post-Civil War era unions were formed by women cigar makers, collar workers, tailoresses and seamstresses, umbrella sewers, cap makers, textile workers, printers, furnishers, laundresses, and shoemakers. A number of organized workingmen, including some prominent trade union leaders, helped them organize, even sometimes going so far as to go out on sympathy strikes when employers tried to ban women trade unionists. A high mark had been set at the founding convention of the National Labor Union in 1866 when—for the first time in American history—a national labor federation resolved "to persuade or force employers to do justice to women by paying them equal pay for equal work."

The difficulties, however, proved too great for the separate women's unions to endure and by 1872 most had disappeared. New hope arose with the founding of the American Federation of Labor in 1886 when it spoke in favor of its affiliates organizing and admitting women to their ranks—but it soon became clear that little would be done to bring this about. Women could make progress only by taking things into their own hands, so Mary Kenney, one of only four women at the A.F.L. convention, founded the Women's Trade Union League and, in succeeding years, trained a good number of women who became outstanding labor leaders.

The problem was that women were largely relegated to less-skilled and unskilled jobs, while the A.F.L., under Samuel Gompers, was oriented toward becoming an aristocracy of labor. By limiting themselves to higher-skilled workers, they could often make deals with employers by failing to protect or by simply neglecting lower paid workers. An historic example of how devastating this policy could be came in the great Lawrence textile strike in the winter of 1911-12, when the strike was finally settled in a deal for the higher skilled workers that abandoned the interests of others. Twenty thousand workers had been involved, half of them women and children, and the bitter outcome had a deeply demoralizing effect.

The lesson was not lost on the many women now developing as effective leaders in the unions and other organizations. Before further and lasting improvements could be won in wages and working conditions, they would have to fight concurrently on all other fronts where they were being denied their rights, with a good possibility of finding progressive men who would lend support.[13]

The Spread of Ancillary Rights

Winning the right to vote in 1920 encouraged women to strike out for other gains. The League of Women Voters, successor to NAWSA, joined with the Women's Joint Congressional Committee (the umbrella organization for the country's principal women's groups) to educate the electorate, democratize politics, and press for reform legislation. Politicians had to respond. In symbolic recognition that politics no longer belonged only to men, officials moved polling places from saloons and barber shops to schools.

Democrats and Republicans both appointed women as equal members of their national committees and named women to government posts. Congress established the Women's Bureau in the Department of Labor 1920 to monitor women's working conditions; passed the Cable Act in 1922 giving women equal citizenship rights with men; and in 1924 sent a child labor amendment to the states for ratification.

Action grew in states also. By 1925, twenty had passed laws letting women serve on juries. Michigan and Montana passed equal-pay laws, and Wisconsin passed an equal rights act. All but four states agreed to limit working women's hours; eighteen states prescribed rest periods and meal hours; sixteen prohibited night work in certain occupations; and thirteen had minimum wage regulations. A few gains were made even in the long resistant South where Virginia, for example, granted reformers eighteen of their twenty-four requests, including a children's code and a vocational education law.[14]

While such gains helped to build a sense of empowerment and elements of progress they did not to any significant extent bring with them the enforcement of equal pay—until the nation came to experience two profound exigencies: the Great Depression and World War II. The first (see chapter 7) made it a life-and-death matter for men and women to cooperate in the bitter class struggle of the time, and the second necessarily opened up extraordinary opportunities.

Secretary of War Stimson was compelled by circumstance to issue a pamphlet to businessmen saying: "You're Going to Employ Women." Women began to handle jobs—and handle them well—that had been thought manageable only by men. There was even an effort to require private military contractors to give women equal pay, as in the case of Brown & Sharp, but such proved to be the exception rather than the rule. In the military itself, however, equal pay did become the rule, applying as it did then to women professionals who had to be brought in as officers.

There were even a number of women pilots, who actually made most of the airplane deliveries. By the end of the war, hundreds of thousands of women were in uniform as clerical workers, nurses and the like, earning equal pay with men in the same rank.

Civilian employers maintained wage differentials every chance they had, even though women became upwardly mobile during wartime's labor scarcity and their median income outside the military rose almost 40 percent. For black women, some minor improvements were also made in job opportunities but discrimination remained rife, notwithstanding the creation in 1941 of the federal Fair Employment Practices Commission. Twenty years later, John F. Kennedy appointed a presidential Commission on the Status of Women, but not much was accomplished by this one either.

All experience in the women's movement pointed to the need for strong independent action, especially through the unions with the support of as many progressive men as could be won to their side. Whatever has been done along these lines has been responsible for reducing the wage differential to its current levels. In the 1990s, the average pay of women appeared to have stabilized at about 70 percent of men's pay for the same or equivalent work.

Setting the Control of a Woman's Body

The sixth concession to women was the most fundamental: the governmental institution of a woman's right to control the use of her body, exemplified in the right to choose whether to proceed with a pregnancy or to abort it in good time. Involved here was more than a grant by a ruling class to an underclass. What remained as a stubborn enemy was the age-old obscurantism of the various religious hierarchies and other male supremacists in which mystical views of the nature of life and society were used to keep women under the control of their male masters.

An enormous amount of struggle was put up but here we can only touch on the highlights, beginning in the turbulent 1960s. After lobbying by women's groups, President Lyndon Johnson signed an executive order in 1967 banning sexual discrimination in federally connected employment and, in the years that followed, women's groups demanded its enforcement.

NOW, the National Organization for Women, which had been formed in 1966, initiated over a thousand lawsuits against corporations charging sexual discrimination.

The right to abortion was made a major issue. Before 1970, about a million abortions were done every year, of which only about ten thousand were legal. Perhaps a third of the women having illegal abortions, mostly poor people, had to be hospitalized for complications. How many thousands died as a result of botched illegal abortions no one really knows. Court actions to do away with the laws against abortion were begun in over twenty states between 1968 and 1970, and public opinion grew stronger, favoring the right of women to decide on this personal matter without government interference. A Harris Poll in the spring of 1969 showed that 64 percent of those polled thought the decision on abortion was a private matter.

Finally, in early 1973, the Supreme Court decided in *Roe v. Wade* that the state could prohibit abortions only in the last three months of pregnancy, that it could regulate abortion for health purposes during the second three months, and that during the first three months a woman and her doctor had the right to decide.

This great breakthrough stimulated the bringing up of other issues. There was a push for child care centers and, although not much help came from government, thousands of cooperative child care centers were set up. Women also began to speak openly about the problem of rape. Fifty thousand rapes were being reported each year and many more went unreported. Many women campaigned to get ERA, the Equal Rights Amendment, passed by enough states to become part of the Constitution but did not succeed.

Much "consciousness-raising" was accomplished in innumerable meetings across the country with frank talk about what had for so long been kept secret, a cause for shame and embarrassment, such as menstruation, masturbation, menopause, abortion, and lesbianism. A highly influential book appeared in the early 1970s, assembled by eleven women in the Boston Women's Health Book Collective, called "Our Bodies, Ourselves."[15]

The Breadwinner Made Permanently Plural

In the middle 1990s the struggle for women's rights found itself facing increased violent and venomous attacks on abortion rights, with threats to women's liberation in general coming from reactionary politicians, right-wing religionists, and other male supremacists. At the same time, the economic struggle had intensified. During the preceding twenty years or so, the real wages (which take inflation into account) had come down about 20 percent for American workers in general. The result was that many women who might have preferred to care for small children at home or to work part-time found themselves forced into the labor force full-time. A significant change in economic relations between men and women was going on.

In the spring of 1995 it could already be reported, that according to a new survey by Louis Harris & Associates Inc., more than half the women surveyed, single and married, said they provided at least half the income of their households—and 18 percent said they were their household's sole provider. Even among married women, 48 percent said they provided half or more of the family income. At the same time, 64 percent of the women in married-couple households said their husbands' jobs offered more financial security than their own jobs.[16]

In the same period, the reason for this had in part been made clear in a report about the "glass ceiling" by a federal commission bearing that name. White men, while only 43 percent of the work force, held about 95 out of 100 senior management positions, defined as vice president and above. White women had taken nearly 40 percent of jobs nationwide, compared with 30 percent three decades before, but they typically counted as less than 5 percent of senior managers in industries across the nation. As for middle management, such as assistant vice presidents and office managers, the 1990 census confirmed that white women held close to 40 percent of those jobs and black women about 5 percent, with black men holding about 4 percent.[17]

Putting the World on Notice

Barbaric practices against girls and women in backward countries have persisted all through the generations in which advances have been won for women in more civilized places. Knowing how arduous its own struggle has been, the women's movement in various advanced countries has learned, at least in the last quarter of the twentieth century, that to fail to act against the barbarism can only endanger their own reforms. After all, the same centers of reactionary male supremacy and right-wing religiosity are active everywhere.

World Press Review reports that the international women's movement grew "dramatically in size, diversity and clout" in the twenty-five years from the first United Nations women's conference in 1975 to the fifth in June of 2000. Although women's Non-Governmental Organizations (NGOs)

> have become key players on the international scene, and are exerting a marked influence on national policies and programs in many countries, women continue to be startlingly underrepresented in elected office. Only 13.5 percent of legislators worldwide are women The parliaments of only nine countries—the five Nordic states, Germany, the Netherlands, South Africa and Mozambique—have female membership of 30 percent or more. (The United States ranks 46th in the world, with 13.3 percent.) [18]

A remarkable Declaration and Platform for Action had been unanimously adopted at the fourth World Conference in Beijing in 1995. As summarized by Katha Pollitt,

> The documents link women's rights to human rights for the first time in UN history and lay out detailed and ambitious plans for the advancement of girls and women on twelve fronts, including health, political decision-making, education and economic opportunity. The platform calls for universal access to family planning, sex education, equal inheritance rights, and the prevention and punishment of rape and domestic violence, and it condemns job discrimination, forced marriage, coercion in family planning and population programs, female infanticide, female genital mutilation, unsafe abortion (although the right to abortion itself is not mentioned), dowry-related violence and other harmful and unjust practices. It connects women's rights to poverty, environmental degradation, global inequality, warfare and various evils that affect women disparately.[19]

There had been a considerable wariness about the fifth women's world conference at the UN in New York, also known as Beijing Plus Five, as reactionary opponents were expected to try to force some backtracking—but such efforts did not work. Instead, the documents supported the entire Beijing platform and even went beyond on some points. There were delegations from 180 nations and representatives of about 1,200 nongovernmental organizations.

They took strong stands against trafficking of women and girls across borders for the sex trade or for domestic or industrial work that often amounts to wage slavery. They called for punishment of domestic violence, including marital rape, which some delegations had argued was essentially a private matter not recognized as a crime in many nations. There were also calls to outlaw the killings of women whose families claim that they have shamed them, so-called "honor" crimes that have drawn attention to countries like Jordan and Pakistan. They demanded more attention be paid to the H.I.V.-AIDS epidemic, especially in Africa, where the sexual rights of women are a matter of life and death—

where traditions within extended families or clans may force girls or women into sexual arrangements they cannot avoid with men they may know to be infected with H.I.V.[20]

One may well expect the internationalization of the women's movement to enhance the struggle for equal rights in individual countries. UN declarations may not have the force of law, but they do carry continuing moral influence. There was great enthusiasm at Beijing and Beijing Plus Five.

Notes

1. Howard Zinn, *A People's History of the United States* (New York: Harper & Row, 1980), 109.
2. Gerda Lerner, *Women and History*, vol. 2, *The Creation of Feminist Consciousness From the Middle Ages to Eighteen-Seventy* (New York: Oxford University Press, 1993), 9.
3. Zinn, *People's History*, 109.
4. Gerda Lerner, *Women and History*, vol. 1, *The Creation of Patriarchy* (New York: Oxford University Press, 1986), 212-13.
5. Rosalind Rosenberg, *Divided Lives: American Women in the Twentieth Century* (New York: Hill and Wang [Farrar, Straus, Giroux], 1992), 72.
6. Philip S. Foner, *History of the Labor Movement in the United States*, vol. 6, *On the Eve of America's Entrance into World War I* (New York: International Publishers, 1982), 230 fn.
7. Lerner, vol. 2, *Feminist Consciousness*, 42-45.
8. Rosenberg, *Divided Lives*, 245-46.
9. Mary Ritter Beard, *Woman as a Force in History* (New York: Macmillan, 1946), 120-21, 20-39.
10. Mary P. Ryan, *Womanhood in America: From Colonial Times to the Present*, 3rd ed. (New York: Franklin Watts, 1983), 20-26.
11. Beard, *Woman as a Force in History*, 130.
12. Ryan, *Womanhood in America*, 84-85.
13. Philip S. Foner, *History of the Labor Movement in the United States*, vol. 1, *From Colonial Times to the Founding of the American Federation of Labor* (New York: International Publishers, 1982), 382-88.
14. Rosenberg, *Divided Lives*, 73-74.
15. Zinn, *People's History*, 499-501.
16. Tamar Lewin, "Women Are Becoming Equal Providers," *New York Times*, 11 May 1995.
17. Peter T. Kilborn, "Women and Minorities Still Face 'Glass Ceiling,'" *New York Times*, 16 March 1995.
18. Margaret Bald, "Women Out Front for Change" *World Press Review* 47, no. 6 (June 2000): 6.
19. Katha Pollitt, "Women: Two Steps Forward, One Step Back?" *Nation* 270, no. 25 (26 June 2000): 10.
20. Barbara Crossette, "Rights Gains are Preserved at U.N. Forum on Women," *New York Times*, 11 June 2000.

Chapter 7

The Movement toward an Economic Bill of Rights

Social Revolt in the Great Depression

The cluster of concessions and reforms which have come to bear the label of the New Deal did not spring full-blown from the brow of Franklin D. Roosevelt. They evolved—as did FDR himself—in the school of hard knocks, the Depression. That unprecedented and comprehensive economic crisis, which refused to behave like an ordinary business cycle, persisted in its devastating damage through the entire decade of the 1930s. The concept of the so-called welfare state which had its difficult birth in those years was equally unprecedented in the century and a half of the nation's previous existence.

Much has been made of Black Thursday, October 24, 1929, when the Wall Street Crash began and was extended in the incredible two-and-a-half-year decline in the stock market. The fact is, however, that the Depression itself began generally six months before and in some parts of the economy even earlier. The facts were not a secret but such was the lustful mood of speculation at the time that the significance of the facts was simply ignored by almost everyone on Wall Street. There were rare exceptions, such as Paul M. Warburg.[1]

John Kenneth Galbraith has analyzed five major reasons for the extraordinary depth and duration of the Depression but it suffices for this study to note only the first of these: in brief, the bad distribution of income. The five percent of the population with the highest incomes in 1929 received approximately one-third of all personal income. And compared with the years following the Second World War, the income of the well-to-do in 1929 was about twice as great.[2]

It seems clear that when FDR presented the New Deal as a campaign slogan he had no definite idea what it would come to mean. His first innovation as president, the National Recovery Act, had little in common with the later concessions. It was more like Mussolini's notions of the corporate state and, fortunately, the Supreme Court declared it unconstitutional—because it would have privatized the law-making right of Congress. Nevertheless, it also seems clear that he did want to find constructive solutions to the vexing social problems of the country. The clamor of the people made it evident he had better do so if the capitalist system itself was to survive.

On March 6, 1930, close to a million people around the country were said to have held demonstrations for unemployment insurance, with the Communists actively involved. From then on, when people unable to pay their rent were evicted and put out on the street with their furniture, there were thousands of instances where spontaneous groups would quickly appear and move them back into their apartments—and if utilities were turned off they would reconnect them. When auctions were scheduled at foreclosed farms, neighbors would gang up with their rifles in hand and prevent the sale. Newspapers were declaiming "insurrection."

Early in 1932, the nation was stunned and angered by the bloodying of the Bonus Army. Twenty thousand veterans of World War I, some alone, some with wives and children, surmounted great difficulty to come to Washington. They brought the certificates for the bonus due them in later years, demanding they be paid now when the money was desperately needed. Some camped in government buildings, but most were in rubbish-rigged lean-tos, crates, and huts across the Potomac, on Anacostia Flats. The House passed such a bill, the Senate refused, and President Hoover ordered the Army to evict them. General Douglas MacArthur and his aide Major Dwight D. Eisenhower led cavalry, infantry, machine gun, and tank detachments, attacking the unarmed veterans and families with tear gas and gunfire and setting fire to the entire encampment, resulting in some deaths and many injuries. To quote a famous FDR phrase out of a very different context nine years later, it was "a day that will live in infamy."

Strikes against wage cuts and other abuses were ever more frequent and often violent. More than a million and a half workers were out on strike in 1934 alone, including hundreds of thousands of textile workers in the South. When the longshoremen all along the west coast went on strike that year against the shape-up[3] and other abuses, they were backed by the teamsters and the maritime workers. When two strikers were killed by police gunfire, there was great protest expressed during the mass funeral processions, leading to a general strike that shut down the entire city of San Francisco. A general strike is politically close enough to revolution to set alarm bells ringing among the powers that be.

The innumerable acts of small and large revolt reflected the cataclysmic nature of the Depression. There was absolutely no cushion, no provision for the 25 percent thrown out of work; for those still on the job facing ruinous wage cuts, speed-up, and long hours; for people whose life savings were lost to venal bankers; for the sick who had no health insurance; for the elderly, both those whose pensions had been robbed and those denied pensions altogether.

People were no longer paying traditional respect to those in high places. This also had its effect on the official leaders of the A.F.L. who could no longer hold workers in check. The Congress of Industrial Organizations (C.I.O.) was becoming too powerful for things to remain as they were in the labor movement—and, heaven forbid, making use of Communists as organizers.

Concessions to Improve Conditions

If Roosevelt's early ventures with the National Recovery Act and the Agricultural Adjustment Administration could be said to have favored big business and the big farmers, it could also be said, on balance, that his venture with the Tennessee Valley Authority was virtually socialistic. Here was the government "going into business," creating a substantial system of dams and hydroelectric plants in seven southern states that gave jobs to the unemployed and lowered electric rates to consumers of all kinds. TVA was a huge success, both for the people and for business development. Utilities who had rooked investors and customers with their innumerable phony holding companies and watered stock issues were in no position to block it.

The New Deal's first major direct concession came in 1935, when making good use of Senator Robert F. Wagner, Roosevelt secured enactment of the National Labor Relations Act, which supported the right of workers to organize trade unions. It remains important even though it was partially gutted twelve years later when the Taft-Hartley Act was passed in 1947 over President Truman's veto. The Wagner Act was intended, and still works to a degree, not only to give labor a badly needed break, but also to promote stability in labor relations.

The second and even more salutary concession came that same year, also with Wagner's help, in the Social Security Act, which provided for employer and employee payments to be put into a retirement fund, federal financing for states to set up unemployment insurance systems, and money to match state funds for mothers and dependent children. Over the years it grew into a highly important social benefit, so firmly entrenched by now that long-continued efforts by reactionaries to dislodge it have not succeeded.

If anything characterizes the "welfare state" at least in elementary ways, it is just such measures as these, among others. It can be argued with some justification that when statesmen like Franklin Roosevelt adopt such measures it is done to save capitalism, but the fact remains that they are not genetic to the economic system, not functionally essential to the profit-making exploitation of labor which is the fundamental operation of a capitalist economy. In a genetic sense, they are normal or essential only in a socialist system, one that exists not for private profit but only for service to its people.

While it is true that the highly industrialized, leading capitalist countries make use of such social welfare measures, developed through generations of class struggle marked by close experience with combative socialist movements, it is also true that there are repressive regimes that abhor even the mention of such measures and manage to exploit labor quite thoroughly without them, proving that the system as such is amoral.

A capitalist ruling class may resolve a conflict of interest with an underclass by adopting socialistic measures that meet people's needs without unraveling democratic capitalist operations or threatening the viability of the system. To do so is only socially mixing the economy. It is not moving fundamentally either to enhance or destroy that economy. More than anything else it is accepting a necessity to make room for the march of civilization.

In 1938, a third and a fourth concession were made as parts of the Fair Labor Standards Act, which established both a minimum wage and a forty-hour work week with time-and-a-half for overtime. The minimum wage then set was paltry, twenty-five cents an hour, but the social justice principle it established for labor relations was as important as it was unprecedented and encouraged the labor movement to force it up from time to time. The importance of the forty-hour work week was obvious, a historic climax to a century and a half of innumerable hard-fought struggles in the Ten-Hour Movement beginning in 1791, and the Eight-Hour Movement that swept across the nation after the Civil War.

Reforms to Solve Social Problems

The administration of FDR initiated an extraordinary series of reforms to counter the social damage done by a dangerously anarchic system of so-called free enterprise. In what became famous as the First Hundred Days came the setting up of the Securities and Exchange Commission to supervise stock market regulation, the creation of the Federal Deposit Insurance Corporation to protect people's savings, and many other reforms.

He could not end the Depression or the full stretch of unemployment resulting from past capitalist savagery, but he did much to ameliorate the condition of the people and prepare the country for the problems it would face in World War II. Young people benefited with moderate pay but healthful outdoor forestry work in the Civilian Conservation Corps. Funds were provided to the states to feed the hungry through the Federal Emergency Relief Administration. Jobs were provided in various ways through the Civil Works Administration, the Public Works Administration, and the Works Project Administration.

One cannot fully appreciate the civilizing aspects of the New Deal without knowing the benefits for a great many people that resulted from funding the Federal Theater Project, the Federal Writers Project, and the Federal Art Project, through the years until they ended in 1939. By 1942, when the C.C.C. ended, three million young people had been involved The many ways in which Roosevelt moved to solve social problems were known by their initials, which reactionaries sneered at as "alphabet soup"—but the millions who benefited made him the first and only president elected four times.

Lessons of a Rare Experience

The concessions to its working people made by the ruling class, some of whom he berated as "economic royalists" and who sneered at him as "that man in the White House," were made by necessity. The people had a life-and-death need for those improvements—and much more, it must be said—while the ruling class stood to lose all its pelf and privilege if it failed to take at least some responsibility for the misery it had caused. A class struggle on the scale it was carried on in the decade of the Depression could not help but present rich lessons for all involved.

For this study, two of those lessons are of prime interest—and clearly they were both learned more profoundly by Roosevelt the more he developed as a statesman. The first was that leaders who concern themselves seriously with the interests of the people in peacetime can rally them to great achievements in a just war. Historians have credited him as a great commander-in-chief but this was possible only because working men and women were willing to contribute an absolutely unparalleled, incredibly enormous production effort notwithstanding rationing and other elements of wartime privation.

Before and during the early "phony war" phase of World War II, imperial circles in the United States, England, and France had been egging Hitler on to destroy the Soviet Union along with socialist influence in Europe and elsewhere. But when they found themselves under full attack and especially when capitalists and communists came to be on the same side in a war for democracy against fascism, it became more evident than ever before in world history that the will of the people can be decisive, warranting respect.

The second lesson, based in good part on that searing experience, was that a narrow social base is dangerous for the capitalist mode of operation, whether it takes the modern fascist form or that of our own past slavocrats; that a broad social base is necessary, not only for capitalist development, but also to bridge the critical difficulties the system itself creates.

The United States became strong because of the way that issue was faced by Jefferson, Madison, Franklin, and Paine when the nation was born, because of the way that issue was faced by Lincoln when the country was being torn apart, and because of the way Roosevelt faced it in the critical years of the Depression and World War II.

The Economic Bill of Rights

There is good reason to believe FDR took that lesson to heart not only for immediate problems but looking far into the future. This became clear in his Annual Message to Congress headed "The Economic Bill of Rights."

A year and a half of fighting still remained, but it had become evident that the way things were going, the war would be won. The tide had turned against the Japanese in the Pacific. During all of 1943, after lifting the siege of Leningrad in January and retaking Stalingrad and other cities in February, the Russians had been destroying the Nazi armies in a sweeping offensive. Roosevelt had every reason to expect that Eisenhower, already in England as Supreme Commander, would within five months lead the Expeditionary Force across the Channel, and less than a year later, share the delivery of the coup de grace.

A large part of the Message was devoted to many proposals to assure an all-out effort to bring victory as soon as possible and thereby hold down casualties. Then he launched into an unprecedented and remarkable set of demands in what is for us today an historic statement of policy and principles. It has never had proper currency in establishmentarian education, probably being deemed potentially subversive, and therefore, appreciating the force of its progressive leadership, deserves full quotation here:

> It is our duty now to begin to lay plans and determine the strategy for the winning of a lasting peace and the establishment of an American standard of living higher than ever before known. We cannot be content, no matter how high that general standard of living may be, if some fraction of our people—whether it be one-third or one-fifth or one-tenth—is ill-fed, ill-clothed, ill-housed and insecure.
>
> This Republic had its beginning, and grew to its present strength, under the protection of certain inalienable political rights—among them the right of

free speech, free press, free worship, trial by jury, freedom from unreasonable searches and seizures. They were our rights to life and liberty.

As our nation has grown in size and stature, however—as our industrial economy expanded—these political rights proved inadequate to assure us equality in the pursuit of happiness.

We have come to a clear realization of the fact that true individual freedom cannot exist without economic security and independence. 'Necessitous men are not free men.' People who are hungry and out of a job are the stuff of which dictatorships are made.

In our day these economic truths have become accepted as self-evident. We have accepted, so to speak, a second Bill of Rights under which a new basis of security and prosperity can be established for all—regardless of station, race or creed. Among these are:

> The right to a useful and remunerative job in the industries or shops or farms or mines of the nation;
>
> The right to earn enough to provide adequate food and clothing and recreation;
>
> The right of every farmer to raise and sell his products at a return which will give him and his family a decent living;
>
> The right of every business man, large and small, to trade in an atmosphere of freedom from unfair competition and domination by monopolies at home or abroad;
>
> The right of every family to a decent home;
>
> The right to adequate medical care and the opportunity to achieve and enjoy good health;
>
> The right to adequate protection from the economic fears of old age, sickness, accident and unemployment;
>
> The right to a good education.

All of these rights spell security. And after this war is won we must be prepared to move forward, in the implementation of these rights, to new goals of human happiness and well-being.

America's own rightful place in the world depends in large part upon how fully these and similar rights have been carried into practice for our citizens. For unless there is security here at home there cannot be lasting peace in the world.

One of the great American industrialists of our day—a man who has rendered yeoman service to his country in this crisis—recently emphasized the grave dangers of 'rightist reaction' in this Nation. All clear-thinking businessmen share his concern. Indeed, if such reaction should develop—if history were to repeat itself and we were to return to the so-called 'normalcy' of the 1920s—then it is certain that even though we shall have conquered our enemies on the battlefields abroad, we shall have yielded to the spirit of Fascism here at home.

I ask the Congress to explore the means for implementing this economic Bill of Rights—for it is definitely the responsibility of Congress so to do. Many of these problems are already before committees of the Congress in the form of proposed legislation. I shall from time to time communicate with the Congress with respect to these and further proposals. In the event that no adequate program of progress is evolved, I am certain that the Nation will be conscious of the fact.

Our fighting men abroad—and their families at home—expect such a program and have the right to insist upon it. It is to their demands that this Government should pay heed, rather than to the whining demands of selfish pressure groups, who seek to feather their nests while young Americans are dying.

Resting in Warm Springs, Georgia, fifteen months later, looking to all who knew him like a man simply worn out by the great challenges he had faced, he died suddenly of a cerebral hemorrhage—less than one month before V-E Day and four months before V-J Day. He had barely begun his last term as President. How differently things might have been done—nationally and internationally—had he lived. His Economic Bill of Rights, consisting mostly of concessions yet to be won, remains a banner for Progressives to this day.

No president can be said to have been more "to the manor born," yet it must be said of this patrician that none since Lincoln had more of the "common touch." He is said to have "saved capitalism," and yet, conceding that even he must have been aware of this, it must be said that he was capable of rising above class to exert a civilizing influence, daring even to embrace such aims of labor as could be called socialistic.

Notes

1. John Kenneth Galbraith, *The Great Crash, 1929* (Boston: Houghton Mifflin, 1988), 72. Galbraith discusses a statement made by Paul M. Warburg, then a banker with the International Acceptance Bank, published in *The Commercial and Financial Chronicle,* March 9, 1929, 1444: "In March of 1929, he called for a stronger Federal Reserve policy and argued that if the present orgy of 'unrestrained speculation' were not brought promptly to a halt there would ultimately be a disastrous collapse. This, he suggested, would be unfortunate not alone for the speculators. It would 'bring about a general depression involving the entire country.'" *(Ed.)*

2. ———, *The Great Crash, 1929*, 177-86.

3. The "shape-up" was a hiring process in which workers assembled and waited to be arbitrarily selected—or not—for that day's work on the docks. Work was available only one day at a time. *(Ed.)*

Chapter 8

The Second Reconstruction

The Civil Rights Explosion

Three more major concessions to African Americans (always subsumed as an underclass decreed by traditional racism) became unavoidable in the 1950s and 1960s. The events of that period seemed to respond to a prophetic 1934 poem by Langston Hughes, "Lenox Avenue Mural," which contained the following lines:

> What happens to a dream deferred?
>   Does it dry up
>   Like a raisin in the sun . . .
> Or does it explode?

A decade later the need to address that question became clear when the deferring of that dream domestically had been assumed necessary in order to carry on the international fight for such freedoms in World War II.

In December 1946, President Truman set up a Committee on Civil Rights. In the committee's report a year later it is significant, that in addition to moral and political considerations, it indicated the financial costs of discrimination to the country and said: "The United States can no longer afford this heavy drain upon its human wealth, its national competence." It urged expansion of the civil rights section of the Department of Justice, establishment of a permanent Commission on Civil Rights, legislation against lynching and voting discrimination, and new laws on fair employment practices, as well as requiring the equitable administration of justice.

Truman asked Congress to act on the report. Congress, still run by Southerners, did nothing. A somewhat better fate came in an executive order Truman issued in July 1948, requiring that a policy of racial equality in the armed forces "be put into effect as rapidly as possible." It took more than twelve years for the armed forces to become entirely desegregated.

The prime example of the many devious ways in which rights—definitively established in post-Civil War amendments and laws—had been evaded under color of legality was the Supreme Court's *Plessy v. Ferguson* decision in 1896. It set up the "separate but equal" principle by stating that requiring the separation of black and white passengers in transportation did not contravene the Fourteenth Amendment.

This principle stood until 1955 when Rosa Parks sat down upon it. As Manning Marable put it: "The Montgomery Bus Boycott, initiated December 1, 1955 by Rosa Parks, was the beginning of the Second Reconstruction, a massive, ethical movement by Blacks and their white liberal allies to destroy racial segregation."[1]

The first of the three concessions had come during the year before. One may well believe it was in anticipation of just such "explosions" that the Supreme Court unanimously rejected the "separate but equal" notion as it applied to public education. The declaration in *Brown v. Board of Education* that racial segregation in public schools is unconstitutional was an important milestone, notwithstanding the way it was marred a year later when the Court provided lower courts with a high-sounding loophole, saying that if they "find that additional time is necessary" they should act "with all deliberate speed." Ten years later, more than 75 percent of the school districts in the South were still segregated.

The second and third concessions in this period were the 1964 Civil Rights Act and the 1965 Voting Rights Act. There had been civil rights acts in 1866, in 1875 and in 1957, but they had been of a general nature and not effectively enforced. The 1964 Act was markedly serious, specifically prohibiting discrimination in voting, education, hiring and promoting of workers, and access to hotels, restaurants, theaters, and other public facilities. It was implemented by the Civil Rights Restoration Act of 1987, and passed in March 1988 over President Reagan's veto—a law which made entire institutions subject to loss of federal funds if they were found to discriminate on the basis of race, sex, age, or physical handicap in any programs, not just those receiving federal funds.

The 1965 Voting Rights Act authorized the U.S. Attorney General to send federal examiners to register black voters in areas where discrimination existed.

It also eliminated all literacy tests and prohibited the use of poll taxes. President Lyndon Johnson had vigorously promoted both laws, even in one speech co-opting the slogan "We Shall Overcome!" In August 1963, over a quarter million black and white Americans gathered in Washington in an unprecedented march for equality, highlighted by Martin Luther King Jr.'s famous "I Have A Dream" speech.

Underneath the nonviolent rights movement black anger had been rising for a long time. It was exactly in those two years in which civil rights legislation reached its highest level that urban riots and rebellions were breaking out spontaneously all over the country, including the highly publicized one in Watts, Los Angeles. In almost all incidents the mass violence was precipitated by some police action which seemed to be, or was, unjustified, usually unnecessarily brutal, occurring much too often not to be seen as typical. Such blatant racist behavior has continued all through the years.[2]

The Aftermath

Two generations later, in observing the rise of celebrations marking the anniversary of *Brown V. Board of Education,* a *New York Times* editorial noted that

> it seems the national consciousness has changed but the reality lags far behind. . . Where statutorially sanctioned segregation once kept the races apart at school, now the trends of suburbanization, white flight, industrial decay and political ennui have combined to keep minority students in poorer districts, in schools with lower expectations for their students' achievements, in communities that are nurseries for failure... Another conspicuously successful product of Brown, the 1965 Voting Rights Act, brought thousands of minorities to elective office. . . The struggle continues. Lawsuits all around the country are now challenging the inherent inequities in the funding of school districts.[3]

There have been many ups and downs in the forward march of civil rights. An interesting example occurred back in 1991. Congress and President Bush finally responded that year to labor and liberal protest against a series of Supreme Court decisions, eight times in a twenty-year period, that obstructed labor action under an 1866 law against racial discrimination on the job. In brief, the court had put the onus on the labor plaintiff to prove that an employer's action was due to discrimination rather than some occupational necessity. The 1991 law reversed this, putting the onus on the employer to prove his case.

It is the landmarks that matter, the major concessions that survive the tug of war between class interests and come to act as milestones of social progress.

Notes

1. Manning Marable, *How Capitalism Underdeveloped Black America* (Boston: South End Press, 1983), 202.

2. Howard Zinn, *Postwar America 1945-1971* (New York: Bobb Merrill, 1973), 120-48.

3. Editorial, *New York Times,* 18 May 1994.

Chapter 9

Health Care as Socialist Intruder

The Nature of the Issues

The latest two major concessions in the United States were Medicare and Medicaid. They can be considered historic steps in the development toward the great concession yet to come and long overdue: universal, government-provided health care. The intrusion of such a socialist practice in a capitalist country cannot be explained by any economic need for it, but only by the persistent pressure of working people who cannot afford it on their own and for whom it is a basic human need. If it is argued that capitalists need it because a healthy worker is more productive than a sick one, the fact can be readily stated that this has never before led employers to take responsibility for it, preferring to leave the burden on the worker by simply denying employment to the unproductive ones.

Medicare may be thought to have originated in Lyndon Johnson's Great Society concept but it did not. He recognized this, having invited former President Harry Truman to attend the signing of the bill July 30, 1965, honoring his effort twenty years earlier to promote a national health insurance program. It had earlier antecedents as well, including its expression as an aim in Franklin Roosevelt's New Deal.

Medicare's potential as a move toward a socially mixed economy was clear to the *Wall Street Journal*. Looking back half a century to what happened when, in the middle of World War II, two senators and a congressman introduced legislation for a compulsory system of health care for everyone covered by Social Security, it reported:

> The American Medical Association exploded with rage. Those charged with running the program would be turned into 'gauleiters,' said Morris Fishbein, editor of the A.M.A. Journal at the time. Those were fighting words: Gauleiters were brutal Nazi district leaders.
>
> The battle to bring compulsory, nationalized health care to the American people is the longest, nastiest, costliest legislative struggle in history.
>
> Of the old, health-care battle cries that echo down the years, none has a more resonant ring than 'socialism.'
>
> National health care was, in fact, an idea that drifted across the Atlantic Ocean from Britain, where a Labor Party—Socialist—government came into power after the war and put into place a health care system that survives intact to this day. . .
>
> In the Senate, the fight against the Truman plan was led by Mr. Conservative himself, Ohio Republican Sen. Robert Taft. When the chairman of the Senate Labor and Education Committee complained about editorials suggesting the idea was socialistic, Sen. Taft interrupted, saying the editorials had it right; it really was socialism. Mr. Conservative then stalked out of the hearings, never to return[1]

The second concession, Medicaid, a system of federal funding for state programs providing medical aid for the poor, was part of the Medicare Act of 1965. Millions look to it for essential, though very limited, medical care. Among other afflictions, the Medicaid program suffers from variety in state programs, much red tape, and inconsiderate handling. One statistic showed that "in 1992 only half the people in families with income below the poverty line received Medicaid benefits; another 18.4 percent had some private insurance."[2]

The Call for Government Health Care

Well before the time the Clinton administration presented the faulty program it claimed would provide universal healthcare, the need for a comprehensive federal program was generally recognized. The country's leading newspaper said:

> Nine out of ten Americans believe the nation's health care system should be fundamentally changed or completely rebuilt. And with good reason. Costs are skyrocketing. Fees appear unfair. And a large segment of the population lacks access to adequate care.
>
> The U.S. is the only major industrialized nation where tens of millions go uninsured—or else cling to unwanted jobs to preserve coverage—and the

> elderly sick routinely go bankrupt in order to qualify for public assistance. Even the American Medical Association now admits the system needs overhaul.[3]

In the same period a crushing indictment of the government's failure to provide adequate health care came from inside the Beltway, from the General Accounting Office, the non-partisan auditing and investigating arm of Congress. Its report, dated June 4, 1991, appeared to favor what had become widely known as the Canadian government's "single-payer plan."

The report concluded that switching to a plan under which state governments pay most medical costs, as the provinces in Canada do, would save more than $75 billion a year. It said that would be enough to cover all 32 million Americans who are now uninsured and make medical care for others available without any insurance deductibles or other payments.[4]

The media, as usual, did not inform the public why the problem was not being solved. It required an unadvertised tribune of the people, Ralph Nader, to set forth such facts as these:

> The largest single source of savings is the $135 billion we pay in unnecessary overhead, profits and administrative costs of paying more than fifteen hundred different private insurance companies. Our private insurance system has made health care in America the most expensive in the world. A public plan like Medicare spends only three cents out of every health care dollar for administration. But the typical commercial insurance company takes an average of 14 percent of premiums for overhead and profit. . . . 24 percent of America's health care dollars go to pay for administration and overhead—by far the largest in the world. Eliminating this waste is our one chance to find the money to pay for a national health care plan that will also truly provide coverage for long-term care.[5]

The Clinton Fiasco and Big Business Strategy

As might have been expected, the Clinton administration was not about to move in that direction. The President and his wife, who took charge, tried with might and main to sustain the insurance industry as part of the solution instead of acknowledging it was the main part of the problem. The result was an incredibly complex program that tried to satisfy everyone and satisfied no one, a mountain of foolishness comprising 1,342 pages with 240,000 words. Presented on October 27, 1993, it was declared dead in Congress exactly eleven months later.

Big capital knew this disposition of the matter was far from final. In the popularity of the single-payer plan it had seen the handwriting on the wall and decided to take matters into its own hands. The basic aim was to consolidate control by means of mergers with and expansion of health maintenance organizations. Hospitals were also merging and forming chains capable of taking doctors' organizations in tow. Throughout the whole complex of the trillion-dollar health business can be traced the fine hand of five leading insurance companies.

No institution is more parasitic than the insurance industry: an aggressive interloper, which stripped of its pretenses, serves no useful purpose whatever in the health field. One reason it has reached such an awesome level of wealth and political influence is that of all major industries it is the most immune to government regulation. This special treatment dates back half a century to the McCarran-Ferguson Act of 1945 which gave it immunity from anti-trust laws. This carries with it such unconscionable pursuits as price-fixing, onerous requirements on consumers, other monopoly practices, and the elements of corruption, which among other things, are part and parcel of a powerful lobby.

People have been puzzled by the failure of so popular a program as the single-payer plan to get beyond the sponsorship of ninety-two congress members. An obvious explanation is that this McDermott-Wellstone bill was snowed under by a financial blizzard of insurance industry lobbying, coupled with a media blitz of false charges against the Canadian prototype plan. However, the fact that there was no effective rebound, no significant public clamor, does require looking at another, a basic and usually hidden reason: the people's distrust of government.

Nobody discredits democracy in the eyes of the people better than democrats in power. That distrust of government, a habit of long standing akin to distrust of politicians, had been fortified by the prodigious blunder of the Clinton program. What had been touted as a proposal for universal health coverage revealed itself to be a program to preserve general profiteering.

Which Role Model?

Americans have much to learn from the international history of such distrust of government and one of its results is the extraordinary success of non-governmental, non-private health programs.

In the standard terms of American policy debate, Canada might seem to offer the only alternative to the American way of providing (and not providing) health care. Canadians use government insurance and are, therefore, very much better off in affordable access to medical care than Americans confronted with private insurance. One is "the state" and the other is "the market" and people take sides depending on what they think—or think they should think—about those labels.

The German form of shared operation, the sickness fund, is not a compromise between the two. It is the superior original to which all others should be compared. It is the highly modernized model of ancient experience and its history is instructive. Here are extracts from a comprehensive study:

> During the Middle Ages . . . guilds of working men—bakers, smiths and the like—created funds to help members with hospital care, to pay for funeral expenses, to help disabled fellows, or to aid bereaved families. Journeymen who did not have guild status formed fraternities for similar purposes, and miners also formed associations . . .
>
> Such community-based insurance had no more to do with the market than with the state. It was not sold on an open market, purchase was compulsory rather than voluntary, and prices were not set in relation to risk but as a flat rate or a share of income. . . .
>
> In the mid-1870s, Germany had about ten thousand relief funds with two million members. In 1883, Chancellor Otto von Bismarck of Germany expanded and systematized this structure. The law provided for employees to contribute two-thirds and employers one-third of the costs and for governance of each fund by a board similarly constituted by representatives of employees and employers. The government set the minimum benefit level by statute, and it included sick pay, medical expenses and hospital treatment. . . .
>
> By 1885, 4.3 million workers were members of the funds. . . . A 1927 law creating unemployment insurance also provided for continuation of membership in the sickness funds for persons who lost their jobs.
>
> Even the Nazis did not threaten the basic benefits, though they did take control . . . purging socialists and Jews. After the Third Reich was destroyed, the victorious allies found little reason to reform the social insurance schemes. In 1951 the contribution rates and representation on the boards of the primary funds were changed to an even split. . . . In 1972 time limits of hospital treatment were abolished; and in 1975 all students were included in the statutory scheme. . . .
>
> Germans pay much less than Americans out-of-pocket for health care—approximately 7.5 percent of the total in 1987. . . . [Extensive detail follows regarding the exemplary fairness of drug and dental coverage and administration, generous benefits for glasses, hearing aids, prostheses, mental health care, etc.]
>
> Education in Germany is funded by state governments, as a right of citizenship, and therefore medical students are able. . . to graduate debt-free. As a result, Germany has 20 percent more physicians per person than either the United States or Canada. . . .
>
> All six other countries [Australia, Canada, England, France, Germany, Japan] . . . have universal systems based on compulsory participation. All are financed not by individual purchases of insurance for fixed prices, but by contribution schemes in which all payers contribute to a fund in proportion to their incomes and withdraw in proportion to their health care needs. In each, smaller families help larger, wealthier people help poorer, and younger (all other things being equal) help older. . . . They limit costs by combinations of fee schedules for some services and budgets for others. Controls on capital investment further limit the proliferation of expensive technology and limit the cost of using the technology that is available.[6]

That international standard has been described by an outstanding authority as a solidarity system, one that, as a leading example, "beginning in the 1880s in Germany made social solidarity official policy and eventually spread it to entire populations."[7]

With respect to the Bismarck initiative, it should be noted that it was politically motivated. He had a felt need to counter the rising strength of the Socialist Party, in the course of which he was not above the hypocrisy of setting the eligibility age for old age pensions at sixty-five, in a time when life expectancy was forty-seven!

The Gathering Storm Over Harmful "Managed Care"

The ruling circles of the highly developed capitalist countries maintaining the solidarity systems described above cannot be totally unaware that the class-leveling procedure of the international standard is comparable to the basic communist principle: From each according to one's ability, to each according to one's need. That doesn't stop them. Why should it stop Americans? How can anyone decently object to the social mixing of an economy by such humane and salutary means?

Even an eminent voice in the establishment academy, the well-known professor of economics at M.I.T., Paul Krugman, could indulge in such musing. In an article discussing the deplorable situation of the elderly under existing health management and imagining the possibility of a society "that provide(s) advanced medical care to everyone and that rations care not by wealth but by other criteria," he ends by saying

> Such an outcome sounds unthinkable in the current political climate, which is dominated by a low-tax, anti-government ideology. But history is not over; ideologies may change. For all we know, the future may belong to the medical welfare state, a state whose slogan might be, "From each according to his ability, to each according to his needs."[8]

Theproblem is too often reduced to the bad-enough situation that there are forty-five million people who cannot afford any health insurance at all and that universal health care is "too much" to handle all at once; and so the situation should be improved incrementally by taking some measures or other, like providing preventive care for children or arranging some payment for pharmaceuticals. What is being evaded is that the general problem of health care in the United States has been steadily getting worse under the "managed care" of so-called Health Maintenance Organizations (HMOs) owned or controlled by the great insurance corporations. Even the number of uninsured people, for example, grew by 4.5 million during the seven years before President Clinton left office in January 2001.[9]

By 1999 the money-grubbing regulations the HMOs had imposed ever more widely and unconscionably caused so much trouble and disgust for those insured, that state legislatures were being flooded with proposed legislation. Being closer to their loudly complaining constituents than the heavily lobbied minions of the insurance trust in Washington, they faced "a greater proportion of bills in state legislatures around the country than any other topic in 1999, about 27,000 bills out of about 140,000." According to Lee Dixon, director of the health policy tracking services of the National Conference of State Legislatures, "It's a populist issue. It's not a Republican or Democratic issue. It's state legislators and legislatures trying to address the needs of their constituents."[10]

There is a great deal more to be dealt with in this obviously gathering storm than can be detailed here. Bob Herbert has clearly summarized some of the major reasons for it:

> Most of the country understands that an unconscionable obsession with the bottom line has resulted in widespread abuses in the managed-care industry. Simply stated, there is big money to be made by denying care. It is now widely known that there are faceless bureaucrats making critical diagnostic and treatment decisions, that some doctors are being retaliated against for dispensing honest advice, that women have had an especially hard time getting the care they need, and that patients have died because they were unable to gain admittance to emergency rooms.[11]

Notes

1. James M. Perry, "In Remembrance of Fiery Battles Past, Cries of 'Socialism' Still Reverberate," *Wall Street Journal,* 23 September 1993.
2. Employee Benefit Research Institute, *Sources of Health Insurance,* Table 14, 33; quoted by Joseph White, *Competing Solutions: American Health Care Proposals and International Experience* (Washington, D.C.: The Brookings Institution, 1995), 38.
3. Editorial, *New York Times*, 4 June 1991.
4. Philip J. Hilts, "Canadian-Style Health System Gains Support," *New York Times,* 4 June 1991.
5. Ralph Nader, *Public Citizen,* letter issued December 10, 1992.
6. Joseph White, *Competing Solutions: American Health Care Proposals and International Experience* (Washington, D.C.: The Brookings Institution, 1995), 72-90.
7. William A. Glaser, *Health Insurance in Practice: International Variations in Financing, Benefits, and Problems* (San Francisco: Jossey-Bass, 1991), 18.

8. Paul Krugman, "Does Getting Old Cost Society Too Much?" *New York Times Magazine* (9 March 1997): 58-60.

9. Robert Pear, "More Americans Were Uninsured in 1998, U.S. Says," *New York Times*, 4 October 1999.

10. Carey Goldberg, "For Many States, Health Care Bills Are Top Priority," *New York Times*, 23 January 2000.

11. Bob Herbert, ("In America" column), "Money vs. Reform," *New York Times Op-Ed*, 15 July 1999.

Chapter 10

The Forty-Four Main Concessions and Some Patterns Observed

Listed here, briefly stated in the order they have appeared in these pages, are the main concessions made to the people by those in power during more than two centuries of capitalist development in the United States. The first twenty-three will be found seriatim in the first ten amendments of the Constitution, the Bill of Rights.

1. No regulation of religion.
2. Free speech.
3. Free press.
4. The right to assemble peacefully.
5. The right to petition for a redress of grievances.
6. No unreasonable searches or seizures.
7. No warrants except on sworn, probable cause, particularized.
8. No indictment for a peacetime capital crime without grand jury action.
9. No double jeopardy.

10. No requirement to be a witness against oneself.
11. No deprivation of life, liberty, or property without due process of law.
12. No taking of private property for public use without just compensation.
13. The right to a speedy and public trial.
14. The right to an impartial jury of the state and district of the alleged crime.
15. The right to be informed of the nature and cause of the accusation.
16. The right to be confronted with the witnesses against one.
17. The right to have compulsory process for obtaining favorable witnesses.
18. The right to have counsel to assist one's defense.
19. The right of trial by jury in suits at common law.
20. No court reexamination of a fact tried by jury except according to common law.
21. No excessive bail.
22. No excessive fines.
23. No cruel and unusual punishment.
24. The shorter work day, first to ten hours, then to eight.
25. The abolition of slavery.
26. The right of African Americans to education and higher education.
27. Full, dual citizenship for Native Americans.
28. Full tribal, ethnic sovereignty on reservations.
29. The right of women to vote.
30. Prohibition of child labor.
31. The right of women to higher education.
32. The right of women to own and control property.
33. The right of women to equal pay, in principle.
34. The right of choice for women concerning abortion.
35. The National Labor Relations Act, legalizing trade unions.
36. The Social Security Act, setting up a retirement fund.

37. The Social Security Act's provision of funds for state unemployment insurance systems.

38. The Fair Labor Standards Act for a minimum wage and the forty-hour workweek.

39. The Federal Deposit Insurance Corporation, to protect personal savings.

40. Racial segregation in public schools declared unconstitutional.

41. The Civil Rights Act, prohibiting discrimination in many specific ways.

42. The Voting Rights Act, with federal registrars for denied black voters.

43. The Medicare Act, funding health care for recipients of Social Security.

44. Medicaid (part of the Social Security Act), funding part of state medical aid for the poor.

Left out of this list are innumerable minor adjustments, both positive and negative, and additional reforms which modify but do not set aside the concessions as such. It is why those listed are referred to as main concessions. This study would not gain from attempting an encyclopedic treatment of all the ins and outs. It is well established that all the concessions have been and remain subject to the flow of struggle.

The first pattern that emerges is that not one of the concessions prevents the accumulation of capital, a fundamental law of motion in a capitalist economy. Even the pro-labor gains, anathema to habitually short-sighted employers at the times they were won, can be seen long-term as often bringing about an increase in productivity as well as purchasing power. This increases the pool of surplus value from which capital can be accumulated.

A second pattern is the changing of a social situation into its opposite. At the nation's outset, all decisions were made by propertied, white, male, English-speaking settlers from Europe. The large noises being made for liberty and equality "for all men" were well understood to be privileged to this minority. The concessions to those beneath them in station, won in two centuries of strenuous struggle, have greatly extended the economic, social, and political participation of all originally barred—but still within some limits—to women, people of color, even the propertyless, and those speaking foreign languages. Notwithstanding the continuing social disease of racism, the country has become broadly multiethnic. The propertied white males who are still making the major decisions in the country have found they cannot survive without closely involving many they have always excluded.

A third pattern is the legalization, virtually as a customary institution, of the labor movement. Where from the beginning the normal way was to suppress trade union action by brutal and military force, it is now the exception rather than the rule. Where it still happens it is sharply and immediately challenged—and not by the labor movement alone. Reacting to a large decline in membership due both to loss of jobs and failure to carry on organization work, there has been a major change in leadership, foreshadowed by the formation of a Labor Party and a resolve to organize the unorganized. This has been recognized as essential to the retention of concessions previously won and the gaining of those still needed, such as repeal of the Taft-Hartley law and the establishment of universal governmental health care.

A fourth pattern is the acceptance as normal of social welfare as a principled practice of government. No matter how repugnant anything of a socialistic nature may be to right-wing capitalist or fundamentalist ideologues, the persistence of the measures which have come to be lumped as social welfare cannot be disputed. They may resist its elevation to the level of principle but its general practice cannot be denied. For Europeans, politically more sophisticated, the socially mixed economy holds no terrors.

Chapter 11

Two Worlds or One?

A Forecast of the Socially Mixed Economy

With reverberations in later years, a very interesting dialogue was recorded in August 1987 between two world-class economists, John Kenneth Galbraith and Stanislav Menshikov, old friends from opposed social systems, stimulated by the Gorbachev initiatives then under way.

After a candid discussion of the different social problems in the United States and the Soviet Union, Menshikov asked:

> What will the world look like in a hundred years? Will it be all capitalist; will it be all socialist? Will it be a kind of mixture of both, as it is now, with the two systems co-existing? Will it be one society that has coalesced as a result of the movement of the systems toward each other or will it be two societies that have become even more different from each other? Will it be a different kind of society we can't even now perceive?
>
> [Galbraith:] . . . I would guess that we would have a mixture. There will be a movement to the market in what is now the socialist world along the lines we have previously discussed. There will be a commitment in the capitalist world to greater social concern. And a hundred years from now there will be countries that are still emerging into this more mature combination of socialism and capitalism.

> [Menshikov:] . . . I generally agree with you that the future will be a mixture of the existing forms, with perhaps some new forms putting in an appearance.[1]

The Socially Mixed Economy Under Socialism

Two and a half years later the matter had become more of a reality for Menshikov, at a time when he was proposing a solution to the Soviet economic crisis they faced. After exploring the theoretical aspects in depth, he summarized his practical position:

> My propositions boil down to the following two major theses:
>
> First, in any decision-making on economic policy it is necessary to bear in mind that socialism has no other way out but a mixed economy. Any deviation from this goal threatens serious complications. A mixed economy for its part inevitably presupposes a private sector freely competing with collective and other socialist forms. The consumer market cannot be satisfied in the near future without the free development of the cooperative and private sectors. This is indispensable if living standards are even to be stabilized, let alone raised. Given the tense sociological situation at present, this becomes a matter of life or death for socialism.
>
> My second thesis is that all proposals to stabilize the economy at the expense of the people, through lowering their living standards, should be discarded.[2]

The Long-Standing Experience of Sweden

In the late 1990s Menshikov's views retained their validity and even a degree of prophetic quality, notwithstanding tumultuous developments he could not have foreseen. This is probably due to the fact that his views are based on real experience. It shows in the way he deals with the question whether there is any guarantee that in a socially mixed economy a minority of private capitalists will not seize political power and that a society with outrageous social inequalities will not emerge. "To answer this question," he says, "I will draw parallels with the Swedish model of socialism, which I saw at first hand during a visit to that country in autumn 1989."

> Sweden is one of the few countries in which evolutionary development led, without any abrupt and violent change of the old system and form of political power, to the establishment of a mixed economy with distinct elements of socialism.
>
> The distinctive features of Sweden's socialism are the high incomes (among the world's highest) of the overwhelming majority of the population and the small income differentials between workers and white-collar employ-

> ees in different occupations and industries; the de facto eradication of poverty; highly developed social security and social services, organized on a social non-market basis; full employment (minimum unemployment); and progressive taxation as a means of further evening out the incomes of most of the population.
>
> At the same time 90 percent of industry and a large part of the rest of the economy are under private control. The dominant force is made up of big corporations such as are typical of the U.S. or West Germany, and in recent years most of these corporations have become transnational and have acquired interests outside Sweden. Of course, this system can be characterized without any reservations as monopolistic capitalism. . . .
>
> Paradoxically, Swedish socialism is a product of the joint efforts of what we have always considered to be the antagonistic classes, the workers and the capitalists. Faced with the prospect of a crisis in the 1930s, they discovered that it was in their common interest to avoid conflicts—strikes and lockouts—through accords on what both sides considered to be a fair distribution of the results of production. It became possible to formulate state policies that satisfied both sides; workers were guaranteed full employment and high pay, and capitalists an efficient use of production capacities and huge profits.
>
> The concentration of economic power in the country is high, and it keeps growing. Three oligarchic financial groups dominate virtually the whole of industry and banking . . . .
>
> The Swedish Social-Democrats . . . left microeconomic regulation to the capitalist and managerial class. Having realized that state enterprises (which in Sweden account for around 10 percent of industry and for a large part of transport and power engineering) usually cannot compete with the private sector, they dropped their original plans for large-scale nationalization and have never revived them. . . .
>
> In sum, the prospects for socialist collectivist forms in the Swedish economy are not altogether bright, which arouses serious fears for the future stability of the system, for the basis of Swedish socialism and social partnership.[3]

It may seem puzzling that an economist who had been the editor of the World Marxist Review should feel free to speak of "the distinctive features of Sweden's socialism" and in the next paragraph say that "Of course, this system can be characterized without any reservations as monopolistic capitalism." What makes this a paradox is the notion often touted by journalists that Sweden is the paradigm of the socially mixed economy, under whatever name devised for it.

Elements of both social systems are present in Sweden but very little political mixture of them. There is in fact a strict separation between their operations, with the tension of an arm's length relationship between the dominant capitalists and the people's administrators of social benefits at the head of government. It is as if a policy of peaceful coexistence has been deliberately enforced for sixty or seventy years and is assumed to be permanent.

Menshikov's "serious fears" began to be validated the year after their publication. Nothing had seemed more stable than the fifty-three-year rule of the Social-Democrats but on September 15, 1991 they were voted out of power. The pendulum swung back again three years later when the conservatives were ousted and Social-Democratic power restored but much had changed and continued to change.

Unrestrained freedom for capital had finally shown how much damage it could do. For years there had been an outflow of capital to European investment, a way to avoid Swedish regulation, and economic growth had fallen to a stagnation level. Inflation and unemployment kept rising, the latter reaching a level of 13 percent, akin to the level throughout Europe.

In an effort to entice capital to invest at home, the top tax rate had been reduced to 51 percent but there was some question whether this would be enough. A rise in interest rates to double digits caused damage. Also, the recession in the early 1990s had been the worst since the 1930s.

It became necessary to make substantial reductions in public outlays. Many minor cutbacks in social benefits were made under the Social-Democrats, then under the conservatives, and then again under the Social-Democrats. While these remained short of a major change in the "welfare state," job security had been dealt a worrisome blow.

By the end of 1999, however, Sweden had bounced back. In its account of this, the *New York Times* referred to the fact that

> This is still, after all, a country where government consumes nearly 60 percent of the national economy, far above the 32 percent share in the United States. Taxes and wages are among the highest in the world. Dismissing a sluggish worker is, in nearly all cases, legally impossible.
>
> And the Swedes are proud of it. When Prime Minister Goran Persson introduced his budget plans in mid-September, he promised that 'Sweden will consolidate its position as a leading welfare nation.' He even pledged to create another entitlement: the right of every person who turns sixty-five to retain a personal assistant.
>
> Yet this largely unreconstructed welfare state is one of Europe's most vibrant economies. . . .
>
> While the government continues to finance health care, education and many social services, Sweden has deregulated industries from telecommunications to airlines and banking. As a result, new companies and high technology have flourished . . . The government, which five years ago carried a deficit equivalent to 11 percent of the gross domestic product, now has a budget surplus."[4]

Notes

1. John Kenneth Galbraith and Stanislav Menshikov, *Capitalism, Communism and Coexistence: From a Bitter Past to a Better Prospect,* (Boston: Houghton, Mifflin, 1988), 110-13.

2. Stanislav Menshikov, *Catastrophe or Catharsis?* (Moscow: Inter-Verso Press, 1990), 12.

3. ———, *Catastrophe or Catharsis?* 146-49.

4. Edmund L. Andrews, "Sweden, the Welfare State, Basks in a New Prosperity," *New York Times,* 8 October 1999.

Chapter 12

The German Model

Some Unique Aspects

Americans seeking precedents or exemplars in the struggle for a higher standard of living would do well to look into the German experience in at least the following respects. In the field of health care (described in the latter part of chapter 9) Germany is more generous and effective than Canada. In the field of labor conditions it is better than Sweden. In the degree of participation of workers in management it is more advanced than any other capitalist country. Its productivity is higher than that of any other country in the world.

While the barbarism of a dozen years of Nazi rule was abysmal and ever unforgettable, the United States should avoid reading moral lectures to Germany in view of its own much more extended history of enslavement, genocide, and other brutal repressions. Americans should also bear in mind that Italian and German fascism, along with other repressive dictatorships, were actively promoted by powerful elements in American, British, and other imperialist circles. In the half-century since the Second World War, Germany has come a long way in what it likes to call "the civilization of capitalism."

Companies are legally obliged to consult with labor representatives on all important decisions. Labor holds seats on the boards of all major companies and is part of the discussion when layoffs or shifts in production locations are being planned. This encourages civility and an atmosphere of reason. True, any such operation "within the existing framework" remains under capitalist control—but the access to internal information and the firmness of strong trade unions combine to restrain the rampant corporate greed often seen in the United States.

The Dedication to Training

In 1999, according to the Organization for Economic Cooperation and Development in Paris, German factory workers were earning an average of $30.20 an hour, the highest paid in the world, and were well ahead of their American counterparts, whose average was $23.60 an hour. It goes without saying that the higher wages and better working conditions would not exist without higher productivity.[1]

This developed in Germany not simply through technology and the increased use of capital-intensive mass production, including robotics. Something more fundamental appears to have been at work, a long-term, thoughtful recognition of the fact that the most productive force of all is labor itself, the creative source of all capital. In line with this, German employers generally prefer to make promotions from within their existing labor force and to bring in new workers usually at the point of entry. That entry is through a rather remarkable, ancient but modernized, system of apprenticeship used all over Germany.

It came up out of the medieval guild system that began in central Europe hundreds of years ago and was brought up to date after World War II by cooperation between government, labor, and industry. It is costly but so beneficial it is considered indispensable. The system is operated by a nonprofit Federal Labor Agency run by people representing government, labor, and business. It employs almost one hundred thousand people at many hundreds of local offices and counseling centers, and actually has a legal monopoly on career counseling. It has a great many psychologists and also does considerable research on economic trends as a guide to industry.

Indoctrination of respect for quality work and its benefits begins early and is accompanied by all necessary information, such for example as how the sickness funds operate. The counselors make it a practice to visit every ninth-grade class and youngsters freely visit the Career Information Centers where they can have individual counseling and take tests. They can enter the apprenticeship system at some company in their chosen field of interest either on graduation from high school or at some later stage in their education. This involves something like three weeks learning on the job, then possibly two more weeks at a specialized school run by the company. After working as an apprentice for three years, if one does well, one can expect a regular job at usually about three times the pay of an apprentice.

Such dedication to training and related matters in the constant effort to improve Germany's ability to cope with economic problems explains in good part how it was possible, shortly after reunification, for Germany's export trade to exceed that of the United States, the leading world power with a population three and a half times Germany's eighty million.

The Role of Germany in Europe

In his insightful study of "the coming economic battle among Japan, Europe, and America," Lester Thurow found good reason to give Europe the edge. Germany is the recognized powerhouse of Europe. There is something more to this than the fact that it is the biggest and economically the strongest.[2]

Without stability the European Community cannot be effective—or even endure—and Germany not only insists on strict adherence to the parameters of economic stability, it is itself the leading example. It is well-known that the inherently anarchic, self-contradictory nature of capitalism produces instability, such as the ups and downs of the business cycles. Like all others, Germany has been subject to this, but unlike the rest, has for many years been relatively and remarkably stable. Two events will illustrate its calculated, reasonable adjustability and a possible special reason for this—one event in which labor collaborated with capital, the other in which labor fought off capital.

There was the special agreement on November 25, 1993, between the powerful metal workers union and the powerful Volkswagen company in which both parties recognized a fundamental economic necessity in their situation. They agreed to reduce their 5-day, 36-hour work week to a 4-day, 28.8-hour work week. They collaborated fifty-fifty on the cost of this 20 percent reduction in working time by the workers accepting a 10 percent reduction in weekly pay. This indirectly amounted to an increase in hourly or daily pay, a "hidden" benefit not likely to be forgotten in better or more productive times by so strong a union.[3]

Then there was the 1996 law passed which allowed employers to cut sick-pay from 100 percent for six weeks to 80 percent for six weeks. When, in the fall of that year, some of the biggest banks and manufacturers announced action along that line, the working class rose up with all manner of opposition: protest demonstrations, walk-outs, shift boycotts, slow-downs, refusal of overtime work, performance by-the-book. Hundreds of thousands were vehement participants. Within two months the business leaders had backed down. Obviously, while such a cut would be felt, it was not a life-or-death matter warranting a mass uprising—but labor correctly sensed it was being "felt out" and this was just the first shot in a possible general attack on living standards—and they would have none of it.[4]

In a relatively favorable situation, stability becomes important. In Germany, if capital would not see to it, labor would. And if in the European Community, others would not see to it, Germany would. In the case of currency, there would be no euro unless it could be as stable as the mark, because, in a sense, the euro would *be* the mark. Capital is concerned in its own way with the exchange value of the currency, but labor is also concerned as changes in the value affect the cost of living and can require difficult social remedies.

The Contribution of the Socially Mixed Economy

Germany presents more of the beginnings of the socially mixed economy as an instrument of social progress than any other capitalist country and this has facilitated its economic and political rise in domestic and international effectiveness. Germany has a long and distinguished history of social thought and it is hard to imagine a German leader in any economic activity unaware of the social significance of an action discussed or taken. Consciousness itself plays a role.

In order to educate the skilled and managerial personnel needed for even the most modern exploitation of labor, a capitalist ruling class need only provide vocational and professional training. When it provides the full range of education freely to all, as in Germany, the fact is that it is doing what capital can manage without—and does manage without in many other countries. It is, in effect, acting on a socialist principle. Of course it is doing it according to its own lights, quite differently from the way it would be done under socialism—but it is doing it. What is happening is what a consciously formed, socially mixed economy would establish as normal.

The German innovation of the "sickness fund" jointly operated by employers and employees in the provision of affordable universal medical care goes far beyond basic capitalist needs. It can be considered a capitalist-socialist cooperative, a joint venture from which both classes draw benefits but which is acting on a socialist principle. It is mixing the economy in such a way that the whole society lives better and operates more efficiently

The shorter work week has always been a socialist aim, an essential way to provide the time needed for creative activity and development of the human personality. The average work week in Germany is thirty-seven hours, shorter than any other country, except for France. It has been proposed to bring it down to thirty-five hours, some major unions urging thirty-two hours, as a means of dealing with the problem of high unemployment. It does not give the appearance of mixing the economy but it has that effect.

The required participation of employee representatives on boards of company management does not equalize control with employers, but does work toward mixing the economy. This is accomplished by placing mutual interest on the order of business, forcing intentions into the open, and thereby inhibiting antagonistic class action.

Finally, such familiar features of the "welfare state" as old age pensions and related benefits known as Social Security, unemployment insurance and related benefits, and miscellaneous aids to the indigent or disabled, are far more extended and generous in Germany than in the United States. They all act to mix the economy because they are not essential to the exploitation of labor and in fact did not even exist in the early stages of the development of capitalism.

Perhaps the most extraordinary characteristic of the German model of the socially mixed economy, at the turn of the century, is the contrast between the instability of its internal politics and the relative stability of its economy. The eighteen-year rule of the Christian Democrats under Helmut Kohl came to an end in the fall of 1998 and he was afflicted with scandals concerning past handling of political funds. The Greens, having switched over to the Social-Democrats, caused a brouhaha with talk about a turn toward the interests of business. A split developed among the Social-Democrats, between Chancellor Schroeder and party head La Fontaine, and the Social-Democrats lost a series of elections. A split developed even in the Party of Democratic Socialism, the successor to the East German Communist Party.

None of this chaotic activity among the politicians was capable of disturbing the remarkable stability of the German economy. How much of this can be attributed to its social mixture? And how far into the twenty-first century can it last?

Notes

1. Edmund L. Andrews, "Strike by Biggest German Union Is Averted," *New York Times*, 18 February 1999.
2. Lester Thurow, *Head to Head: The Coming Economic Battle Among Japan, Europe, and America* (New York: William Morrow, 1992), 252-53.
3. Ferdinand Protzman, "VW Plan for 4-Day Workweek Is Adopted," *New York Times*, 26 November 1993.
4. Edmund L. Andrews, "German Industry Losing Appetite for Labor Struggle," *New York Times*, 10 December 1996.

Chapter 13

French and Italian Statism

Does Statism Serve Capitalism or Socialism?

On February 1, 2000, France became the first country in world history to establish the thirty-five-hour workweek. To reduce the double-digit unemployment afflicting the people, the law had been initiated two years before by the leader of the Socialist Party, Prime Minister Lionel Jospin. It was neither a pro-capitalist nor a pro-socialist measure but one to benefit the country as a whole. Why then was it met with loud protests by a number of both employer and employee organizations? Apparently, even a non-class statist measure can be interpreted as having the thrust of a class interest, depending only on one's point of view.

Among capitalist countries, statist activity has been most effective in the European Economic Community (EEC) as a whole and especially in those countries with socially mixed economies, such as France and Italy. Austria and Sweden could also be listed among these countries but they have not been involved much in the extensive inter-governmental economic arrangements in the European Community. Such arrangements have been decried as statist by the American authorities, complaining of improper competition, subsidies, etc.

Europeans have long considered Americans who are taken in by such fulminations as politically infantile, noting the extensive help given American big business by the Pentagon's special sustaining contracts, the long-standing government subsidies to big agribusiness, and the enormously expensive bailing out of owners (and swindlers) of failed savings and loan banks, not to mention export facilities and loan guarantees. The key to American authorities' concern over statism, completely without candor, is that approval of it implies approval of socialism.

This charge is worth examination. Historically, those industries or big companies which have been nationalized have usually been the ones that private capitalists have been unable to operate profitably, but which have some importance in the national economy. Governments provide the required capital and the basic reorganization needed to stabilize them, and in those cases which do not become immediately profitable, simply subsidize them.

In such instances what the government is actually doing is rendering an essential public service. It is using income from the taxation of successful sectors of the economy and the public to sustain unprofitable but essential sectors on behalf of the people of the country as a whole. In addition to its use value there may be other benefits such as continued employment.

This is not yet socialism—bearing in mind that such state-operated enterprises move in collaboration with the general run of private capitalist business—but it is an obvious recognition that private enterprise has failed and has been remedied by socialized enterprise. It holds the promise of the possible advent of socialism, hinting at benefits making it superior to capitalism. Contributing to such thinking is the fact that the labor movement in such countries has been able to make use of the involvement in politics of the managers of statist enterprises to enhance wages and working conditions, and even to prevent such privatization as has been consonant with an attack on living standards.

France, a country in which about a third of the economy is state-operated and accounts for about half its production, provides interesting examples of this. Two of these occurred at Air France, the enormous airline which had been losing money and concerning which there had been much talk of privatization but no action. In October 1993, a plan to restructure the company and lay off 4,000 workers brought on a violent strike which shut down the two main airports in Paris for more than a week. It resulted in the withdrawal of the layoff plan and the resignation of the company chairman, Bernard Attali.

He was replaced by Christian Blanc, who in a contrary example, managed in April 1994 to win the approval of the strongly unionized employees for a restructuring to avoid bankruptcy without any layoffs whatever. Instead, wages were frozen for a time and 5,000 jobs were gradually eliminated by attrition. The government then undertook a financing package of up to 20 billion francs (about $3.4 billion). A number of key managers were to be replaced by ones prepared to cut costs by 30 percent by 1997.

A third rebuff to those who would solve a budget deficit problem at the expense of the working class came in October 1995 when President Jacques

Chirac, conservative successor to socialist Mitterand, attempted once again to freeze wages as in 1986 when Chirac had been Prime Minister. In this confrontation, all seven government service unions united for the first time since 1986 and five million workers walked out, shutting down all transport, communications, schools, and other vital services for more than a day. The freeze had to be withdrawn in the face of threats of more strikes, demonstrations, and slowdowns if necessary. It was clear other ways would have to be found to solve economic problems.

These and even more dramatic events of a similar nature in later years reflect the fact that concessions won from the ruling class in France are deemed irreversible. The relatively high standard of living of the working French is considered a normal entitlement, a condition they refer to sometimes as *le contrat sociale,* sometimes simply as *la civilisation.* Note that, unlike the western Germans, they have no need to tack on an attribution to capitalism. Much the same sophisticated air of normality characterizes the French attitude toward statist activity in the economy: it does not seem to take on one or another political coloration.

The European Community as a Cooperative

The freedom with which statist and private managements join forces to accomplish aims which private capitalism cannot fulfill on its own brings to the fore the unique value of the socially mixed economy; of the special ways of benefiting from advances made both in a capitalist and a socialist way, regardless whether so labeled. A substantial social benefit derives, for example, from changes in military planning which depart from traditional nationalistic ways of operating.

In one way this was shown in 1994 when Italy, France and England, each having separately decided it needed a new naval destroyer, set aside old-fashioned notions of secrecy and isolation in such matters. The three nations organized a consortium of shipbuilding, electronics, and armaments companies to build three "Eurofrigates" at a cost of up to $12 billion, much less than it would have cost them the traditional way.

The companies given military contracts for intergovernmental projects do not usually merge; they remain independent national entities, free to compete in other activities. They simply make their resources available in consortiums which divide production responsibilities according to best abilities and logistics, thereby eliminating the great costs of wasteful duplication.

This is how Germany, England, Italy, and Spain undertook a $50 billion European fighter aircraft project; how France, Germany, England and Spain planned a new military transport plane; how France and Germany worked on an armored personnel carrier; and how France, Germany, Italy, and the Netherlands planned the development of a military helicopter. The point of these examples is that having overcome the hindrance of traditional rivalries and mistrust on the military level, they could all the more freely cooperate on other levels.

It also worked the other way around. In the domestic aircraft field, there was the extraordinary success of the Airbus, which incidentally, took more than twenty persistent years to accomplish, challenging Boeing for the number one position in the world. The way they did it was to have Deutsche Aerospace in Germany make the fuselage for each of the five or six types of jet, British Aerospace make the wings, Casa in Spain make the tailfins, and have big transports called "Super Guppies" fly the parts to Toulouse, France, the base where Aérospatiale did the assembly. The complaint of their American competitors was that the four countries had poured $26 billion into the project. Naturally.

An even more startling success of European industrial cooperation, also as it happens French-led, is Arianespace, a partnership of forty European aerospace companies. Number one in the world, well beyond the United States, Russia, and China, it is the product of constant development ever since it sent up its first rocket in 1979, and already by 1994 was accounting for about half of all commercial launchings. As if to call the attention of Americans to its world position, Aérospatiale operates its launching pad in the western hemisphere, in French Guiana.

There have been both failures, like the French-British Concorde, and other successes, like the $180 billion *Train à Grande Vitesse*, the European high-speed train. Many other examples exist that point to the special value of government participation in both internal and cross-border operations of the economy. Public-private cooperation in the drive for economic development is not practical or durable without conformity to the separate interests of the capital and labor involved, and therefore takes on the aura of the socially mixed economy. In that spirit it seeks protection through joint action.

The "single market" was officially born January 1, 1993 when all tariff and customs barriers were eliminated among the 345 million people of the twelve nations then making up the European Economic Community. It was well understood that the free trade advantages were to be limited to these countries and those they would invite in, thereby strengthening the EEC competitively against the imperial economic thrusts of the United States and Japan. *Le Monde* stated this in its usual candid fashion:

> We would do well to deny our market to nations to which we owe nothing and that can do nothing for us or against us. Prussia's choice of a protectionist system 160 years ago enabled it to form the German state. A similar move by Japan some 50 years ago enabled it to become . . . [a] leading economic power.

> Europe will not exist unless it follows the same course, establishing itself as a trading bloc—reserving its market first for its founding members, then for those aspiring to raise themselves to its level (Eastern Europe), and finally for those whose underdevelopment is also a European problem. Such a greater European zone would be so large that—provided it is fully deregulated and compliance with the rules of competition is strictly monitored—there would be no danger of the harmful effects that classical economic theory assumes the establishment of trading blocs will generate.[1]

Special Problems in Statist Italy

Shipbuilding, steel, banking, mining, energy, aerospace, utilities, and railways are among the sectors in which the Italian state is either the sole owner or the dominant force. Close to half the economy is operated by the government. Through the years, especially 1992-1995, there has been an ebb and flow of austerity plans at the expense of the working class, in order to reduce the enormous national debt and budget deficits. These plans included pressures for privatization ostensibly to accomplish the same result—but not a great deal has changed. Protests in which millions of workers have taken to the streets have time and again been politically effective, with the administration of any party attempting such a plan finding itself out of power within a year.

During the same years it became no longer possible to cover up the incredibly widespread corruption among leading business and political figures. One exposé led to another, resulting in some three thousand arrests in high places, the disintegration of the Christian Democratic Party and the flight from prosecution into self-exile of the long-time leader of the Socialist Party. With former prime ministers, cabinet ministers, and important business leaders under investigation or arrest, the revulsion of the people expressed itself in the 1995 regional elections. There was an upsurge of support for the largest leftist organization, the Party of the Democratic Left, successor to the Communist Party of Italy, which had been the largest of Europe's communist parties. In those elections it gained 26 percent of the total vote.

A Personification of the Socially Mixed Economy

Under these circumstances, the Left proved able to stimulate and maintain organization of a new Center-Left coalition, gaining for the first time even the support of the hard-line Communist Refoundation, and quite broadly, some elements of the old Christian Democrats, some from the set back Socialist Party, and some others. Appropriately, a new type of unaffiliated politician came forward as spokesman of the coalition, a progressive professor of economics at the University of Bologna—Romano Prodi.

Non-partisan to a fault, Prodi himself is unique. Without having campaigned for it, he was endorsed by two of Italy's three large labor unions and some parts of the Catholic press. He spent time at the London School of Economics, at Harvard, and at Stanford but has shown he is not limited to the academy. In 1982 he was called in to rescue Italy's largest publicly owned company, IRI, which was near bankruptcy. In seven years as chairman, he turned it to profit, shedding more than a fifth of its 550,000 employees by selling off steel, banking, and automobile subsidiaries. And yet, when called to head the new organization called "The Italy We Want" he was only fifty-five.

It is a sign of the times that such a man, sufficiently respected by General Electric, IBM, and Goldman Sachs to have been on their international advisory boards, is unimpressed by his own standing, rides a bicycle, has a modest office, and feels completely at home with his colleagues on the Left. Perhaps it is the *Emilio Romagna* air, "the way people just are" in Bologna, which has always been a unique place, a comfortable, politically clean, well-kept city with a relatively high standard of living, run continuously by communists for about fifty years. The whole province has been known as a "red belt."

Perhaps it is something else, a duality, a kind of natural evolution through a learned life in both upper and lower classes to function as a personification of the socially mixed economy. It seemed inevitable he would be ultimately recruited into the leadership of the European Community, itself a developing socially mixed economy.

In the year 2000, as President of the European Commission, he was busy working with a Council of Sages he created to carry out the mandate of the EU special summit meeting held in October 1999 in Tampere, Finland. Their task was to work toward a European constitution with rules governing legal rights, penal codes, border security, asylum policies, and other matters, without destroying existing national achievements.[2]

First in Health Care

On June 20, 2000, the World Health Organization issued rankings in health care for the 191 nations that are its members, disregarding relative sizes of population. France and Italy were at the head of the top five, along with San Marino, Andorra, and Malta.

The report measured not just overall spending on health but also how health care was distributed among different groups in each population. It found, for example, that the United States outspends the world and ranks near the top in average health measures, but fails to deliver good health care to a large proportion of its population and distributes the cost relatively unfairly, leaving it at number thirty-seven in the rankings. European health systems, according to the report, are generally performing best.[3]

The indication is that countries with socially mixed economies are more oriented toward caring for the health of their people as a whole than other countries. The direct relation may not be provable but the opinion is reasonable.

Notes

1. Alain Gomez, "The Folly in Free Trade," *Le Monde*, Paris, quoted in *World Press Review* 40, no. 2 (February 1993) 52.

2. Torsten Wohlert, "Limitless Growth", *Freitag*, Berlin, 22 October 1999, quoted in *World Press Review* 47, no. 1 (January 2000) 4.

3. Philip J. Hilts, "Europeans Perform Highest in Ranking of World Health," *New York Times*, 21 June 2000.

Chapter 14

The Wayward Six in Eastern Europe

The Common Problem

Although more than six other European countries happen to be located east of Western Europe, because of a common history those usually referred to as Eastern Europe were six in number. They remained six, as listed below, even though the German Democratic Republic was lost by fusion with the Federal Republic of Germany on October 3, 1990, that event having been followed by the fission of Czechoslovakia on January 1, 1993.

Their socialist identity had not derived from socialist revolutions or any other national initiatives, but only from their having been so declared by the Soviet Union when occupied by the Red Army as World War II was ending. Their main commonality lay in the fact that they had functioned as members of Comecon, the Council of Mutual Economic Assistance, in which they benefited from subsidized arrangements with the Soviet Union, while subservient to it, and operated their economies in an imposed division of labor, which while helpful in some ways, limited their development.

For some forty-five years they were all called socialist countries and carried on as such, with social benefits but also with the deficiencies of command administrations. It cannot be said that they followed Lenin's thinking that "socialism without democracy is unthinkable." There were also some problems related to their diversity—ethnic, economic, political, and demographic. Their approximate populations: forty million in Poland, twenty-three million in Romania, nine million in Bulgaria, ten million in Hungary, ten million in the Czech Republic, and five million in Slovakia.

Those who were adults in 1989, when Gorbachev's drive toward democratization had undone the dominance of Soviet rule over them, found themselves virtually suspended between social systems, unable through inexperience to make optimal choices, reaching out therefore to have the best of both worlds, perhaps as in an imagined socially mixed economy.

They had not experienced socialism in the idealized form that was claimed for it, but only its deformation under Stalinism. They had not experienced capitalism as it really existed in the West, only the rosy deceptions mass-produced by television, Hollywood movies, and other guided media. They had heard of something in both systems called "reforms" and another mysterious thing called a "market economy." They were left with an intuition that capitalism had something they needed, something that socialism as they knew it could not provide.

What these otherwise intelligent, educated people didn't understand, for lack of direct knowledge, was that the nature of a market economy is determined by the social system controlling it; that in and of itself a market is nothing more than a facility for the purchase and sale of things and services; and that markets had existed from time immemorial and could exist under capitalism, socialism, or any other system. What they couldn't know in advance was that the glib promoters bearing gifts of promise really sought to exploit the people and any resources they might have for at least as high a profit as could be gained elsewhere.

Their intuition, however, was correct. Capitalism did have something they needed: in one word, capital; in three words, means of production. Eastern Europeans had been in the same predicament as all others who had established socialist systems, whether after revolutions or otherwise: in no such country had there been a sufficient prior accumulation of capital—that full development of the capitalist system Marx had envisioned as the necessary foundation for the building of a true socialist structure.

Another factor is important to bear in mind. In the modern world, in which technology often runs ahead of existing national economic structures and competitive abilities, no country, not even the well-endowed United States, is entirely self-sufficient. Every country wishing to move forward finds itself dependent on specific imports of one kind or another, with payment usually required in hard currency. Eastern European countries could not rely for this, in any adequate way, on tourism or remittances from relatives in the West, as did some other underprivileged nations. Exports were the answer, exports to this rich West—and these Easterners, for the most part, could produce goods for this purpose. The trouble was that the West appeared more interested in selling than buying.

Into this dilemma came a Sir Galahad riding from the West, a galloping knight-errant who would perform wondrous deeds to bring prosperity. It would occasion some pain for a little while, it was true, but only pain for the common people who, after all, were accustomed to deprivation. This guru of political economy, Jeffrey Sachs, was more than just a Harvard professor. He had written a trail-blazing article in a 1990 issue of *The Economist* which outlined the entire strategy later to be known as "shock therapy," following it up with articles in other prestigious journals and some books. His proposals were highly praised by other establishment economists and had the strong backing of leading spokesmen among the G-7 powers. He was therefore in much demand among the so-called reformers who had taken power in the East.

In short order he became an official consultant in Yugoslavia, then in Poland, where the uneducated Lech Walesa obviously needed his tutoring, and then in Russia, where Yeltsin's pro-capitalist economists Yegor Gaidar and Boris Fyodorov, didn't need educating but valued his suggestions. The word spread and much happened as a result, albeit in half-baked fashion, throughout the East.

Within a few years, however, the people became so fed up with the gross inequities and deprivations of shock therapy that Sachs found himself out of the picture, the people having ousted Walesa, Gaidar, Fyodorov and the reform nabobs in all the Eastern European countries except the Czech Republic. Instead, in all those five Eastern countries, they voted in former Communist Party leaders, who favored continued moves toward a market economy which the people also appeared to favor, but who also pledged to slow the process down to a reasonable pace. The main thing pledged was that they would use the government to run the economy for the people's benefit, safeguarding traditional social services and democratic rights. What brought about this drastic political change?

Lessons of the Experience with Reform

The fundamental problem from which other evils flowed had been the break-up of Comecon, which Sachs had sneered at as a "community of the poor," and a break in essential economic activity between the six Eastern European countries and those in what was then the Soviet Union and later the Commonwealth of Independent States. The Gorbachev government and even the French government had favored the retention of the Comecon economic conveniences as a way of making Eastern Europe's moves toward a market economy far less painful and much more constructive. Sachs and his yea-sayers, however, were adamantly opposed, insisting that utter destruction of that system was the absolute condition for gaining the benefits of relations with the West, from whom great gobs of investment could be expected.

The East conformed, their tongues hanging out for the much-needed capital. They even tried to go along with his main aim, privatization, to an extent that would be going far beyond anything they could realistically accomplish, and even beyond anything Western Europe itself had ever accomplished. It was a maximum program, reflecting more than anything else the sheer arrogance, hypocrisy, and typical inhumanity of imperialist ideologues. At one point there was even the galling suggestion that they should begin to charge for higher schooling, surely a ludicrous notion for people well aware that even advanced capitalist countries like Germany and France provided free university tuition and even stipends where needed.

The "rapid transformation," involved instruments such as destatization of some industries, questionable and often corrupt privatization, deregulation of prices inducing inflation, bankruptcies and shut-downs caused by the termination of subsidies, and the ham-fisted actions of some foreign entrepreneurs. All combined to devastate the economies, causing high unemployment, a loss of social services, and widespread impoverishment. Even within the first year the people could see they were getting, as many said, shock without therapy.[1]

What about the promised capital, the all-important foreign direct investment? The sad lesson learned was that capitalists like to buy everything on the cheap. Many business purchases were made but the total capital involved was relatively small. Here are the totals for the period of the first four years as a whole[2]:

Hungary	$5.50 billion
Poland	3.04
Czech Republic	2.30
Romania	0.76
Bulgaria	0.24
Slovenia	0.14
Slovakia	0.13

Leaving out Slovenia, which is in Central rather than Eastern Europe, the combined total comes to $11.97 billion. To realize how skimpy this is, scattered unevenly among six countries, compare this $12 billion with the $150 billion invested by West Germany in the conversion of East Germany alone, with its population of sixteen million, only one-sixth that of the combined six Eastern countries.

Another sad lesson learned was just how crassly capitalists can behave when allowed to act as economic occupiers. There is the case in Hungary of Tungsram, a successful, diversified company especially well-known for its large-scale production of light bulbs. General Electric, whose unexpressed interest was apparently limited to extending its international leadership in light bulbs, bought the whole company in order to have a free hand—and then promptly shut down its production of vacuum equipment, electronic components, floppy disks, and magnetic tape products, all of which had been found profitable by the Tungsram management. What matter to General Electric the havoc and privation this would cause!

Finally, what became of the alluring prospect of the access trumpeted by Jeffrey Sachs, access to the promised land of trade with the European Community? The EC extended a warm invitation. There was just one little problem however: any products competitive with those produced by EC member companies could not be admitted to its so-called free market. Was this to be a new kind of iron curtain between Eastern and Western Europe?

The New Roads of the Eastern Countries

As one reads what Eastern European activists came generally to be discussing, people who are surely not unsophisticated, one notices an apparent reluctance to deal with systemic aspects of socialism and capitalism. Instead, there appears to be a preference for the term "a third way." It is not just a convenient phrase but a developing reality. Through all the storm and stress what emerges most persistently is a reaching out for the best things available in both systems, as if to probe the unprecedented possibilities of the socially mixed economy. Daniel Singer summarized it well in 1994:

> What we have been watching in the past five years throughout the East is a battle for power and property between privileged elites, with the working people occasionally striking to defend their own immediate position and at other moments being used as electoral fodder. Yet sooner or later they should enter the stage as the main actors, with their fundamental interests reflected in their own vision of society. If, or rather when, they do so, they will probably seek what they should have been looking for from the start: their own forms of management and democracy, a third way, their own, as strikingly distant from the Stalinist heritage as from capitalism with its inevitably inhuman face.[3]

In the second half of the 1990s each of the six countries became so concentrated on its own problems that the very concept of Eastern Europe began to disappear and finally ceased even being mentioned in the Western press. It is as if they were behaving like Stephen Leacock's rider who "flung himself upon his horse and rode madly off in all directions." Their individual propensities had been forced by circumstance to become decisive.

The freedom to move toward the West, which they appeared to have gained from the relaxation of Soviet control, did not carry with it a full sense of security. Three of these—Poland, the Czech Republic, and Hungary had painful memories of military action against them, and weak as it may have become economically and politically, the Russian bear was still there, militarily poised as a nuclear power.

Russian influence and potential power was a matter of concern in the West, especially for the United States, which wished to extend its military suzerainty in Europe through NATO. And so, by 1999, all three found their applications for membership in NATO accepted, effective at a time when they could make the required military contributions. The embrace of the West, however, did not prove as felicitous for the disparate economic needs of each of the three.

As for the others—Romania, Bulgaria, and Slovakia—who were aware of the lack of felicity in the Western relationship, there was neither the same orientation toward the West nor respect by NATO for their possible value to it. The three-for-three diversity, however, did not keep the six from making the effort to maintain normal economic relations among themselves. The trend toward the socially mixed economy varies among the six just as they differ in other ways, never having had good historical reasons for being considered a political unit. Comecon had only been an economic convenience.

In Poland, Andrej Lepper, the leader of an opposition called Self-Defense, displayed in his office a quotation from Pope John Paul II: "It is unacceptable to claim that after the fall of Communism, capitalism is the only alternative." Ten years after the Communist head of government, General Wojciech Jaruzelski, peacefully turned over power to Solidarity's Lech Walesa, which is what Poles refer to as "the revolution," there was great discontent with the rapid rise of capitalism. In September 1999, about fifty thousand gathered in a protest demonstration in central Warsaw, including farmers, miners, the unemployed, underpaid teachers and nurses, steelworkers, and arms industry employees.[4]

Anna Walentynowicz, a former welder at the famous Gdansk Shipyard, is an instructive symbol. She had been fired for criticizing directors and for making candles commemorating forty-four workers killed in a strike ten years earlier. She was popular and the resulting successful strike demanding her reinstatement and a pay raise led to the extraordinary grass roots movement called Solidarity in 1980. She says now: "We wanted better money, improved work safety, a free trade union, and my job back. Nobody wanted a revolution. And when I see what the so-called revolution has brought—mass poverty, homelessness, self-styled capitalists selling off our plants and pocketing the money—I think we were right."

Her interviewer adds: "There are millions like her. Pensioners eking out a living on $200 a month; the unemployed; those nostalgic for the predictable security, closer communities and free day-care centers of old; the disillusioned who believed capitalism was actually good in some moral sense and now recoil at the egotism of what many former East Germans call 'the elbow society'." Further on he mentions that Walentinowic, who spent nineteen months in jail during martial law, had, "like others in the former Soviet bloc, actually dreamed of some sort of 'Third Way,' a true socialism."[5]

Under the existing realities, that would have to take the form of a socially mixed economy. Poles might not have this term in mind, but known for their national pride, might very well, like the Russians who look forward to "the Russian way," make use of the term "the Polish way." In mid-2000, considerable speculation developed as to Poland's future, arising from a split between the main Solidarity Party and its junior partner, the Freedom Party. Most polls indicated that elections scheduled for the fall of 2001 would be easily won by the Democratic Left Alliance, a cohesive group made up mostly of former Communists. "The Polish way" would have to be its order of business.[6]

In Hungary, where a surface doom-and-gloom apprehension appears to be a national trait born out of a long, unbroken history of military defeats, there is a talent for survival, along with above-average talents in the arts and sciences, marked by an older and stronger orientation to the West than in any other Eastern European country. Even during the Cold War years, Hungary had been hospitable to Western economic ideas.

That is when Yuri Andropov, Soviet KGB head who became General Secretary of the CPSU, chose Hungary to experiment with market reforms such as Gorbachev later undertook, and loosened control of the economy to let some free enterprise take hold. The result was that while about 97 percent of Czechoslovakia's economy was state-owned before the fall of the Berlin Wall, in Hungary the number never topped 80 percent.[7]

Early in the post-Soviet period, here is how Roger Cohen described the nature of things:

> It has been a terrible three years for Eastern Europe. The economies of the region have shrunk by almost 25 percent, since the painful transition to capitalism began. But in Hungary, where the model that served post-war Italy well appears to be finding favor, the faint outlines of a success story are beginning to appear.
>
> The Hungarians have long prided themselves on being shrewd, practical people. When the country was part of the Soviet Bloc, it was sometimes described as 'the West of the East' because of its ability to circumvent Moscow by quietly introducing, from 1968 onward, elements of a market economy. Now that same pragmatism is being applied in a way that may one day turn the country into the Italy of the East.
>
> 'In the rapid growth of small and medium-sized enterprises, in the development of a huge underground economy, in our widespread evasion of taxes and even in our slow-moving government, we have a sort of Italian system taking shape here,' said Eva Voska, a prominent economist here and an expert on privatization.
>
> Over the past three years, the number of legally registered private companies has shot up to 57,000 from 5,000. Beside this, said Gyorgy Suranyi, for-

> mer governor of the central bank, 'there are tens of thousands, perhaps hundreds of thousands, of small, family businesses operating outside the official economy.' In a sign of this activity, savings have been rising sharply, a development not usually associated with a steep recession such as Hungary's last year.
>
> A chief attraction [to major foreign investors] appears to be Hungary's pragmatism. Unlike Czechoslovakia and Poland, which opted for sweeping 'shock' programs to introduce market economies, Hungary has taken a more gradualist approach. In part, this choice reflected the fact that the country had already moved some way toward a mixed economy before 1989. Private holdings in the countryside and small businesses were already widely tolerated when the Communist government fell.[8]

The next national election on May 8, 1994 brought a big swing back toward the left. The Socialist Party, chiefly people who had been Communists, emerged as the largest single party with 33 percent of a relatively high vote, in first-round elections. The Hungarian Democratic Forum, the conservatives who had ruled since 1990, wound up with only 12 percent of the vote. The country's gross domestic product had fallen 20 percent. A poll in the month before the election showed barely 50 percent favoring private ownership of large companies, while less than 30 percent approved any foreign control of privatized assets. Foreign takeovers were particularly held to account for much of Hungarian unemployment, then about 12.2 percent.[9]

Gyula Horn, who was the last Communist foreign minister, became the new Prime Minister, and even though he had a clear enough majority in Parliament to rule without them, negotiated and signed a coalition agreement with the opposition liberals, the Free Democrats. He was under pressure from the International Monetary Fund and was trying to resist the cuts in social welfare demanded by the I.M.F. He was also slowing up the moves toward market reforms.

As might have been expected, he could not satisfactorily solve the economic problems brought on by market reforms, while remaining pledged to such reforms, nor maintain Hungary's relatively generous social welfare measures, to which he also remained pledged, while meeting I.M.F. demands. Amid all the public dissatisfaction, a new center-right movement was growing rapidly by virtue of ingeniously (and temporarily) limiting membership to those under thirty-five, who had therefore no first-hand experience with socialism, which could be falsely held responsible for current problems, while promoting the rosy-hued promise of a faster path to Western prosperity.

The result was that in the next elections, May 24, 1998, the center-right Young Democrats-Civic Party became the leading party and the thirty-four-year old Victor Orban became prime minister. He was quick to say he would continue talks aimed at gaining membership in the European Union. A degree of balance was possible though not easy to establish between the Young Democrats with 149 seats and the Socialists with 133 seats, but they would have to take into account that 14 seats were won by the extreme rightist Hungarian Truth and Life Party, known for its anti-Semitic and racist positions.[10]

One thing appeared certain, due to strong public insistence. The network of social welfare measures would remain and, along these lines at least, Hungary was continuing its socially mixed economy in the same taken-for-granted manner as in the Western European countries it admires.

Social unrest in the Czech Republic makes pendulum swings in electoral politics to be expected there also, either in one direction as in Poland, or in the other as in Hungary. *Le Monde Diplomatique* was struck by it in April 2000:

> A specter haunted November's celebrations of the tenth anniversary of the 'velvet revolution.' After years on the margins, the Communist Party of Bohemia and Moravia (KSCM) had suddenly doubled its rating in opinion polls, to the dismay of the Czech Social Democratic Party (CSSD), which came to power in 1989. . . . KSCM Party Chairman Miroslav Grebenicek is clear about the reasons:
>
> > 'The brand-new capitalist system is not working. That is to say, it's working very well for the lucky 10,000 at the top of the social pyramid and very badly for the rest of us.'. . . The CSSD's opinion poll rating fell from 26 percent in mid-1998 to 15 percent last November. In the same period, support for the communists rose from 12 percent to 24.5 percent. . . .
> >
> > This puts the KSCM in an almost ideal situation. The social democrats and their friends in the trade union leadership are embarrassed by demonstrations of laid-off workers demanding their few months' wages. The communists, excluded from the democratic bloc, are riding the wave of growing anger and frustration, and their proposed policy of job creation through virtual re-nationalization is strengthening their image as the 'workers' party.
> >
> > 'We intend to give the state the enterprises it needs in order to play its proper role,' says Vojtech Filip, coordinator of the communist parliamentary group. 'We are thinking in terms of creating new enterprises. But compulsory repurchase—re-nationalization, if you like—is also an option.'
>
> Among the general public, anticommunism is not what it was. . . . 43 percent of voters say they are prepared to accept communist participation in the government. . . .
>
> Finally, anticommunism has no deep roots among the under-twenty-fives, who never really lived under the old regime. What is more, a growing minority among the young are attracted to the idea of communism, to communist ethics and commitment.[11]

Two months earlier in 2000, the Foreign Service of the *Washington Post* was also struck by the relatively strong upsurge in popularity of the Czech Communist Party (Communist Party of Bohemia and Moravia, so renamed because of opposition to the January 1, 1993 division of Czechoslovakia into two republics):

> Ten years after the Velvet Revolution toppled one of the most oppressive of Eastern Europe's Soviet-era governments, a largely unreformed Communist Party has surged in opinion polls to become one of the two most popular parties in the Czech Republic, which is a new member of NATO and a leading candidate for membership in the European Union. . . . some analysts are raising a once-unthinkable possibility: the Communists could return to power. . . .
>
> The current minority Social Democratic government, in return for the support of the rightist Civic Democratic Party, is committed to passing electoral reform legislation by July that would boost the parliamentary representation of the larger parties beyond their share of the electoral vote. The details of the measure are still to be determined, but it is designed to effectively create a two-party system composed of the Social Democratic Party and Civic Democratic Party. It could instead propel the Communists into government. 'Both parties are blind enough to pave the way for them,' said Jiri Pehe, a former dissident and adviser to President Vaclav Havel who heads the Prague campus of New York University. 'Who can say that the Communist Party will not get 30 percent of the vote [in elections two years away] and end up with 45 percent of the seats?'. . . .
>
> The Communists have benefited from the hardship of three years of recession here and a growing sense that the two main parties are wedded to the trappings of power rather than to the Czech Republic's economic progress. In recent opinion polls, 80 percent of the Czechs said they were 'disgusted' with the practice of politics in the country. And one hundred thousand workers in failing state enterprises have not been paid for months. . . .
>
> The Social Democrats, who have fallen to between 11 and 15 percent in polls from 32 percent in the last election, say they can climb out of the trough. But so far, the numbers favor the Communists, who are in a virtual dead heat with the Civic Democrats in polls. In one October 1999 survey, the Communist Party polled 23 percent and the Civic Democrats 21 percent. Since then, the Communists have trailed just behind the Civic Democrats with 20 percent. . . .
>
> Analysts such as Keith Crawford, a lecturer in politics at Charles University in Prague, say that . . . the return of hard-line communism is inconceivable: 'There is a lot of paranoia about them, but strip away the word Communist, look at their policies, and what you've got is a heavy dose of welfarism,' he said. 'I believe their support is dissatisfaction looking for something to hook onto. Support for the Communist Party is not support for communism but for a social net.' [12]

All through the decade since the end of Soviet power in Czechia—to which these analysts have been referring—whether within Czechoslovakia or separated from Slovakia, the "welfarism" mentioned above has been extensively maintained and is an important element of the country's socially mixed economy. Popular insistence on its retention was to be expected in a country where incomes, for example, were generally higher than in Poland or Hungary, a country which had always been noted for its relatively higher-skilled labor and technical expertise than the rest of Eastern Europe, and a country more involved in European culture.

In the decade since Eastern Europe began its systemic change-over, it has become very evident that the West has settled on Poland, Czechia, and Hungary as its favored three, the "sphere of influence" in which to extend the military power of NATO and the economic power of its capital investments. It has expressed hospitality to similar future relations with the unfavored three: Romania, Bulgaria, and Slovakia, as in the encouraging speech President Clinton made in Bulgaria when passing through there in November 1999, but that is all it amounts to.

In the first half of that decade, while it is true the population of the unfavored three stood at little more than 60 percent that of the favored three, the amount of foreign direct investment stood at only 10 percent, only one-sixth as much! So great a disproportion could only be the result of deliberate choices. The labor skills, the industrial experience, the hunger for employment, the willingness to protect investment were all there, comparably, in all six countries.

Big problems in the unfavored three were the resistance to rapid privatization, expressed suspicion of Western motivation, and strong objection to cuts in social welfare that the International Monetary Fund was in the habit of requiring. Lacking also the previous trade and economic support from the East, the result was deep poverty. A socially mixed economy without funds cannot provide benefits. It may remain in form, demanding future substance, but that can only be a call to such action as people are prepared to take.

Notes

1. Peter Gowan, *New Left Review* no. 213 (September-October 1995): 3-60.

2. *New York Times*, "Foreign Investment: Eastern Europe 1990—January 1994," *New York Times*, 3 May 1994.

3. Daniel Singer, "Ex-Communists and Rough Beasts," *Nation* 259, no. 16 (14 November 1994) 580-82.

4. Roger Cohen, "Poland's Glossy Capitalism Displays a Darker Underside," *New York Times*, 30 September 1999.

5. Roger Cohen, "The Accommodations of Adam Michnik," *New York Times Magazine* (7 November 1999): 71.

6. Associated Press, "Liberal Partner Bolts Coalition Leading Poland," *New York Times,* 7 June 2000.

7. Kyle Pope, "Hungary's Privatization Czar Is Unloaded," *Wall Street Journal,* 21 October 1996.

8. Roger Cohen, "Smaller Companies Grease the Wheels in Hungary," *New York Times,* 3 May 1992.

9. William Pomeroy, "Hungarian Election Turns Out Right-Wing Regime," *People's Weekly World,* 28 May 1994.

10. Associated Press, "Center-Right Coalition Beats Hungary Socialists," *New York Times,* 25 May 1998.

11. Adam Novak, *Le Monde Diplomatique*, April 2000, "Return of the Communists," in *World Press Review* 47, no. 7 (July 2000): 33-34.

12. Peter Finn, *Washington Post Foreign Service,* 20 February 2000, 30(A), E-mail from philipoke@earthlink.net (February 22, 2000).

Chapter 15

The Vietnamese and Cuban Models

Two Davids and Their Goliath

Vietnam and Cuba, the smallest of the four countries which made and sustained socialist revolutions, have provided world history with its most startling incarnations of the David and Goliath legend, having for decades fended off the aggressive power of U.S. imperialism.

Consider the incredible disproportions: There are currently about eighty million Vietnamese, and many fewer during what they call "the American War" when half their number in the South were held back from support, with a total land mass only the size of New Mexico; and about eleven million Cubans in one-third that land mass, about the size of Pennsylvania. Both countries with very poor economies are pitted against the world's greatest military and economic force with over three times their combined population.

To top this off, they are proceeding to milk the capitalist cow with all manner of joint ventures, bringing in a growing number of direct foreign investments, albeit cautiously, to build up their variously damaged productive forces. No deception is involved in this, both countries having made clear their dedication to maintaining socialist control of the commanding heights of their economies. Participating capitalists, on the other hand, undoubtedly have their own convictions as to the ultimate effects of their own operations within these socially mixed economies.

It is true, of course, that Vietnam and Cuba could not have survived the most crucial years of their struggles, both in war and peace, without the substantial materiel supplied by the Soviet Union, and to a lesser but significant extent, by China as well. But they bore the main brunt themselves and after 1990 had to operate very much on their own.

The Trend toward the Socially Mixed Economy

Their moves toward mixing the economy, especially in the case of Vietnam, began well before the end of substantial Soviet and Chinese aid. The ideological stimulus and the acceptance in socialist theory of making use of a market economy arose from Mikhail Gorbachev's program of perestroika and glasnost all through the latter 1980s. The remarks disparaging him that can be heard in Vietnamese and Cuban circles relate not to the program as much as to his inability to maintain control, and especially to his indication that they would have to be pretty much on their own. The fact is, however, they came to apply much of his program in their own ways.

Capitalist leaders, who find it necessary for the political health of their systems to adopt reforms of a putatively socialist nature are not inclined, as this study does, to identify such measures as socialistic in their nature. They try to claim them as their own under the catch-all ambiguities of the much-abused words "democracy" or "the free world" or other euphemisms of establishment rhetoric. This makes it possible to treat socialism as an obvious enemy of all that is good.

A somewhat similar evasion is practiced along opposite lines among the countries that made socialist revolutions. Since none of them was favored at the outset with the capital needed for the construction of socialism, all are now, each in its own way, reaching out for it. Albeit under socialist or statist control, this process does involve engaging in some capitalist practices—but this is not to be advertised. It is, however, only technically true to say, in Fidel Castro's phrase, that "capital is not capitalism."[1]

The ways in which socialism could be preserved and enhanced, while making use of market practices to solve their economic problems, has been the subject of deep discussion and sharp dispute in the Communist Party congresses of both Vietnam and Cuba.

The Trend in Vietnam

Vietnam began the process of mixing the economy well before Cuba—at a party congress in December 1986. Political anxiety caused a slow-down in the process around 1989, but in 1991 it was decided to move ahead with it more boldly. To formalize it, a law was enacted that year giving all Vietnamese citizens eighteen and older the right to open private businesses, with only certain environmentally and socially critical operations subject to approval.

Another important step taken in 1991 was to set up a Western-style central bank and five competitive commercial banks, four of which are state-owned and one privately owned, each with an initial capital of about thirty million dollars. In addition to encouraging domestic private enterprise, Vietnam warmly welcomed direct foreign investment, with the result that by 1993 the figure of four billion dollars had been reached, spread among industry, oil and gas, and hotels and tourism. At least ten countries were represented by investments over one hundred million dollars. By then, Vietnam had become the world's third largest exporter of rice, after Thailand and the United States.

Pravda in Moscow gave it high marks:

> The paradise of a socialist market economy has not arrived in Vietnam. But reforms are gaining tremendous momentum, and the movement seems unstoppable. In 1988, the Vietnamese radically changed the agricultural system, allowing peasants to receive land from the state on long-term lease and giving them full autonomy for managing it. Just two years later, the first fruits of the new policy appeared: for the first time Vietnam became self-sufficient in food. A new economic "dragon" is rising in Asia and should achieve full strength in ten to fifteen years. The lion's share of the projects are concentrated in Ho Chi Minh City. . . .Vietnam has made the transition to a market economy while maintaining its previous course toward socialism. The country has achieved success in diverse areas by relying above all on its own resources and only later on foreign investment.[2]

Expansion continued in 1994. The Singer Company, from its base in Hong Kong, announced a plan to open as many as one hundred stores in Vietnam over a three to four year period and to manufacture sewing machines through a joint venture in Ho Chi Minh City. Its new plant, when fully operating early in 1995, would be making 250,000 machines a year as well as assembling durable goods ranging from televisions to refrigerators. Singer planned to make credit available to consumers as it had been doing with great success in China.[3]

Vietnam is no small entrepreneur in its own right. Vietnam Airlines was talked about in 1994 as the coming leading regional carrier, already profitable in 1993 when it carried over a million passengers to fourteen domestic and seventeen foreign cities, with seats filled to 75 percent capacity. Knowing its expansion plans, Boeing, McDonnell Douglas, and Airbus offered discounts on new planes and asked their governments to provide attractive financing with help from banks. Vietnam considered a plan to raise expansion money by offering domestic and foreign investors a minority stake in the airline.[4]

After the United States faced reality and ended its thirty-year-old trade embargo in 1994, quite a few American companies came to compete with those of other countries and entered into all manner of joint ventures. The World Bank was sufficiently impressed to make a $150 million loan, its fourth to Vietnam. By 1995 the United States had opened a liaison office in Hanoi and signed an agreement to exchange diplomats, having reached a settlement on private and government claims.

With so many foreign entrepreneurs coming in, abuses of workers by exploitative managers were bound to develop and the trade union movement pressed for legislation. In June 1994 a comprehensive labor law was passed by the National Assembly. It provided for compulsory unionization of every shop floor in the country, protection against wrongful dismissal, allowed for unemployment benefits, retrenchment packages, maternity leave, sickness benefits, new technology allowances, skill training, courts of conciliation and arbitration—even enterprise bargaining.

Most importantly, at a time when Vietnam's workers were beginning to fight back against exploitative managers, it enshrined in law the right to strike. Companies that failed to respect the rights of their workers could, under that law, have their licenses revoked, be reported to their respective embassies, and see their actions reported in the media.[5]

By the middle of 1995 it became possible to report that over 50 countries with more than 1,200 investment licenses worth more than $14 billion were active, that Japan had become the largest single investing country, and that the United States had already come up from nowhere to fifth place.[6]

Near the end of 1995 came news of an especially important event. China and Vietnam agreed to reopen rail links severed in the late 1970s during a brief border war. Jiang Zemin, General Secretary of China's Communist Party, and Do Moui, his Vietnamese counterpart, issued a communiqué pointing to the "immense potential for the two countries to expand economic and trade cooperation." The report stated that trade that year was expected to pass one billion dollars, more than doubling the previous year's total—and that Beijing had proposed joint exploitation of the Spratly Islands.[7]

The dual nature of Vietnam's socially mixed economy was illustrated in 1996, on the one hand, by a statement at the Communist Party congress that year that "the state sector is the leading sector of the economy and together with the collective sector makes up the foundation of the economy" and, on the other hand, announcing an impressive list of the main foreign investors (slightly shifted in standing from a year before):[8]

	No. of Projects	Value in Billions
Taiwan	272	$4.09
Japan	167	2.69
Singapore	146	2.49
Hong Kong	188	2.39
South Korea	171	2.32
United States	63	1.32
Malaysia	51	1.01
France	80	0.76
Thailand	66	0.70
British Virgin Is.	38	0.69

On May 9, 1997, ending a twenty-two-year hiatus, Pete Peterson was warmly greeted on his arrival in Hanoi as U.S. Ambassador. He had spent six-and-a-half years there as a prisoner after his plane had been shot down in the war. On September 7, 1999, a new U.S. consular building in Ho Chi Minh City was dedicated on the very same site where twenty-four years before the then U.S. Ambassador had fled by helicopter from the roof of the Embassy.

Such dramatic echoes of this modest hero-country's remarkable history point to the respect in which it is broadly held. But what is most impressive is its unrelenting dedication to social progress, to the task at hand even when slammed by such great natural disasters as the punishing drought and lethal flooding that marked the late 1990s. Vietnam finds it right to build anything that appears necessary for the socially mixed economy, even experimenting with something so alien to traditional socialist practice as a stock market. Testing for systems to run the country's first stock market actually began in June 2000.

Most typical and most easily appreciated, is the large-scale project for the transformation of the Ho Chi Minh Trail into a modern national highway. It started out in 1959 as little more than a muddy path for shuttling supplies on foot and bicycle. By the end of the war in 1975, it had become five main, roughly parallel roads and twenty-one crossroads that covered nearly 12,500 miles, passing also through neighboring Laos and Cambodia. In defiance of heavy bombing, the North Vietnamese kept the trail open and it played an important role in defeating the U.S.-backed government in South Vietnam in 1975.

On February 18, 2000 Hanoi announced plans to turn it into a modern two-lane highway, later to be widened to six lanes, between the northern province of Ha Tay and the southern hub of Ho Chi Minh City. A North-South road the length of the country already exists, but it is congested and suffers floods during monsoon season. The planned two-lane road, scheduled for completion in 2003 at a cost of $375 million, will be 1,000 miles long and cut through ten provinces and dense jungle in less flood-prone territory.[9]

The Trend in Cuba

Cuba has also had a long and heroic history of determined resistance to imperialist domination, but having had to face four decades of an economic blockade of a most threatening sort, along with other great deprivations, it finds it necessary to move more cautiously toward a socially mixed economy, even to the point of vacillation. For example, free peasant markets which had been allowed before 1986 were abolished that year, but late in 1990 the private ownership and sale of pork was reinstated.

In the fall of 1991 a Communist Party congress approved the launching of small private-sector enterprises, such as mechanics, carpenters, and other tradesmen working for individual gain. There was also a government assurance to prospective investors that it would allow total repatriation of profits. This updated the 1982 legislation which approved of mixed enterprises with 50 percent of foreign capital. According to the President of the Cuban Chamber of Commerce, joint ventures amounting to about twelve billion dollars were being negotiated.[10]

A year later, a little improvement in relations with Russia became possible when Cuba agreed to keep a former Soviet electronic intelligence gathering station on the island and Russia agreed to resume trading oil for sugar. The trade-off, however, was much smaller than previously: in the first half of 1982 Cuba supplied a million tons of sugar for only 1.8 million tons of oil. Joint work on a nuclear reactor in Cuba, stalled at 70 percent of completion, would not be resumed until a third party investor could be found.

Innovative work in biotechnology had raised income in that field to more than one hundred million dollars in 1991 but much more could be expected from developing tourism. To this end, it was decided to offer arrangements in which foreign partners could own 50 percent of projects and possibly more. They could also hire and fire workers, import supplies duty free, ignore taxes for a decade, and repatriate all their profits. By 1992 the tourism industry earned $400 million, up from $250 million in 1990, with a gross operating profit of more than 40 percent.

On June 15, 1993, as at other times, Cuban officials expressed a willingness to negotiate reparations for American properties confiscated in the 1960s, to no avail, as usual. Washington's appetite, apparently, was for nothing less than total capitulation. Its obduracy has its tragi-comic aspect in the Guantanamo Naval Base. This petty imperial infliction serves no military purpose that could not be as readily served by the Roosevelt Roads Naval Base in Puerto Rico—and the United States would save $36 million a year by eliminating it. Each year the United States sends Cuba a ridiculous check for about four thousand dollars on its ancient and obsolete lease and each year Cuba refuses to cash it.

The year 1993 saw a number of steps taken to open the Cuban economy and to mix it in constructive ways. Cubans were permitted to hold dollars. Foreigners were allowed to open joint-venture banks. Arrangements were made to expedite visas for exiles visiting relatives in Cuba, with no longer any limit on the dollars they could bring in, giving them the right to host relatives in tourist hotels and the right to return as often as they like. Cubans could also open bank accounts in convertible currencies like dollars. Reuters reported that "Cuba took another step toward establishing a mixed economy today by authorizing limited, individual private enterprise. . . . More than one hundred trades and services were declared open."[11]

The year 1993 also marked the first time drug-smuggling suspects, two Americans, were handed over by Cuba in a cooperation which authorities in both countries said has grown quietly but steadily since the late 1980s. U.S. officials had provided Cuba in 1992 with evidence to convict a smuggler caught in its waters. Cooperation was reflected in another way under an arrangement in 1984, renewed in 1993, to repatriate Cuban inmates of U.S. Federal prisons at the rate of fifty a month.

A higher level of cooperation was reached when American doctors came to join Cuban medical authorities in searching out the mysterious cause of an epidemic that swept the island, seriously sickening ultimately some fifty thousand people. When the epidemic subsided, a team of epidemiologists from the Federal Centers for Disease Control and Prevention in Atlanta came to work with the Cubans in a six-month study of 150 of the patients.

There was also other evidence in the United States of a growing civilized attitude toward Cuba. Organizations expressed solidarity with it, and one such, the Inter-religious Foundation for Community Organization (IFCO), gained special attention because its aid to the Cuban people took the form of a successful challenge to the embargo. IFCO, also known as Pastors for Peace, reported to its nationwide membership on December 23, 1995 that in the past three years it had organized five "Friendshipment Caravans" through which more than five thousand volunteers collected and delivered eight hundred tons of aid to Cuba: medicines, school buses, solar panels, thousands of bicycles, and other items. It also organized hundreds of Congressional visits with scores of delegations, work brigades, and educational projects.

Popular protest finally reached a level where it could be voiced significantly in Congress. Rep. Charles Rangel introduced a bill with numerous cosponsors to repeal the 1992 Torricelli Law, saying that the Cubans have a right to their own form of government, that the blockade is immoral, and that it is wrong to refuse to allow shipment of food and medicine there. This law imposed penalties on third nations trading with Cuba and all such nations have strongly denounced it as a violation of international law.

As if to drive home the interdependence of nations, when Argentina, especially in Buenos Aires, experienced an epidemic of meningitis-B, Cuba provided the vaccine. Cuba was the only source, having created this vaccine for a disease that had also been ravaging poor communities in Brazil and Colombia. The disease had been virtually eliminated in Cuba where it had reached near-epidemic proportions in the early 1980s.

The Cuban pharmaceutical industry operates four manufacturing plants, producing over 350 million doses each year of twelve different vaccines, both for its own immunization program and for export. In 1993, Cuba's vaccines earned over $200 million abroad.

The United States had been pressing the members of the Organization of American States to isolate Cuba economically and politically but Cuba fought back, and in the years leading up to 1994, managed to triple its trade with Latin America, going from 7 percent to 21 percent. On June 15, 1994, the leaders of Spain, Portugal and nineteen Latin American nations approved a communiqué calling for the elimination "of unilateral coercive economic trade measures."[12]

By the end of 1994 Cuba had signed deals for 185 joint ventures. Tourism was rapidly increasing and business arrangements to expand it were being made with Canadians, Spaniards, Germans, and other Europeans. The first foreign financial institution, the Dutch ING Bank, arrived in June. Mitsubishi and Nissan were selling cars in Havana. Joint venture deals to explore for nickel, gold, silver, copper, lead, and zinc had been signed with Canadian and Australian companies. Hoping to do business in a post-embargo Cuba, more than one hundred American firms had visited there within the preceding year, twenty-six of whom signed non-binding letters of intent looking toward post-embargo tourism, medicine, and biotechnology. In an interview, Fidel Castro specified Cuba's particular aims and methods in utilizing the socially mixed economy:

> I am still a communist. . . . I was among those who proposed joint ventures even before the collapse of the Soviet Union because we had resources that we could not make use of. We have factories that need raw materials, such as fuel, or some more updated technology so we may accept a joint venture. . . . But we are not implementing a privatization policy. For domestic consumption, we prefer our own industries. And in the case of the enterprises that are functioning, we prefer that they continue being state-owned. . . . We have not

> renounced socialism as our common objective. Now we are introducing reforms to develop the country during the 'special period' because the socialist camp has disappeared. We have lost more than 70 percent of our imports. We were left without credits, without capital, without technology and without markets. . . . What we are doing will continue. The commitments we make here now will be fulfilled. There is no going back."[13]

In 1995 the private farmers' markets legalized in October 1994 doubled to more than 250 and continued to increase. Operations of self-employed workers, street vendors, garage repair shops, and the like were spreading. Family-run restaurants, outlawed the previous year, were allowed to re-open. On a more ambitious level, a law was passed in September after more than a year of concerned debate which allowed foreign investors access to all economic sectors other than defense, health care, and education—with the right of full ownership of their businesses, either individually or corporately, and with guarantees as in other countries for transfer of capital and compensation. Foreign investments were exceeding the two billion dollar mark and tourism became the second largest source of foreign exchange with some 800,000 tourists spending about one billion dollars a year.

In 1996, Cubans began paying income tax for the first time. In an effort to reduce the great inequality developing between those with dollar income and those without, the tax excludes both those with peso income and those receiving dollar remittances from abroad, and for those earning dollars in Cuba, is levied at 10 percent up to $2,400 and up to 50 percent for more than $60,000 a year. The peso is officially worth a dollar but its street value has been only a small fraction of that.[14]

Improvements in the economy, resulting gradually in improvements in the Cuban standard of living during succeeding years, reflected ever closer trade and fraternal relations everywhere from Latin America through Europe and Asia. But it was Canada that provided leadership. It denounced the Helms-Burton Law of 1996 as a violation of the North American Free Trade Agreement, and along with others, rejected the U.S. embargo and its blockade measures as violations of international law. All fifteen countries in the European Union angrily denounced the U.S. attempt to dictate to other countries and threatened counter-measures. But the most dramatic public events were the friendly and economically cooperative visits to Cuba by Canada's foreign minister, Lloyd Axworthy, in January 1997, and by its prime minister, Jean Chrétien in April 1998.

Between those two demonstrations of international goodwill, there was the visit by Cuba's foreign investment and economic cooperation minister, Ibrahim Ferradaz, to Paris, in which he and Franck Borotra, France's minister of industry, posts, and telecommunications, signed a bilateral accord on protection and mutual promotion of investments in April 1997. Borotra made it clear that, if necessary, France is prepared to haul the United States before a panel of the World Trade Agreement for its violations of that agreement.[15]

The trend to a socially mixed economy featured a remarkable transformation in agriculture from the rigidly large-scale Soviet model to flexibly small-scale operations involving private interests in a program called "linking people with the land." The crisis in Cuban productivity that came with the loss in 1989-90 of essential Soviet inputs forced a reconsideration of the traditional socialist structure in agriculture.

Planners had already begun to be aware several years before that the organization of work on state farms was profoundly alienating in the relationship between the agricultural worker and the land. Large farms of thousands of acres had their work forces in teams that would prepare the soil in one area, move on to plant another, weed still another, and later harvest an altogether different area. Almost never would the same person both plant and harvest the same area. Significantly, no one ever had to confront the consequences of doing something badly, or conversely, enjoy the fruits of his or her own labor.

The new system had been tried before the Special Period on a number of state farms and had rapidly led to enormous increases in production but had not been widely implemented. With this in mind, in 1993 the Cuban government terminated the existence of state farms, turning them into Basic Units of Cooperative Production (UBPCs), a form of worker-owned enterprise or cooperative. The 80 percent of all farmland once held by the state, including sugar cane plantations, was essentially turned over to the workers.

The UBPCs allowed collectives of workers to lease state farmlands rent free, in perpetuity. Members elect management teams that determine the division of jobs, what crops will be planted on which parcels, and how much credit will be taken out to pay for the purchase of inputs. Property rights remain in the hands of the state, and the UBPCs must still meet production quotas for their key crops, but the collectives are owners of what they produce. What they produce in excess of their quotas can be freely sold on the farmers' markets.

By mid-1995 the food shortage had been overcome. In the 1996-97 growing season Cuba recorded its highest-ever production levels for ten of the thirteen basic food items in the Cuban diet. The production increases came primarily from small farms, and in the case of eggs and pork, from booming backyard production. The earlier food shortages and the rise in food prices suddenly turned urban agriculture into a very profitable activity for Cubans. The result has been that urban farming, relying almost exclusively on organic techniques, played a key role in succeeding years in assuring the food security of

Cuban families. A new paradigm had come into use: linking people with the land.

It meant that when tractors and their repair parts could no longer be imported, or fueled, raising oxen could prove productive in cash-poor farming, very suitable for small-scale operations. Agro-ecological technology could substitute for, and even be preferable to, unavailable chemicals. For instance, Cuba has used intercropping, locally produced biopesticides, compost and other alternatives to synthetic pesticides and fertilizers. Given the incentive of proper prices, farmers produce regardless of the conditions under which that production must take place. Smaller farms worldwide produce more per unit area than do large farms. In Cuba that redistribution was relatively easy because there were no landlords there to resist change. Local production, including urban agriculture, offers great potential.[16]

Popular support for a socially mixed economy may require non-economic approaches such as hospitality to religious practice. It was of no small importance that Fidel Castro went to the Vatican in 1996 to invite John Paul II to visit Cuba, and significant when he responded by making a five-day visit in January 1998. Among the things that impressed the Cuban people and Castro himself, was the Pope's statement against the embargo:

> In our day, no nation can live in isolation. The Cuban people, therefore, cannot be denied the contacts with other peoples necessary for economic, social and cultural development, especially when the imposed isolation strikes the population indiscriminately, making it ever more difficult for the weakest to enjoy the bare essentials of decent living—things such as food, health and education.[17]

It became evident in 1998 that there was a growing impatience with Washington's pointless persistence with the blockade. There was the dinner in March with Fidel Castro in Havana, attended by several leading businessmen including the Caterpillar Company's C.E.O. There was the statement by John Howard, director of international policy of the U.S. Chamber of Commerce, that "There is a widespread and growing sentiment that our policy toward Cuba makes no sense." There was also the fact, according to the U.S.-Cuba Trade and Economic Council of New York, that the number of American businessmen traveling to Cuba—legally but in most cases without State Department sanction—had quadrupled to two thousand in 1998 from five hundred in 1994.[18]

One of Cuba's long-standing top priorities has been to reduce its dependence on foreign oil. Recent developments are encouraging. On January 19, 1999, the Caribbean & Central America Report stated that domestic oil production in 1998 increased by 12 percent to 1.65 million metric tons and was expected to rise in 1999 by 21 percent to 2 million tons. However, most of the finds so far have been heavy oils—which poses extra problems for refining—but the government is predicting a 130 percent increase in refining in 1999. Finds of natural gas have led ministers to forecast a fourfold increase in output. Since the beginning of the decade, the share of electricity generated with Cuba's own energy resources has doubled to 40 percent.[19]

A bit of promise for future relations between the United States and Cuba came in a public statement on May 6, 1999 by General Barry McCaffrey, U.S. drug policy director, who said that Cuba is not involved in drug trafficking and is cooperating with the United States in fighting the illegal trade in the Caribbean.[20]

On August 3, 1999, the Clinton Administration announced that it would permit direct flights to Cuba from New York's Kennedy International Airport and Los Angeles' International Airport, in addition to flights already operating from Miami.

In January 2000 nearly one hundred companies lavishly took part in the United States Health Care Exhibition in Havana, the first American tradeshow held there in four decades. It drew great interest from Cubans, both lay and professional, as if they were viewing a mirage. While the sale of medical goods and food are permitted despite the embargo because they are considered humanitarian aid, they have failed to materialize. American officials said they had approved $45 million in medical sales in the last eighteen months, but that only meant approval to begin negotiations. Cuban officials said none had taken place because of bureaucratic and other hindrances, including such inhumanly ridiculous requirements as documentation that medicines and equipment supplies have not been used to treat foreigners and hence earn hard currency.[21]

On June 28, 2000, six-year old Elian Gonzalez and his father flew home to Cuba after seven months of unnecessary U.S. dalliance with legalistic and other outrageous ploys by distant right-wing relatives in Miami. As Wayne S. Smith, former head of the U.S. mission in Havana, said: "Most Americans realized that if this small minority is controlling U.S. policy, then no wonder it is so screwed up."[22]

It was also reported in June 2000, that as Treasury Department officials said, the number of Americans traveling legally to Cuba had surged by 10 percent a year in the preceding five years and that the number traveling there on the sly had more than doubled in the same period. Regarding U.S. relations with Cuba, it was apparent that ever more Americans were voting with their feet.[23]

Worldwide Repudiation of U.S. Policy toward Cuba

In Latin America, which Henry Kissinger legally claimed as the United States' "backyard," the great power had to face the painful fact, that where in the past all had respected its blockade, by 1995 all were ignoring it. Moreover, all but four very small countries were maintaining full diplomatic relations with Cuba, where thirty years before only Mexico had done so. Cuba's airline, Cuba de Aviación, was already flying to ten Latin American countries and some 220,000 people could be counted on, from those countries alone, as visitors in 1995. To make matters worse for Washington, all but three had switched from abstention to an outright vote for the U.N.'s resolution condemning the embargo and demanding its elimination.

American imperial arrogance faced extraordinary denunciation in the United Nations Assembly when the vote favoring condemnation and lifting of the embargo rose steadily each year through the decade. It climbed from 59 in favor and 3 against including the United States itself, all the way up to 157 for and 2 against. It was understandable that a substantial number of countries would find it advisable not to offend the United States—they would abstain rather than vote to condemn—but even that number changed dramatically, dropping from 79 to only 12.

The embargo is generally considered a violation of international law and its operation as a blockade technically an act of war. Was the hateful Senator Helms declaring economic war against the whole world, against all who might defy the threats of punishment in the Helms-Burton Law? The many angry responses and expressions of contempt should have taught him that his was not the only fist that could be shaken. At the very least, one would have to agree with the judgment of the late Francois Mitterand—when he was president of France—that the embargo is "stupid."

The Outlook

The general import of the data thus far gathered concerning the economic operations of Vietnam and Cuba as socialist countries in relation to the capitalist world appears to be that they are developing, each in its own way, what may come to be recognized as classic examples of the socially mixed economy; systems in which the mixture of socialistic and capitalistic economic activities works to develop productive forces in ways which advance the standard of living of the population as a whole. In Cuba and Vietnam, the social and political dominance of socialist aims in this process appears to remain firm, reflected in the singular operations of their communist parties.

What is not yet clear is the extent to be expected of their successes along these lines over time, their durability as stabilized exemplars, and therefore what their influence is likely to be among the countries in which the elements of a socially mixed economy are still embryonic—or only a gleam in the eye.

On July 13, 2000, after five years of difficult on-and-off negotiations, a 150 page trade agreement was signed by the United States trade representative, Charlene Barshefsky, and Vietnam's trade minister, Vu Khoan. Congressional approval was scheduled for 2001. It covers bank branches, customs fees, publication of laws and regulations, and tariffs on onions, garlic, potatoes, and cheese among many other goods and services, and investment protections—with some indications Vietnam is willing to curtail Communist Party control over the economy.

A comfortable grace period allows Vietnamese companies to adjust to foreign competition. American retailers can enter the market there for the first time but will be limited to single retail stores indefinitely. American financial companies are allowed to issue credit cards but only eight years after the agreement takes effect. In businesses that might affect Vietnam's ability to exercise political control, including phone and internet services, foreign companies will have to wait at least three years before they can begin to enter joint-venture agreements with local partners, and then they will be allowed to take only minority equity stakes.

The changes Vietnam agreed to undertake are similar to those China pledged, but the pace is often slower. There are a few exceptions. Vietnam agreed to allow foreign banks to take deposits and make loans in local currency, the dong, relatively quickly. For the agreement to take effect, Congress will not only have to approve it but also award Vietnam normal trade relations, which can be subject to annual review.[24]

The details provided above illustrate the complexities that inevitably develop when opposed systems cooperate in the forward movement of a socially mixed economy. The experiences of China and Vietnam are undoubtedly being studied by Cuba, in anticipation of the day if and when it succeeds in normalizing relations with the United States.

Notes

1. Howard W. French, "Castro, Looking for Investors, Courts Executives from U.S.," *New York Times*, 12 June 1992.

2. Viktor Linnick and Viktor Pritula, "Old Soldiers in a New War," *Pravda*, translated in *World Press Review* 40, no. 7 (July 1993): 9-10.

3. Bloomberg Business News, "Singer To Make Sewing Machines in Vietnam," *New York Times*, 16 February 1994.

4. Miriam Jordan, "Vietnam Airlines Makes a Flying Start in Its Effort to be a Leading Carrier," *Wall Street Journal*, 23 May 1994.

5. Bruce Dovier, "The Workers Unite," *The Australian*, in *World Press Review* 41, no. 12 (December, 1994): 37.

6. Edward A. Gargan, "For U.S. Business, A Hard Road to Vietnam," *New York Times*, 14 July 1995.

7. World International, "China and Vietnam to Reopen Rail Link," September, 1995, in *People's Weekly World*, 9 December 1995.

8. Reginald Chua, Hanoi, "Vietnam Frustrates Foreign Investors as Leaders Waffle on Market Economy," *Wall Street Journal*, 25 November 1996.

9. Associated Press, Hanoi, "Ho Chi Minh Trail to Be a National Highway," *New York Times*, 19 February 2000.

10. Miguel de León, "Cuba Expands Its Economic Horizons," *People's Weekly World*, 16 November 1991.

11. Reuters, "Havana Will Permit Some Private Enterprise," *New York Times*, 10 September 1993.

12. James Brooks, "Castro Dons Civvies for Latin Conference," *New York Times*, 16 June 1994.

13. Time's Editors, "Castro's Compromises," *Time, The Lion in Winter*, Special Issue (20 February 1995): 57-59.

14. Reuters, "Well-to-Do in Cuba to Pay an Income Tax," *New York Times*, 26 November 1995.

15. Craig R. Whitney, "France Signals Its Displeasure at U.S. Over Cuba Trade Policy," *New York Times*, 25 April 1997.

16. Peter M. Rosset, "Alternative Agriculture Works: The Case of Cuba," *Monthly Review* 50, no. 3 (July-August 1998): 145.

17. Larry Rohter, "Pope Asks Cubans to Seek New Path Toward Freedom," *New York Times*, 26 January 1998.

18. Jim Carrier, "Wish You Were Here," *New York Times*, 22 April 1998.

19. Caribbean & Central America Report, 19 January 1999, in "Sea Changes: The New Cuban Economy," *NACLA Report on the Americas* (March-April 1999): 28.

20. Reuters, "Cuba Cooperating to Combat Drug Trade, U.S. Official Says," *New York Times*, 8 May 1999.

21. David Gonzalez, "On Show in Cuba: Marvels of American Medicine," *New York Times*, 28 January 2000.

22. Paul Magnusson, "Cuba: Why the Big Thaw Is Happening Now," *Business Week* (10 July 2000): 56.

23. Christopher Marquis, "Despite U.S. Restrictions Against Cuba, Door Opens Wider for Visits by Americans," *New York Times*, 19 June 2000.

24. Joseph Kahn, "U.S. and Vietnam Are Said to Agree on Normal Trade," *New York Times*, 14 July 2000.

Chapter 16

India's Special Ways toward the Mix

Taking Socialism for Granted

India, a country that has never actually had a systemically socialist government, has been referred to in that vein so often and for so long, that it presents a classic case of conceptual confusion between statism and socialism. This is true for those of its greatest leaders who were inspired by socialistic ideas, and of the general run of commentators on their work. Though not identified as such, the actual performance of those leaders shows that they were in fact promoting the embryonic elements of a socially mixed economy—as if it would be possible to create socialism and capitalism at the same time. Though unexpressed, this idea appears to be as prevalent in India as predestination.

How the socialist label came to be attached in the absence of the systemic reality is aptly described by Ramesh Thakur:

> In India, the Congress Party and Jawaharlal Nehru, with strong views on poverty eradication, were committed to planned economic change even before independence. Ownership and control of key industries, resources and services by the state was adopted as a strategic goal by the Congress Party at its 1931 session in Karachi.
>
> At independence in 1947, the private sector in India had neither the money nor the expertise to finance industrial development on the scale and at the pace of the government's ambitions. The more visible hand of the state

would be used to create socialism in the industrial vacuum: the state, not the private sector, would play the decisive role in the production and distribution of material goods. But because the existing private sector would be left to get on with the business of creating wealth, a command economy on the Soviet model was rejected initially in favour of a state-directed economy: public-sector corporations would act as transmission mechanisms for state plans to oversee the flow of investment through the right channels. That is, the strategic points of the economy would remain under state control; agricultural farming, consumer goods and services were left in private hands.

The consensus was expressed in the constitution in the form of the Directive Principles of State Policy which proclaimed the right of all citizens to an adequate means of livelihood. The socialist influence was evident in the assertion that the ownership and control of the material resources of the community should be distributed so as to best serve the common good, and that the state should not permit a concentration of wealth and the means of production to the common detriment

The ten-point economic programme of May 1967 as well as reiterating earlier slogans on land reforms and consumer cooperatives, extended state control into banking, insurance, export-import and foodgrains distribution. The fourteen leading domestic banks were nationalized by presidential ordinance in July 1969.[1]

Some Realities of the Situation

The self-contradictory nature of the national polity in its existing form became ever clearer as time passed. Under Nehru's leadership, the previous economic stagnation was broken, the national income per capita was raised, the infrastructure was strengthened, and in the 1950s and 1960s, the economy grew three times as fast as during British rule. In the first forty years of independence, infant mortality was cut in half, life expectancy nearly doubled, and adult literacy nearly tripled—but vast numbers of the poorest Indians remained in miserable conditions. It simply meant that a large number gained access to health and education benefits that had been previously restricted to the privileged elite.

Two conditioning factors must be taken into account. The first is Hinduism, peculiarly a great religion that does not hold itself the only true faith. In its inherent diversity it was capable of uniting the deeply religious Mahatma Gandhi with his second in command, the atheist Jawaharlal Nehru. Characteristically, both men considered themselves democratic-socialists, each in his own way, but neither one actually instituted full-scale democracy or real socialism. In the circumstances in which the country found itself in their time, such dispensations would have required a genuine socialist revolution—which neither man nor their successors in power ever favored for India or presumably would have known how to effectuate.

The second is the caste system, practiced by all the religionists, not only the 80 percent deemed Hindu. It has been and remains a formidable obstacle in the struggle for social justice. Some further inroads have been made beyond the example set when Nehru, pressing for a secular society, brought a lawyer who was an untouchable into his cabinet. In recent times political positions have been gained by lower caste people, especially in Communist-controlled states, and a high point was reached in 1997 when an untouchable, K. P. Narayanan, was elected President of India—but these are all rare exceptions. The worst part of the problem, one that has not changed much in more than a half-century of the country's independent existence, is the poverty of half the entire population.

British imperialists had extracted wealth for 150 years out of this mélange of tribalism, feudalism, and capitalism. The situation obviously cried out for drastic change when the liberals who won independence took over in 1947—but old afflictions remained for many years. For example, it was not until the twenty-fourth amendment to the constitution in December 1971 that some 250 former princes were stripped of the privy purses they had been receiving tax-free, in varying amounts as much as $330,000 a year, along with other privileges.

The Mentality of the Nehru Dynasty

In the oppressive atmosphere of India's social and economic backwardness, every statist move for modernization was magnified into a move toward socialism. This incorrectness had its social and political benefits, ideologically stimulating movements for gains in social welfare.

The fact remains, however, that when Nehru or when his daughter, Prime Minister Indira Gandhi (no relation to the Mahatma), nationalized certain industries, this did not result in systemic socialism any more than when such actions were taken in England or other capitalist countries. In instances where sick industries were taken over, statism more often than not moved the burdens of loss-prone companies onto the backs of the people until such time as a more favorable circumstance arose and the devotees of capitalist anarchy would clamor for privatization. Witness this exchange between Prime Minister Indira Gandhi and her interviewer, Professor Mary C. Carras:

> M.C.C: Would you comment on how a leader who is publicly committed to socialism and has referred to private enterprise as a necessary (though temporary) evil could sanction the undertaking of a private-enterprise project in her own immediate family (her son Sanjay's auto company)?

I.G: I am not against all private enterprise. As you know our system is based on a mixed economy; but I do believe that private enterprise should be under control. . . . Where it goes wrong is where there are monopolies, and the profit motive becomes so dominant that it overrides social interests. But I don't believe the two are incompatible.

M.C.C: Nevertheless you have said that you are committed to socialism.

I.G: Yes, but our socialism is not what other countries call socialism. In no two countries is socialism interpreted in the same way. Our major aim is not socialism but how to remove the poverty of the people. Socialism is a tool or a path because it seems necessary for what we have to do; and in any case, the development of any system has to be by trial and error. We have to see what actually solves problems. We nationalized yarn and still have not been able to solve the problem of our weavers; we complicated it. On the other hand, nationalization of coal was an essential step because the owners of the mines were not looking after the workers and exploiting mines in such a way that workers suffered and mines themselves were deteriorating.[2]

One can understand how Jawaharlal Nehru and his daughter, possessing that interesting amalgam of Eastern and Western philosophic strains, could come to be dubbed Fabian socialists—but it is not quite right since they did not limit themselves to the notion that all things could be accomplished by persuasion, although they often behaved that way. Nehru took his education and a law degree in England but he also visited and was impressed by the Soviet Union.

Influence of the Soviet Union and China

Of special importance was the fact that Indian independence came in the wake of the Soviet Union's demolition of the fascist phase of world capitalism. The British empire had been greatly weakened and U.S. imperialism had begun to anticipate the advantages of financial penetration over the costly and questionable burdens of military colonialism. There was also the influence of the socialist revolution in India's other and closer neighbor, China, in a stunning victory that shook the world in 1949. In the main, however, it was its friendly political and close economic relations with the Soviet Union from which India benefited all through the years, until the 1991 cabal that broke up the Soviet Union.

Often compared to China, it should be noted that the customary reference to India as a vast sub-continent is a bit misleading. The word vast does properly apply to the comparable size of its population, about a billion, increasing at the rate of some twenty million a year. Yet the astonishing fact is that India's land mass is only 43 percent of China's—or of the United States'. It is roughly half the size of Australia (53 percent) and of Brazil (48 percent). The point is that

India's population density is much higher than that of any other large country, with no national program yet underway to deal with the problem.

Highlights of the Nehru Dynasty's Work

No lack of problems awaited Nehru when he became India's first prime minister. The British had left no instrumentalities for social progress, only the dubious value of a thoroughly class-conscious bureaucracy; nor was the nationalist movement itself geared for anything more than the grand symbols of independence and the earnestly expressed social welfare aims that inspirited mass support.

Private Indian capital, such as it was, could not be much relied upon either for the promotion of such aims, or the building of the country's desperately needed economic strength. With three-quarters of the population scattered in backward villages and with little hope that foreign capital could be drawn into constructive cooperation, it was inevitable that Nehru and his followers would turn to the use of statist measures.

Fired up by the extraordinary achievements in large-scale, rapid industrialization of the Soviet Five-Year Plans, Nehru undertook three Five-Year Plans of his own and succeeded in reaching considerable increases in the means of production, notwithstanding strenuous opposition by private capital to the development of public industry. Although state-managed business never became dominant, his initiatives and those of his successors were highly influential in improving labor relations, social controls in industry and agriculture, and in the conduct of joint ventures with foreign capital.

All through Nehru's seventeen years and Indira Gandhi's fifteen years as Prime Ministers, their efforts to move India along lines of social progress were fought bitterly by private capitalists, rich peasants, and the conservative and religious parties. The Supreme Court supported the views of the right wing from the beginning, arbitrarily applying uniquely Indian obscurantist precepts. One would imagine that a Supreme Court would base itself on the constitution as the law of the land but India was not so blessed.

It had been clearly stated that the constitution's Directive Principles of State Policy were "fundamental to the governance of the country" and it directed the state as a matter of duty "to apply these principles in making laws." The Supreme Court held, however, that these principles were "subsidiary" to the individual's fundamental rights, these rights having a "transcendental" nature that put them beyond the reach of the amending power of Parliament. Having said this in the Court's 1967 decision and elsewhere, Chief Justice K. Subba

Rao went on to say that "the concept of fundamental rights is rooted in the doctrine of natural law."

During the 1967 election campaign the right-wing Swatranta and Jana Sangh leaders said that dharma, as the law of God, is superior to man-made laws. Specifically, Swatranta had designated for repeal those amendments that had "abridged or taken away" the fundamental right to private property. Such were the ways used to render all the economic rights guaranteed to the individual meaningless to the poor and to nullify all land-reform legislation passed since the early 1950s.

The people reacted. Circumstance forces oppressed people to be pragmatic, to be concerned not with purity of program but with its material import. It did not matter whether the Congress Party principles were truly socialist or only protosocialist or even pseudosocialist—nor did it matter whether they failed to respect some obscure supernatural pronouncement. They felt the Congress Party was campaigning in their interest and they supported its democratic and progressive moves against high privilege.

It is to the credit of Indira Gandhi that, riding an electoral wave of popularity, she was able to put through a number of reforms, that for a time at least, set the conservatives back on their heels. She secured the passage of the twenty-fourth amendment in 1971 which restored the right of Parliament to amend even the "fundamental rights" which had been a code term for property rights. The twenty-fifth amendment later that year knocked down the Supreme Court's ruling that compensation to property owners had to be at market value, a prohibitive requirement, instead allowing Parliament to set guidelines making nationalization possible as a practical matter. It also provided that laws aimed at preventing the concentration of economic power, in accordance with Directive principles, could not be challenged by the courts.

In 1972, the twenty-ninth amendment protected the Kerala Land Reform Act which had been enacted by the Communists in charge there in 1963 and amended in 1969 and 1971. This was a law that the Supreme Court had tried to destroy by rendering vital provisions of it ineffective. In 1973, she broke the long-standing precedent of appointing the most senior judge Chief Justice, and to protect progressive legislation, appointed a liberal judge instead, which caused three judges to resign in protest.

She nationalized the coking-coal industry and the general insurance companies in 1972. That year she also tackled the two largest steel producing companies, nationalizing one without compensation—the Indian Iron & Steel Company—and gaining a say in management of the other, the Tata Iron & Steel Company. The latter was a part of the Tata conglomerate, the largest business house in the country. In December 1973 she nationalized two more large companies, in steel and railway car construction. Other actions were also taken. The cascade of leftist policies provoked energetic opposition by conservative business and landed interests.

Then came a series of overwhelming difficulties, beginning with a severe economic crisis in 1972, on top of the strain of caring for ten million refugees from the 1971 Pakistani civil war. There was a severe drought, lasting through the spring of 1974. The tremendous financial burdens of India's own war with Pakistan were made heavier by the developing world oil crisis. Spiraling prices which resulted from increased government spending caused food riots and other difficulties in 1973.

A railwaymen's strike prevented food grains from getting to scarcity areas, a situation made worse by rich peasants hoarding grain in anticipation of higher prices. By 1975, after an electoral defeat in Gujarat and other political reverses, the prime minister was no longer able to withstand the sustained economic and political pressures. She declared a state of emergency and began to build an authoritarian structure.

She tried to mollify the opposition. As far back as the 1971 Election Manifesto of the Indian National Congress, she had assured capitalists that the Congress "has no intention of abolishing the institution of private property," but this had obviously satisfied no one. She had committed too many sins for the conservatives to forgive and it was now a fight to the finish.

As long as she was alive, however, Indira Gandhi could not be put down for long. Defeated at the polls in 1977, she maintained her leadership of the Congress Party, manipulated a split in the opposition, and was reelected in 1980. She could no longer advance her program of social progress as effectively as before, but maintained her emphasis on the problems of the poor. The victim of a misdirected act of religious revenge, she was assassinated on the morning of October 31, 1984.

That evening, in a groundswell of support for the Congress Party, her son Rajiv was sworn in as prime minister. He was not equal to the strength of purpose of his mother and his grandfather but he did continue their drive for modernization until his electoral defeat five years later, in 1989. Two years after that, Rajiv Gandhi was also assassinated. Amazingly enough, he was still not the last of the remarkable Nehru dynasty to serve as a political leader.

After a long hiatus, in which the Congress Party had its up and downs under various leaders, the Party elected Sonia Gandhi as its President on March 15, 1998. She was Rajiv's 5l-year-old Italian-born widow. When she began activity after having withdrawn for a period, she found herself mocked as just a "housewife" and a "foreigner" even though she had been a citizen since 1984. With courage and dedication to the dynasty's long-standing social program, she rose above political setbacks and programmatic opposition both within and outside the Congress Party, becoming a vibrant, popular leader working to keep the socially mixed economy moving forward.

The Continuing Struggle

In 1991, when P. V. Narasimha Rao succeeded Rajiv Gandhi as parliamentary leader of the Congress Party and became prime minister, a serious governmental effort was undertaken to undo the Nehru program. Rao began a planned revisionist program intended to do away with the apparatus of controls, to end the subsidies to unprofitable enterprises in the public sector, and to open the country more actively to foreign enterprise. Determined to promote private domestic and foreign capital, the Rao forces moved ahead but found it necessary to tack against the wind of leftist opposition.

In July his finance minister, Manmohan Singh, acted to allow foreign investors to hold more than the previously allowed 40 percent stake in domestic companies—but had to limit it to 51 percent. Direct investment would be permitted in as many as thirty-four important industries such as transportation, food processing, hotels, tourism and electrical equipment—but the government would keep controls in the manufacture of hazardous chemicals, motor vehicles, coal, petroleum, arms, atomic energy, and drugs. He proposed to reduce the fiscal deficit by increasing corporate taxes and taxes on cigarettes, fertilizer, recorders, cameras, refrigerators, and entertainment. He met an I.M.F. demand by ending subsidies on fertilizers and sugar—but increased subsidies for food production. Singh also announced a 20 percent increase in the prices of gasoline, aviation fuel, and cooking gas, which stirred up trouble even in some business circles.

One effect of Rao's campaign was to galvanize action by the various communist parties. They came together in January 1992 and agreed to launch a nationwide united movement against the Rao program and especially against his demand for a two-year ban on strikes. The occasion was the Madras congress of the largest party, the Communist Party of India (Marxist) which had thirty-five elected members of the Indian Parliament and is the governing party in West Bengal Province, the capital of which is Calcutta. Some 650 delegates attended from all over India, with delegations from communist parties in five other countries. Nine months after launching Rao's so-called market reforms, the strength of the resistance was very evident, as noted by an American reporter in 1992:

> The Finance Minister has observed that it is still not clear how the government will close the 90 that are completely bankrupt of India's 244 enormous state-owned industries; these 'patently unviable' enterprises, to use Mr. Singh's

phrase, employ some 800,000 people and taxed state coffers $750 million in 1990. Although Mr. Singh has said they must shut down, India's socialist traditions have made industrial layoffs all but impossible.

To that end, the World Bank has agreed to provide $500 million to create a National Renewal Fund, which would be used to re-train laid-off workers. But India's powerful trade unions, many organized over the years by the country's left-wing parties, have taken to the streets frequently in the last few months to protest any dismissals"[3]

Special problems complicate the struggle of the contending parties in India, as noted by another international correspondent in 1994: "In India, the bureaucracy still paralyzes day-to-day business operations. Customs duties are still high; and the tax system is still irrational. Only 2 percent of Indians pay direct taxes. Entrepreneurs must pay comparatively high taxes, while the agricultural sector escapes taxation. India also has made little progress in privatizing its unwieldy and unprofitable public sector. Two-thirds of industrial capital lies in the hands of the government, where it earns an average return of just 2.6 percent. Public-sector reform would mean losing some jobs, but loud union protests and strict labor laws make it almost impossible to lay off workers. Rules that prevent firms operating at a loss from closing and that guarantee job security diminish India's attractiveness to foreign investors.

The infrastructure is also far from sufficiently developed. Trains, for example, travel on average at less than 10 miles per hour. Electric-power supply is so erratic that it limits big industrial projects largely to Bombay (where electric power supply is privately organized) and a few other cities; even in New Delhi and Calcutta, energy-intensive enterprises must build their own private power generators. . . .

A large problem with India's economic reform is that it does not reach the lower levels of the bureaucracy and lacks an enthusiastic base of popular support. Resistance comes not only from bureaucrats, union members, and farmers, but also from some industrialists who have lived comfortably behind protective tariff walls that excluded competition. . . . India is the fifth largest economy in the world."[4]

The Way India's Communists Operate

Although the communists have gained electoral power in only three of India's thirty-two states and have won only about 10 percent of the seats in Parliament, their influence extends substantially beyond West Bengal, Kerala, and Tripura, due to the respect they have gained for achievements in office. Kerala, for example, where they have been a leading force since 1957, was singled out as a model for the Third World by the United Nations Population Fund in 1992.

Its report said Kerala's fertility rate has dropped to 2.3 children per woman, lower than that of China, Ireland, the former Soviet Union, and Thailand. Also, Kerala has the lowest infant mortality rate in India, only 26 per 1,000 live births. While 27 percent of the Kerala population live in poverty, in northern India two-thirds to one-half the people do. And, helped by a relative shortage of labor, they were able to get wages raised over 3 percent a year in Kerala between 1970 and 1985, compared to little or no rise in most northern states.

State governments in India are very limited in what they can do, as the national government has much more say in the regulation of the economy. However, leaders who want to improve living conditions in a country so heavily weighed down by poverty and underdevelopment must reach out on both levels for capital. The communists have come to understand this and go along with promotion of market activity, but unlike procapitalists of the Rao type, work at the same time to protect working people and to use gains in production to enhance social welfare. In a sense, they are cultivating the seeds of a socially mixed economy similar to Nehru's vision.

The Socially Mixed Economy Also Requires Control

Joint ventures became the order of the day some years ago. In October 1995, for example, three such projects were approved by the Indian government: a fifty-fifty partnership between Mahindra & Mahindra of India and the Ford Motor Company for a venture to cost about $250 million, a joint venture between Siel Ltd. and Honda Motor of Japan costing $31 million, and one between Hindusthan Motors Ltd. and Mitsubishi Motor Corporation of Japan in a project valued at about $174 million.

There have been times when Indian leaders, on a state level more so than national, have found it necessary to rap the knuckles of Western industrialists whose greed becomes excessive. An important case in point was the Enron dispute, involving the centerpiece of India's plan for a 50 percent increase in electric power by the year 2000. In August 1995, after Enron and its partners had spent $300 million, the Maharashtra authorities in Bombay abruptly cancelled the project, accusing Enron of padding its costs and overcharging for electricity to be supplied.

These are no small operators—the giant Enron held an 80 percent interest in the plant with Bechtel Enterprises and General Electric splitting the rest, but after wrestling with Indian authorities for five months they had to come to terms. Together with their partners in the Dabhol Power Company—the Indian subsidiary that was building the plant—they cut $300 million from the original figure of $2.8 billion, agreed to increase the project's size to 2,450 megawatts from 2,000, and brought the cost of electric power down substantially, from the initially set price of 6.7 cents a kilowatt/hour to 5.2 cents. Other improvements were also made.

A probable factor in resolving the dispute was that, like many others, they had been charged with corrupting officials at a time when national scandals were erupting. So many accusations of corruption had been leveled at the Rao government that seven cabinet officers had to resign, facing indictment. The revulsion in the country was so general, that in the elections of May 1996, the Congress Party lost half its political strength. Left with only 25 percent of the seats in Parliament, now a minority among 20 minority parties, Rao had to resign as prime minister and was himself eventually indicted.

The situation had become one in which no one could rule except by representing a coalition of parties and much political parrying and thrusting went on. For a time, backed by a coalition, there was even a proposal that the new Prime Minister be Jyoti Basu, the communist Chief Minister of West Bengal, but he decided he would be able to carry out his program without majority control by his party.

President Sharma picked Atal Bihari Vajpayee as head of now the largest of the minority parties, the right-wing, nationalist Bharatiya Janata (or Indian People's Party) to form a government. Within two weeks following induction he resigned, knowing his coalition would fail a scheduled confidence vote. The President, accordingly, turned in the other direction, a center-left coalition, and asked H. D. Deve Gowda, Chief Minister of Karnataka State, to form a government.

Now this was something that could happen only in India, where thirty-five languages are spoken, each by no less than a million people, with seventeen of these languages declared official in the Constitution. Deve Gowda knew no Hindi or English, only his native Kannada, the language of Karnataka State—yet he accepted the post. When a speech was required to be made in Hindi, it was transcribed in Kannada script and he would speak it, the words making no sense to him at all! He lasted eleven months.

In April 1997, the centrist Janata Dal party, heading a similar left-center coalition, furnished a far more competent and durable prime minister in I. K. Gujral. In the course of government service since the 1970s, he had built a considerable reputation for personal integrity, essential when charges were being brought against at least fifty-six other politicians, including the head of his own party, Laloo P. Yadav, chief of Bihar State, who by July 30, 1997, would find himself jailed to await hearings. Gujral had served twice as foreign minister and was respected for having improved relations with Pakistan, Bangladesh, and Nepal. Fluent in Pakistan's Urdu, among other languages, he was ambitious enough to bring that key neighbor closer. Domestically, his program for economic development, which included continued market reforms and alleviation of poverty, drew support from both business and the people.

But even so acceptable a politician as Gujral could not last in the highly contentious, fragmented politics that followed exposure of widespread corruption, both left and right. On November 29, 1997, after only seven months in office, he became the fourth Prime Minister in a year and a half to be forced to resign. The last straw had been the withdrawal from his coalition of the Congress Party because of strong suspicion that Gujral's party had been involved in guiding Rajiv Gandhi's assassination six years earlier.

Sonia Gandhi was consolidating her control of the Congress Party, having taken over as parliamentary leader even though not holding a seat. She was looked upon by many as a possible future Prime Minister but had not yet gained sufficient public favor to warrant such an effort. She was not a demagogue and demagogy was now the order of the day. The man for that was Atal Bihari Vajpayee, the right-wing Hinduist who had been building a reputation for himself as a moderate.

Vajpayee backed away from the extremists in his Hindu nationalist Eharatiya Janata Party, saying their razing of the Muslim Ayodhya mosque had been "a blunder of Himalayan proportions." He spoke reverently of Gandhi and Nehru, avoided unreasonable hostility to the Congress Party and made strong speeches against ethnic and religious discrimination of any kind. He wanted only the best for India—as a strong nuclear power. On March 19, 1998, he was sworn in as prime minister, his political comeback having been so well managed that his coalition virtually walked over the Congress Party, now reduced in political strength to about 25 percent.

Eight months later the Bharatiya Janata Party suffered landslide losses in a number of state elections—the people having become infuriated by spiraling prices of onions, tomatoes and potatoes, essentials of the Indian diet. The Congress Party, on the other hand, went through a resurrection, maintaining and gaining strength. Four and a half months later, on April 17, 1999, Vajpayee's coalition narrowly lost a vote of confidence and his one-year regime appeared at an end. But it was clear that centrist coalitions were now the order of the day. Several smart new alliances with rising state-level parties resulted in such a coalition—consisting of twenty-four parties—that on October 7, 1999, Vajpayee was back in power with a more substantial majority in Parliament, one that might provide a more durable shot at the normal five-year term.

Such a normality, however, was not to be taken for granted. Profound changes at the grass roots level had to first be taken into account, changes which for centuries had been so well suppressed as not to be even a matter of conjecture until recently.

Nowhere to Go but Up

A token of class consciousness in lowest-caste Indians is the unwillingness to refer to themselves that way and surely not as "untouchables" or even by the indulgent term "Harijans" (Children of God) as Gandhi used to refer to them. Rather they prefer the blunt term "Dalit" which means oppressed or ground-down in Hindi. Celia Dugger tells us that

> Researchers have learned from election and survey data that in the 1990s the country's most oppressed people—the low castes, the poor, the illiterate—have been voting and joining political parties in growing proportions, as have women, who were long at the fringes of the nation's political life.
>
> Many of these voters are flocking to the caste-based and regional parties that more directly reflect their own identities and interests and that now hold the power to make and to break governments. . . .
>
> Remarkably, the poorest Indians are now more likely to vote than the richest ones. This turns on its head what was true here only a quarter of a century ago, and what is still true of American and European democracies: namely, that the prosperous are more likely to vote than the disadvantaged. . . .
>
> As an example of the trends, the percentage of people from formerly untouchable castes who said they were members of political parties rose from 13 percent in 1971 to 19 percent in 1996, while the percentage from the upper castes who said they belonged to a party declined from 36 percent to 28 percent.
>
> The percentage of very poor people who believe voting makes a difference rose from 38 percent in 1971 to 51 percent in 1996, and jumped from 42 percent to 60 percent for low caste people. . . .
>
> Scholars say politics has also provided a route to something less tangible but perhaps even more potent politically: pride, dignity and the confidence to fight back against the kinds of indignities the low castes have suffered for millenia—of being beaten for sitting on a chair instead of on the ground, of being contemptuously called by their caste names, of being forbidden to draw water from the same wells as the upper castes, of being denied the right to ride a horse in a wedding procession like an upper caste groom.[5]

In a region here and there, some Dalits have gained political prominence and are effective in building the movement for their social progress but its momentum has yet to reach the level of national prominence. A number of Dalits have also gained university degrees as a result of the affirmative action principles in the Constitution and this quickens political action.

The movement is gaining strength, and in the broadly democratic atmosphere that the Nehru dynasty cultivated through the decades, apparently cannot be put down. As in all political movements, it has a future which runs the risk of corruption or diversion, but its value remains as the only solution to their great problems. As the Dalits have always been denied the group experience and ideology of either capitalist or socialist programs, their programs center on their urgent human needs. This conditions their development much along the lines of the socially mixed economy, whether so identified or not. Their action, unless it becomes outright revolutionary, moves along within existing conditions.

Notes

1. Ramesh Thakur, *The Government and Politics of India* (London: Macmillan, 1995), 308-309.
2. Mary C. Carras, *Indira Gandhi: In the Crucible of Leadership, A Political Biography* (Boston: Beacon, 1979), 251.
3. Edward A. Gargan, "India's Revolution: Socialism Out, Free Market In," *New York Times*, 29 March 1992.
4. Andreas Bänzer, (*Tages-Anzeiger*), "India: A Caged Tiger Freed?" *World Press Review* 41, no. 4 (April 1994): 34-35.
5. Celia W. Dugger, "New Delhi," *New York Times*, 25 April 1999.

Chapter 17

The Portent of "Chinese Characteristics"

A Socially Mixed Economy Changing World Leadership

The outlook for the world economy is for a change, early in this century, from one that is tripolar to one that is quadripolar. This is derived long-term from the extraordinary and relatively high degree of expansion of the Chinese economy. Based on what has been happening consistently for a number of years, it is now reasonable to expect that in the not distant future China will become generally equal as an economic world power to the United States or Europe or Japan, possibly even first among equals.

Such a prediction was in fact ventured back in early 1993—and by an institution hardly likely to be partisan to China. Noting that the prodigious growth of its economy had already made it the third largest, the World Bank estimated that if this continued, the combined economies of China, Hong Kong, and Taiwan would become larger than the United States economy in less than a decade.[1]

That growth did continue. Moreover, with reversion of the territory of Hong Kong in 1997 and of Macao in 1999, the reversion of Taiwan came to be held in closer prospect. This belief was stimulated not by national pride alone, but also in good part by the large investments already made on the mainland by entrepreneurs in Taiwan, many of whose companies have offices and enterprises on the mainland. When retaking Hong Kong, China agreed to allow enterprises in that developed economy to remain capitalistic for fifty years, which gave rise to the unprecedented, somewhat oversimplified, shorthand slogan "One country, two systems." It may, one way or another, also come into play when working out a peaceful reversion of Taiwan.

Significant for this study is the fact that this remarkable growth of Chinese industry and commerce stems from a deliberate, even if not so identified, policy of creating a socially mixed economy. That policy, under the engaging disguise of "Socialism with Chinese Characteristics," appears to have come into force beginning in the late 1970s. It appears to have been necessitated as a means of surviving the colossal human damage done by Mao Zedong's economic failures and arbitrary dogma.

Aims and Purposes

The passing of Mao in 1976 made it possible to set in motion a sharp departure from past practice, a change initiated in the main by Deng Xiaoping. For the edification of capitalists and other non-believers in socialism, the term used all along for the new policy has simply been *reforms,* with no purpose stated other than to gain the purported benefits of a market economy. For those in the know, socialism has always been the express aim of the party and government leaders. The Chinese version is not easy to define. Here is how it was put by Sidney J. Gluck, a long-standing expert on China, in an article in the *Beijing Review:*

> The essence of socialism, Deng has said, is the liberation and development of the productive forces, the elimination of exploitation and polarization between rich and poor, and the final achievement of common prosperity. . . . What makes socialism different from capitalism is the development of the productive forces to enhance the overall national strength and raise the living standards of the people.[2]

Elsewhere in this article subtitled "China in a Foreigner's Eyes," Professor Gluck mentions that "most people in the West, regardless of political orientation, believe that the institution of market relations, notwithstanding the social content of government relations, put China on the capitalist road."

What is significant is that the Chinese leaders appear content with letting this misunderstanding prevail. Is this a pragmatic policy on their part, aimed at avoiding ideological obstacles to the flow of foreign capital? It brings to mind Deng's pragmatic aphorism: "It does not matter whether a cat is black or white as long as it catches mice."

What does matter, it was to be understood, is that two significant things result from joint ventures with world-class corporations from other countries. The first is a required level of development of productive forces without which socialism is impossible. The second is a concurrent rise in the standard of living. As to the latter, a report could already state in 1994: "The World Bank calculates that since the reform era began in 1978 a total of 170 million Chinese have risen from absolute poverty. That marks a 60 percent decline in the number of the destitute in China—impressive by any standard."[3]

Obviously a special factor had been involved. When a backward socialist country gets foreign capital to participate in its market economy, the genius of the arrangement lies in its ability thereby to leap-frog a half-century or more of the difficult, stressful, and expensive creation of high technology. Technology which—when it cannot be gained directly by purchase—can be acquired indirectly through joint ventures. Add to this essential factor the dedication and organizing ability of the membership of the Chinese Communist Party, which had grown rapidly and by the year 2000 numbered 67 million, and it becomes clear how the effectiveness of the leadership came to be consistently above average.

Nature and Scope of Economic Activity

It is no simple matter to stimulate an economy to keep on growing at the rate of 7 to 10 percent a year. By 1995 it was possible to report that "China has exploded into a global export power," pointing to various examples such as its production of half the world's toys, two-thirds of its shoes, and most of the world's bicycles, lamps, power tools, and sweaters. Big increases had also taken place in high-end products such as video camcorders, facsimile machines and other electronic goods, including military equipment.[4]

The Three Gorges Dam has been called the most important construction in Chinese history since the Great Wall and will come to be known as the biggest dam in the world. Its merits and demerits having been debated since it was first proposed in 1919, it was finally approved in 1992 and active work began in 1993 with completion expected between 2005 and 2010.

It will not be the highest, nor will its reservoir be the largest, but it will become by far the largest hydroelectric project in the world, producing seventeen to eighteren thousand megawatts. That is nearly three times as much as the Grand Coulée Dam, the biggest in the United States. At a towering height of 607 feet, it will stretch 1.2 miles along the third of the three famous gorges and will create a lake 350 miles long. The cost is estimated at $30 billion and involves moving 1.25 million people out of the area to promised fertile farmland, profitable new factories, improved homes, and good-paying jobs. The dam will tame the mighty Yangtse River and save millions of people from the constant threat of massive flooding. More than a third of the population lives in its basin.

The other multi-billion-dollar undertaking, one of the largest public works projects ever conceived, was brought up for discussion in 1995. Called officially the South-North Water Diversion Project, an aqueduct would carry water 860 miles from the huge reservoir at Danjiangkou to the two great political and commercial centers in the north, Beijing and Tianjin, a necessity to rescue them from droughts expected in this century. It requires a six-year operation to increase the reservoir to the size of the one planned for the Three Gorges Dam and it involves the properly organized transfer of 225,000 people, mostly farmers, out of the provinces of Hubei and Henan.

Americans can visualize it as an aqueduct reaching from the Mississippi River to Washington, D.C., carrying four trillion gallons of water annually, a volume seven times greater than that used by New York City and twice as large as the amount delivered by California's largest water diversion system. Plans like this solve only part of China's water problem. Half of its 570 cities suffer water shortages.

Aside from the paramount human needs requiring action, it is estimated by officials that this costs the country nearly $14 billion a year in lost economic output. Necessity, not ambition alone, explains China's hard drive to mix the economy with foreign capital. To supplement what could be drawn from general revenues for such infrastructure purposes, China made its first global issue on February 2, 1994: ten-year bonds priced to yield 6.583 percent, only 85 basis points above U.S. ten-year Treasury securities. They sold well.

That month, Goldman, Sachs and Company opened its first China office in Beijing, planning to open one in Shanghai also. The New China News Agency reported that this leading investment bank had in 1993 co-managed eleven bond issues for Chinese companies that raised $2 billion in Europe, the United States, and Asia. The news agency said there were sixty-two other foreign investment banks with offices in Beijing and that more than one hundred foreign banks have offices or branches in China. Complex arrangements often develop but are usually well balanced.

For example, a year and a half later, on August 11, 1995, Morgan Stanley Group and a Chinese partner started China's first international investment banking company, the China International Capital Corporation. They based it in Beijing with a capitalization of $100 million. Morgan Stanley holds 35 percent, the People's Construction Bank of China has 42.5 percent and the other shareholders, each with 7.5 percent, are the China National Investment and Guarantee Corporation, the Singapore Government and the Mingly Corporation, a Hong Kong holding company. Ten Morgan executives were to be stationed there, the largest presence in Beijing of any American investment bank.

In China, not just industry and commerce, but even finance itself will be socially mixed and the mixture's caliber world-class. Note that in the above complex the control is fifty-fifty between socialist and non-socialist participants. It is as if to say: domination is not the order of the day. Either there will be cooperation or there will be nothing. It is this generally practiced understanding, this *realpolitik,* that makes it possible in some other joint business ventures for unequal controls to be set up wherever particular circumstances make it more equitable to do so.

The automotive field exemplifies this more substantially than most others. All manner of practical arrangements were made throughout the 1990s with such large and competitive foreign car-makers and parts suppliers as General Motors, Volkswagen, Chrysler, Citroen, Peugeot, Audi, Ford, Mitsubishi, Toyota, Nissan, Mercedes-Benz, and possibly others. One aim was to modernize and combine China's own 120 less-endowed automakers, hopefully ending up with half a dozen large entities and the resulting economies of scale. Another aim, much planned but necessarily postponed, was the achievement of a small "people's car" that would be up-to-date in all respects but affordable at a price between $5,000 and $10,000. There would obviously be an enormous market for it in China, let alone abroad, provided that road building would proceed apace, given the extremely poor condition of China's roads.

The Twin Problems of Energy and Pollution

Other countries have not failed to notice China's favorable relations with Germany, its largest European trading partner and one more open to concepts of the socially mixed economy. When it partnered up with Siemens A.G., the electronics and industrial conglomerate, to develop power stations and airports—a deal which could be worth more than $1 billion—the message for the United States was unmistakable.

U.S. Energy Secretary Hazel R. O'Leary had made a six-day visit to China five months earlier, in February 1995, in which for the first time since 1989 an American company was allowed to sell high-technology components for a Chinese nuclear power plant. Other deals for electrical power had also been made and more could be expected—but not taken for granted. China's eggs would not be entrusted to any one basket.

In the midst of all the progress a vexing problem kept forcing attention: China's rampant industrial growth caused growing pollution as a result of traditional reliance on the country's enormous coal reserves for its surging energy needs. The socially mixed economy can expect hydroelectric and nuclear power installations to alleviate the problem eventually, but by no means solve it, as these are devilishly expensive, long-term, and problematic methods. The main

main approach, therefore, must be modernization of the coal resource. While China is the world's largest coal producer it has not been its most efficient.

An interesting effort, among others, was the project of a consortium led by Custom Coals Corporation of Pittsburgh and by MRL Ltd. of Australia to build a coal slurry pipeline in northern China costing $888.6 million. The consortium owns 51 percent and a government organization 49 percent. The 500-mile-long underground pipeline, originally scheduled for completion late in 1997, runs from landlocked Shanxi Province to Shandong Province on the coast. A big problem has been that more than 80 percent of the coal China burns is not being cleaned of pollutants like sulfur—but this pipeline, at long last, does remove this and other pollutants from the coal.

Solving the Communications Problem

Some problems cannot wait for others to solve. In the field of communications the problem was monumental. In 1993, for example, the Chinese Ministry of Posts and Telecommunications reported that in 1991 there were 8.5 million telephone lines, up 24 percent. With an estimated 282 million households, this indicates that there was one telephone for every thirty-three Chinese households. This contrasted all too sharply with the United States and other developed countries which average almost one telephone per household.

The American Telephone and Telegraph Company joined with a Chinese company in 1993 to market telephones, facsimile machines, and other telecommunications products. A.T.&T. and its manufacturing partner for cordless phones, the Hong Kong-based S. Megga International Holdings, formed this joint venture with the China National Posts and Telecommunications Industry Corporation. It would obviously tax even the giant A.T.&T.'s ability to meet the colossal, pressing demand.

A sense of the great reach of Chinese projects can be gained from a 1995 report that "China's longest on-land fiber-optic cable passed inspection and will vastly improve long-distance telephone service to the northwest part of the country. The Xian Lanzhou-Urumqui line, more than 1,860 miles long, connects 39 cities in four provinces and regions. . . . Built for 790 million yuan ($94.9 million), it offers the shortest path between East Asia and Europe."[5]

As if to top this, it was reported in 1995 that

> Teleglobe Canada Inc and a Chinese telecommunications company are negotiating a $500 million project to build the first fiber-optic link between China and North America, to carry voice, video and data communications. . . . Lian-Tong Communications is backed by China's Ministry of Electronics Industries [and] said it planned to invest at least $1.1 billion each year during the next five years to finance its development plans.[6]

High-Flying Ambitions in Aircraft

China's predilection for the joint venture is a way to gain high technology and the means of high-grade production, in addition to sharing in the profits. This is translated by the quick-study chiefs of foreign corporations to mean you had better be on the inside if you want to seize the best opportunities. This applies even in the aircraft industry, a very difficult one in which to develop sharing. Significantly in this respect, it was reported in 1994 that

> Boeing said . . . it would invest $100 million in a plant in China to make tail sections for 737 jetliners, build a spare-parts service center and finance training programs for Chinese flight crews and maintenance workers. . . . The investment increases Boeing's spending in China to a projected $600 million [by the year] 2000. . . .
>
> The Boeing 737 tails, one of the most difficult parts of the plane to make, are currently manufactured in a plant in Wichita, Kansas. In three or four years, they will be built as well by Xian Aircraft Company in the central Chinese city of Xian, Mr. Ron Woodard [president of Boeing Commercial Airplane Group] said. 'Our thinking is, once that is built, Xian and Chinese industry will be able to build anything to world standards.'[7]

From 1994 to 1996, China was shopping around and negotiating with possible partners for the means of building its own commercial aircraft industry to meet its own needs and to operate in the enormous market for suitable planes in Asia. The focus was on a 100-seat plane that would meet international standards and excel at a competitive price. Early in that period the state-run Aviation Industries, Inc. said that this near-term aim was to be followed by developing a high-quality 180-passenger plane.

And so, on April 11, 1996, in Paris:

> China and France signed a preliminary agreement today to study development of a 100-seat jet, dealing a blow to American companies that were also seeking to team up with the Chinese to build a new plane.
>
> Aérospatiale, a state-owned French company, signed the agreement with Aviation Industries of China . . . [and] the fact that both Prime Minister Li Peng of China and President Jacques Chirac of France presided over the signing made it clear that the preliminary agreement was significant A final accord would include South Korean and Singapore companies working with the Chinese, and Aérospatiale's partners, British Aerospace and Alenia of Italy. . . .
>
> It also comes a day after China awarded Airbus Industrie, the European consortium that is the Boeing Company's biggest competitor, a $1.5 billion order for 30 jetliners.[8]

Some Planned and Unplanned "Characteristics"

Foreign trade had actually begun to be significant following Nixon's visit in 1972 and was further stimulated by China's own Statute of Joint Venture in 1980. It developed as rapidly as it did in the late 1980s and all through the 1990s due to the deliberate fashioning of a socially mixed economy, one which leading communists were pleased to call a "socialist market economy." It is an environment in which foreign capital and its auxiliaries are freely employed in concert with uninhibited Chinese entrepreneurs, professionals, technicians, and workers. For such a mode of operations to move forward, all Chinese had to be free, in the Chinese vernacular, to "jump into the sea," meaning to go into business.

Other characteristics also had to develop. In a socialist society, the least a government could do was to match the work-time arrangements workers had won in capitalist countries—and so, effective at the beginning of 1995, the government established the eight-hour day as the norm, and in May 1995 did away with the six-day week, establishing the five-day week as standard. Chinese people made other positive gains from the mixing of the economy and many, albeit a minority, prospered from all manner of commercial activity.

There was, however, a deeply disturbing development arising from the promotion of private gain in a society which, for more than a generation, had been assumed to be dedicated to community welfare: a sharp increase in corruption and crime. In a society controlled not by rule of law as much as by Communist Party rules of conduct, there had been no experience or even acquaintanceship with the large body of judicial, legislative, and civil legalities built up through the centuries in the capitalist world—legal controls to suppress the disorderly or disruptive practices generated by the driving acquisitiveness and greed typical anywhere the social product is privately appropriated.

Unaccustomed to such restraints or even to acquisition as a way of life, when the Chinese people were signaled by Deng Xiaoping's crude—some would say crass—slogan "Getting rich is glorious!" they can be forgiven for mistaking this to mean "anything goes." This is not to say moral purity previously reigned supreme. From time immemorial, in every type of propertied society, there had been paid favors, nepotism, social preferences, the privileges of power, and much criminality. Under socialism in China, for example, the old tradition persisted of "*guanxi*" or connections, meaning "pull" or it's whom you know—but major graft and crime generally had been greatly reduced after 1949. In fact, people had little recourse for the handling of grievances other than the use of such *guanxi* as one might have.

Western businessmen had long been accustomed to kickbacks and bribes, to government bailouts for banks and corporations criminally mismanaged, as well as lawyerly evasion of taxes, and of penalties for embezzlement. They would have preferred to operate without bribery in China but were perfectly ready to use it anywhere necessary to make or improve a deal—and the word quickly spread. So sharp an increase in corruption developed in the flourishing of the market economy, that the Chinese people expressed their disgust with it; so much so that American reporters were impressed by its intensity, especially when the disease was found to have reached into high places. It had to be dealt with.

The War against Corruption

In August 1993, President Jiang Zemin found it necessary to undertake an anti-corruption drive, saying "the corruption phenomenon is a virus that is invading the healthy flesh of the party and state institutions." He told the Central Discipline Inspection Committee that "if we lapse into soft-heartedness, if we allow it to run rampant, it could spell an end to our party."

Apparently not enough was done, because a year and a half later, on February 25, 1995, a dozen prominent intellectuals presented a 2,000-word petition to China's parliamentary bodies calling for an independent investigation into corruption in the Chinese leadership. The 4,500 delegates at this annual session were bound to pay attention as the twelve scholars and writers included two former top editors of *The People's Daily,* the official Communist Party newspaper. Two and a half months later, in May 1995, it was dramatically reported that in Beijing:

> Dozens of top city officials, their secretaries and, in some cases their relatives, are under arrest or investigation in a broadening anti-corruption campaign that has seized public attention. It began after the death, apparently by suicide, of the Executive Deputy Mayor, Wang Baosen, on April 4 and the dismissal of the Beijing Communist Party Secretary, Chen Xitong, on April 27. . . .
>
> [T]op party officials have acknowledged that earlier this year they broke up another large corruption ring in southwestern Guizhou Province, a case that led to the dismissal of the party secretary and the execution—ordered from Beijing—of his wife. . . .
>
> President Jiang's handling of this politically charged case has demonstrated that the top level of the party is united behind him. In what appeared to be a show of solidarity, China's Parliament, the National People's Congress, announced last week that it was drafting legislation to apply the death penalty for some financial crimes.[9]

So much for the vertical extent of the campaign against corruption. A report three months later, on August 9, 1995, describes its horizontal extent:

> Last week the authorities announced that more than 47,000 officials had been disciplined on corruption charges in the first half of this year, an increase of 7.8 percent over the same period last year. Of those punished, official news reports said, more than 1,801 were division chiefs or magistrates or higher, a 44 percent increase.
>
> Large cases are more common, too. In July, investigators publicized the outline of the largest corruption scandal yet in 46 years of Communist Party rule, a case involving central government as well as provincial officials.
>
> A well-connected woman in Wexi, 100 miles west of Shanghai, bilked government officials and private investors of more than $380 million over five years in a pyramid scheme built on imaginary investments. . . .
>
> The woman, Deng Bin, 57, was accused of running an operation that bribed officials in dozens of cities to invest in her company, Xinxing Industrial Corporation, sometimes offering profits in advance. The operation even reached into Beijing's Municipal State Security Bureau, where a senior official lured high-ranking customers into the scheme, before it collapsed last summer when the Wexi authorities arrested Ms. Deng. She now faces the death penalty.[10]

On September 1, 1995, a final episode in this continuing drama was reported:

> Five men charged with embezzling more than $22.7 million in public funds face death in China's biggest stock-fraud trial. The men are accused of stealing from accounts under their trusteeship. The bulk of the money was recovered but about $900,000 in public money was lost. Under Chinese law, those who fail to pay back embezzled money face the death penalty. The charges stem from a probe of other economic crimes in Jiaxing, south of Shanghai.[11]

Where crime is not involved, by and large the incentive of personal gain that a market economy normally makes possible has worked well in China. This is because national, provincial and local governing bodies have been learning that for a socially mixed economy to be successful, socialist authorities must operate flexibly, even hospitably, with capitalist participants, whether domestic or foreign. The Chinese have been observed providing such facilities, legal protections, and promotional opportunities as nourish mutual interest. Observers also agree that the number of Chinese who are prospering as a result, both in town and country, has been continually growing, although more so in the cities.

The Challenge of Agriculture

The lagging behind of the countryside is by no means unique to China. So universal has this been historically that it has always been an express aim in socialist programs to overcome the disparity between town and country. The initial capital for industrial and urban development in burgeoning capitalist countries became available through "primitive accumulation"—the forced extraction of commodities from peasant production. Something similar, albeit with different driving forces, came to pass under the exigencies of socialist rule in economically backward, largely peasant countries like China and Russia, as monstrously under Mao as under Stalin.

Efforts were made to solve the problem. There was much improvement in the rural standard of living after Mao's disastrous communes were dissolved to be replaced by household farming and village-owned cooperative operations, a movement genially termed self-emancipation. There were instances, however, where the countryside felt damaged and discriminated against. In the early 1990s, for example, a government newspaper reported that angry peasants attacked post offices in eleven provinces because a sudden cash shortage had made it impossible to cash postal money orders sent home by relatives working in cities. In Sichuan, thousands of enraged peasants rioted for five days to protest excessively high taxes, arbitrary government fees, and official corruption, put down finally by armed military police using tear gas. In Guangdong Province, angry peasants snarled traffic for hours when they blockaded a main highway to protest expropriation of their fields for a road improvement project. Numerous other protest actions were also reported.[12]

Industrial production has continued to grow at a higher rate than agricultural, although bumper crops did materialize in some years. The market system has been working in agriculture, which means in the first place that the family contract system has been working. The latter is a system which itself reflects a feature of the socially mixed economy, the blending of private interest and societal interest.

The government has wisely encouraged not only farming initiatives on the family level but also all manner of village-owned cooperative enterprises—industrial, commercial, agricultural, etc. These have become responsible for a substantial part of the gross national product and some have prospered substantially.

A peculiar practice develops in such instances. Village-owned enterprises are usually operated democratically as cooperatives, with equal votes and equal shares, except for such uneven rewards as they may jointly decide for special responsibilities or services. Besides assuring full employment, all village dependents are cared for equally, along with facilities for education, medical care, recreation, or whatever else can be provided with or without resort to higher government. But when expansion requires bringing in outside workers, a two-tier situation develops. The outsider is accorded the same labor rights as the villager but not the right to vote or to share in owners' benefits except as they alone may decide, if at all. Whether this is just or unjust is a matter for future theoreticians to mull over. Such are the riddles of the socially mixed economy.

The greatest challenge of agriculture lies within the greater challenge of expanding social progress to the whole territory of China; thus defeating the centuries-old practical limitation of restricting most economic activity to a North-South coastal swath only 1,000 miles wide. This area is one in which nearly four-fifths of the harvest comes from irrigated land and where water shortages, both urban and rural, still exist.

Taming the Wild West

China's agriculture has been marked by ingenuity throughout its history. Is it possible for China to prevail in the daunting task 'to make the desert bloom," innovating adjustments to its specific soil, climate, and water conditions in its own way as California and Israel did in theirs? The cost of acquiring the required water supply would no doubt be huge, but gaining needed money is a prime purpose of the socially mixed economy; and what could be more valuable than China's "winning of the west?" An interesting, somewhat startling possibility along these lines was discussed in a 1996 scientific article concerning China's interest, notwithstanding Western opposition, in the technology of nuclear explosions for peaceful purposes:

> China's northwest territory, which includes the Gobi desert, contains almost half that country's landmass but only 7 percent of its freshwater. Recently, some Chinese engineers proposed diverting water into this arid area from the Brabmaputra River, which skirts China's southern border before dipping into India and Bangladesh. Such a feat would be 'impossible' with conventional methods, engineers stated at a meeting . . . at the Chinese Academy of Engineering Physics in Beijing. But they added that 'we can certainly accomplish this project' with nuclear explosives."13

It is questionable whether such giant projects can be undertaken before China is over the hump with such prior giant projects as the Three Gorges Dam, but half a century ago much smaller efforts did begin. A prime example occurred in the furthest western province of Xinjiang, which consists almost entirely of desert and mountain terrain. It accounts for one-sixth of China's land area, yet even now has a population of little more than seventeen million. Over the last two centuries there have been repeated revolts by Muslim Uighurs against Chinese overlords there. After the 1949 revolution, the Chinese Communists took steps to assure control of its northwestern frontier bordering Kazakhstan, Kirgyzstan, and Tajikistan—territories in Stalin's not-so-friendly

Soviet Union. They formed a paramilitary organization called the Xinjiang Production and Conservation Corps, made up of cashiered soldiers, convicts, and volunteers, to settle, make secure, and develop this alien region.

Operating out of Aksu, an ancient camel stop on the Silk Road, the Corps, as it is known, has built whole cities and hundreds of farms and factories producing more than one-third of the province's cotton and other goods. With workers and their families numbering 2.4 million, 97 percent of them ethnic Chinese, it runs its own university and television station, and its own militias and prison camps. In 1949 there were just 300,000 Chinese, but by 1997 there were more than six million, 38 percent of the population, according to official figures. Uighurs number eight million, 47 percent of the total, while 1.2 million Kazakhs and numerous smaller groups round out the total.

Especially important, the Corps still reclaims more than 100,000 acres from the desert each year, usually expanding from existing farms. In the new, more market-oriented China, even the Corps is trying to transform itself into a corporate conglomerate, battling low farm prices and obsolete factories by avidly seeking foreign investors. Its Agricultural Division has even sold shares on the Shanghai exchange to raise money for new desert development.[14]

The region contains huge coal and oil reserves—the latter believed to be three times those of the United States—that are only now being exploited. Xianjiang holds much promise as a base for taming the rest of China's wild west.[15]

In the Spring 2000 session of the National People's Congress (NPC) the highest priority was given to implementing the government's decision to shift the focus of economic construction from the eastern coastal provinces to the western region. It was recalled that in the 1980s when Deng Xiaoping suggested opening up and developing the eastern regions first, he promised that the western region would be accorded similar preferential policies when the time was right; as Jiang Zhenghua, Vice-Chairman of the NPC Standing Committee put it, "The right time has come."

After twenty years of opening-up and reform, the eastern region has established a fairly good infrastructure and a strong economy. The western region has also advanced quite a bit, with its problem of subsistence basically resolved. This, said Jiang, made it possible to start the development of the western region. A difficult region in which to operate, with more than half the country's verified natural resources covering 57 percent of its land area, the region has a population of 285 million, only 23 percent of the national total—and includes 90 percent of its poorest people.

Jiang made the point that the development of the western region is necessary for further development of the national economy. The eastern provinces need to find venues for their extra capital and commodities. The western region, which badly needs investment, can complement the east since it has rich resources and a large potential market. With the two joining forces, the country's economic and social development will be raised to a higher level. But the solving of such large-scale infrastructure problems as reforestation to overcome erosion and desertification, the provision of water and other resource availability, road and rail construction, communication facilities, and whatever else makes for modernization all calls for intensive action within long-term planning. It includes pipelining natural gas west to east.

Zeng Peiyan, Minister of the State Development Planning Commission, estimated that the arduous task of developing China's great western region would not be finished within one or even several five-year plan periods, saying "It might even take several generations." That there is every desire to expedite the process is clear from the fact that even though in 1999 the government invested in the west 60 percent of the money raised from bond issuance, in 2000 it scheduled 70 percent of the 100 billion yuan being raised from government bonds. Furthermore, 70 percent of the 440 billion yuan of financial support to local governments was headed west, along with investment of 70 percent of international loans.[16]

The Chinese government has evidently decided, difficult as the task may be, that in time it can raise the entire territory and population of China to the level of social progress, perhaps the leading level, warranted by its ancient civilization. During the last two decades of the twentieth century, concentrating in the east, the main structural instrument used in the rapid and unprecedented increase in productive forces was the deliberate development of the socially mixed economy. China will have every reason to apply this approach to the taming of the west and thereby move the whole nation forward in the early decades of this century.

Notes

1. Steven Greenhouse, "New Tally of World's Economies Catapults China Into Third Place," *New York Times*, 20 May 1993.
2. Sidney J. Gluck, "The Socialist Path in China." *Beijing Review* (September 1993): 20-26.
3. Shirley WuDunn and Nicholas D. Kristof, "China's Rush to Riches," (from their book, *China Wakes*), *New York Times Magazine* (4 September 1994).
4. Joseph Kahn, "China Swiftly Becomes an Exporting Colossus," *Wall Street Journal*, 13 November 1995.
5. Unsigned item, "China's Biggest Stock-Fraud Trial," *Wall Street Journal*, 1 September 1995.

6. Bloomberg Business News, "Teleglobe Canada Talks of China Project," *New York Times,* 7 October 1995.

7. Associated Press, "Boeing Planning to Invest $100 Million for China Plant," *New York Times,* 9 August 1994.

8. Bloomberg Business News, "China and France Will Study Developing a 100-Seat Jet," *New York Times* 12 April 1996.

9. Patrick E. Tyler, "Beijing Party 'Decapitated' by President," *New York Times,* 8 May 1995.

10. Seth Faison, "China's Anti-Graft Drive Grows, So Does Graft," *New York Times,* 10 August 1995.

11. Unsigned item, "China Clears Phone Cable Service," *Wall Street Journal,* 1 September 1995.

12. Peter Goodspeed, (*Toronto Star*), "Left of the Boom," *World Press Review,* 40, no. 10 (October 1993): 31.

13. John Horgan, "'Peaceful' Nuclear Explosions," *Scientific American* 274, no. 6 (June 1996): 14-16.

14. Seth Faison, "Major Shift for Communist China: Big State Industries Will Be Sold," *New York Times,* 12 September 1997.

15. Jeffrey Tayler, "China's Wild West," *Atlantic Monthly* 284, no. 3 (September 1999): 22-29.

16. "Focusing on Western China," *Beijing Review* (10 April 2000).

Chapter 18

Four Mixtures Made in Russia

The Historic Trend

In the country where the world's first socialist revolution took place in 1917, the long agony of the turbulent twentieth century was destined to pass into the twenty-first without Russia ever establishing a successful socialist system in unadulterated form. Nor, despite eventual misguided efforts, did it ever establish in its place a prevailing capitalist system. It seemed destined instead, in at least four historic efforts, to keep trying to solve its problems by fashioning a socially mixed economy. Influenced differently each time by existing circumstance, it was always seeking, without any well-worked-out theoretical basis, to co-opt the best features of both systems.

Did anyone have the blithe notion that a snap-convergence could be made between opposed social systems? Hardly. The proponents of both were dedicated to their distinctive material purposes and conformed ideologies, not to convergence as such. For the great mass of people however, especially after the dissolution of the Soviet Union and even before it, the prime interest was not in form, including such labels as "socialism" and "capitalism," but in the content of programs—how their material way of life was affected by so-called reforms.

Aware as they were of the general march of civilization, being an educated people, they were also deeply aware of the uniqueness of their own history, culture, and customs. They were "different." It seems almost inevitable that with respect to acceptable social change, they would come more and more to speak of "the Russian way."

This is not to imply that there was at any time a dominant view of this concept, one that might provide a lasting connection among the elements of the four efforts, a possible developing program, even if only in potential. Nor was there any precedent elsewhere that might be applicable to Russia, except that around the turn of the century, social engineers were finding the remarkable success of "the Chinese way" worth close study.

Lenin's First Effort

The first and obviously most urgent time was at the actual birth of Soviet Russia. How do you build socialism when you have nothing with which to build it, when history has bestowed the first socialist revolution on a vastly backward peasant and petty bourgeois country devastated by war?

There was not even a plan, let alone the material means, as Lenin and his little political party of 20,000 had never expected such rapid success. Shortly after the Brest treaty in March 1918 ended Russia's part in World War I, it became evident that the valiant attempt to operate as a workers' state was only going from bad to worse. We are fortunate to have available an objective historian's briefly incisive account of Russia's first socially mixed economy:

> Lenin reacted to the worsening situation with characteristic decisiveness, announcing in early April 1918 his determination to change course. His plan called for an end to nationalization and expropriation and provided *a modus vivendi* with large private capital. The new economic order would rely on limited state ownership while preserving private (or joint) ownership and management in most enterprises. The Soviet state would regulate the private sector through financial and political suasion.
>
> The survival of his government, Lenin reasoned, required the technical collaboration of the large bourgeoisie, the termination of the revolution's destructive phase and the re-imposition of managerial authority. Centralized control was to be established over local soviets [councils]; labor discipline was to supplant workers' control. Lenin's commitment to economic recovery was absolute; wage incentives were to be restored. In short, as he frankly acknowledged, there was to be a 'suspension of the offensive against capital.'
>
> Searching for a conceptual definition of his proposals, Lenin described the projected socially mixed economy as 'state capitalism,' his model being Germany's wartime economy. State capitalism, he argued, would represent an

> enormous step forward for backward, petty bourgeois Russia, a giant step toward socialism.[1]

War Communism

Though furiously debated, this first planned effort at a socially mixed economy was firmly established and taken seriously—but it could not last. Within two months after its inception, beginning in June and July, civil war began to rage, started by "White" (anti-Red) armies and the troops of Japan and many Western powers.

All high aims had to give way to martial law and severe command administration, The policies which later came to be known as War Communism gained victory at great cost after three years. Also later, these years came to be known among Russians as "the heroic period."

Lenin had no love for War Communism, and though he well understood its necessity, bluntly disposed of it as a failure as soon as peace came. Again the need to achieve a socially mixed economy had become unavoidable.

Lenin's Second Effort

For an excellent summary, written in the context of its significance in 1985, we do well to turn again to Professor Stephen F. Cohen:

> Remembered as the period of the New Economic Policy, or NEP, the years between the end of the Russian Civil War in 1921 and the coming of Stalin's revolution from above in 1929 represent the first and still most far-reaching liberalization in Soviet political history—a kind of Moscow Spring.
>
> The policies introduced by Lenin in 1921 were new in that they broke sharply with the extremist measures and coercive ideas of the civil war. They gave birth to the first dual economy in the history of Communist movements, combining a public and private sector, socialist aspirations and capitalist practices, plan and market. The Soviet state retained control of heavy industry, foreign trade, banking and transportation. . . . But lesser enterprises were denationalized, the principle of private peasant farming reaffirmed, and market relations, which had been suppressed during the civil war, restored.
>
> NEP brought also a new, more conciliatory politics. The Communist Party maintained its dictatorship, but the Soviet party-state of the 1920s was limited and relatively tolerant, allowing a greater degree of social, cultural, and intellectual pluralism than has ever existed since in that country. As in economic life, the excesses of statism and coercion were deplored. Social harmony and class collaboration, rather than strife and terror, became the principles of NEP. The Soviet 1920s were neither democratic nor, in our sense,

> liberal. But when Stalin unleashed a virtual civil war against the peasantry and the private sector in 1929, repudiating NEP as 'rotten liberalism,' he destroyed a model of Communist politics and economics that many citizens would long remember as the 'golden era' in Soviet history and in which, decades later, Communist reformers in the USSR, Eastern Europe, and elsewhere would find a lost alternative to Stalinism.[2]

In Russia, and after 1922 in the other republics which then joined it in forming the Union of Soviet Socialist Republics (USSR), the New Economic Policy was slowly bringing constructive results, with the possibility of realizing high hopes if allowed to continue for the long time expected to be required. As we now know, a prime requisite would have been to follow Lenin's warning, given in vain shortly before his death in 1924, against allowing Stalin to continue as the Communist Party's general secretary. Unfortunately, at that time his insight carried little of the importance that it later acquired. It staggers the imagination to speculate how differently life would have been in Russia if, instead of Stalin, someone like Nikolai Bukharin had prevailed, the man Lenin called the Party's "greatest theorist."

The Basic Problems Created by Stalin

It is impossible to understand why things took the sharp turns they did in recent times without assessing the history of the murderously despotic and unprecedented pseudosocialism which was so persuasively and deceptively paraded by Stalin as "Marxism-Leninism." A full assessment is not possible here. It is available in an extraordinarily insightful book by a fine historian, Roy Medvedev, *Let History Judge: The Origins and Consequences of Stalinism.*[3]

Here we need primarily deal with three aspects of the Stalinist legacy burdening Russia's third and fourth efforts at forming a socially mixed economy. First, is the vast and all-too-durable bureaucracy of self-serving, dutifully rigid underlings needed and preferred by Stalin for his monarchial control of central planning and political domination. Some change has proved possible in quantity but far from enough in quality.

Second, is the very lop-sided domination of the economy by the military-industrial complex created by Stalin's paranoia. This was stupidly extended by his successors until the time Mikhail Gorbachev took steps to counter it. Very little conversion to constructive civilian purposes has been accomplished.

Third, is the deliberate habituation of the people, enforced over two or three generations, to direction from above in virtually all matters. Reminiscent of prerevolutionary custom, it is almost as if people continued to believe, even after perestroika and glasnost, that they had nothing to say about anything of social consequence.

All along, the fundamental problem afflicting the Soviet Union and now Russia individually has been its very method of governance: systematic command administration. Through eight five-year plans of forced march to heavy industrialization, productive forces had expanded along those lines but not to create an economy of abundance which should be the aim of a truly socialist country. Central planning of that sort had to find itself eventually overgrown and inefficient, crippled by sclerosis. The point at which serious deterioration of the economy set in has been fixed in time as the beginning of the ninth five-year plan in 1972 by that keenest of observers, Georgi Arbatov.[4]

Minor reforms had been attempted by Kosygin, by Khrushchev, and others, only to be sponged up by the bureaucracy. There had even been some discussion of perestroika-like ideas by the famous sociologist Tatiana Zaslavskaya in conversations with Gorbachev a few years before he became General Secretary of the Communist Party of the Soviet Union (CPSU).[5]

The Third Effort, by Gorbachev

Mikhail Sergeyevich Gorbachev took on the leading role of General Secretary in March 1985 and dedicated himself to a virtually revolutionary change in domestic and international affairs. In a book published in the United States in 1987, he made a succinct statement of the basic problem he had been facing:

> Our past experience, in which repeated attempts to reform the upper management levels without support from below were unsuccessful because of the stubborn resistance of the management apparatus, which did not want to part with its numerous rights and prerogatives. We have recently encountered that resistance, and still encounter it now. Here too, as in all other areas of restructuring, we must combine what comes from above with the movement from below, i.e., give the structuring effort a profoundly democratic nature.
>
> What is the main shortcoming of the old economic machinery?
>
> It is above all the lack of inner stimuli for self-development. Indeed, through the system of plan indices, the enterprise receives assignments and resources. Practically all expenses are covered, sales of products are essentially guaranteed and, most importantly, the employees' incomes do not depend on the end result of the collective's work, the fulfillment of contract commitments, production quality and profits. Such a mechanism is likely to produce medium or even poor quality work, whether we like it or not. How can the economy advance if it creates preferential conditions for backward enterprises and penalizes the foremost ones?
>
> We can no longer run our affairs like that.[6]

Four years later, in 1991, at another Central Committee plenum, Gorbachev made it clear that he and the party definitely opposed a changeover to a capitalist system:

> Giving full consideration to the special features and traditions of our society, we are against replacing 100% state ownership with 100% private ownership.
>
> The matter at hand is nothing other than the creation of a mixed economy. Plus the free development of all types of ownership, with emphasis on the conversion of enterprises to joint-stock ownership and the leasing of enterprises which will make it possible to include ever wider strata of the working people among leaseholders, proprietors and owners.[7]

Why a socially mixed economy? Why not simply an elimination of bad practices and a further direct march toward full socialism, an aim to which Mikhail Gorbachev has always remained dedicated? After all, there was a world of difference between the great power the Soviet Union had become and the impoverished backwardness with which Lenin and his small band of Bolsheviks had been confronted back in the 1920s. If the problem was that they did not have the potential for a socialist economy of abundance which Marxists had expected advanced capitalism to provide, did not the Soviet Union now have that potential?

The answer came through authoritative analysis, beginning with the realization that "the economic situation was very serious, and more so than had been thought in 1985." Leaving aside oil production, there had been virtually no growth at all in industrial production, and the income from oil export had been squandered on importing grain—grain which the country should have been able to produce, having the largest farmland in the world and the world record for the production of chemical fertilizers. "In short, this was no economy, but rather an elaborate fiction. . . . For twenty years the USSR had achieved absolutely no growth in national income. . . . Juggling the books was common practice. . . . However, the most serious problem was human resources . . . the unpreparedness of the cadres.[8]

Was it possible to rally the human resources, the cadres, the essential "support from below," to activate the "inner stimuli for self-development" in a people habituated for generations to political passivity, accustomed to leadership by a "strong man" as the norm, having had no experience with democratic government for a thousand years? A people, in fact, educated to consider Western displays of democracy as a sham.

It is to Mikhail Gorbachev's everlasting credit that he made it his highest priority to act creatively on Lenin's precept that "socialism without democracy is unthinkable." Firmly pushing through the party and the government his policies of glasnost (openness) and political democratization, he started the long educational process to develop the self-empowerment of the people, that exercise of political initiative, of "pressure from below" without which the economy would not be changed.

With the general practice of Gorbachev's innovations of free speech, a free press, free assembly, and free elections, it would become possible to throw off the dead hand of bureaucracy and work to build a better life. But to what extent—and when--would that broadly develop? Not sufficiently during the short—and very busy—six and a half years that history would allot Gorbachev to remain in power.

There was also the "new thinking" in foreign affairs. With his abandonment of the Brezhnev Doctrine and the withdrawal of troops from central Europe, with his bold initiatives for nuclear disarmament at nine summits, would not Gorbachev then be able to cut the military-industrial complex down to size and convert to the production of much-needed consumer goods? Again, for this also his time in power proved too short. Even so, Gorbachev, virtually single-handedly, forced an end to the Cold War which deservedly won him the Nobel Peace Prize. What a magnificent contribution to world peace!

Tbere was another obstacle to the restructuring called perestroika. Ethnic grievances and nationalist strivings had long existed—and been repressed—during Stalin's time and after. With democratization and glasnost, they gained expression. Gorbachev could manage while this involved only the Baltics and other small republics in the Caucasus, but a problem that would become insuperable was created when Boris Yeltsin's lust for power led him down the road to separatism for Russia, that vastness with more than half the population of the Soviet Union and its major resources.

Others, the Ukrainian leader for example, were quick to see possible benefits for themselves in asserting independence. To preserve national unity in the face of the separatist threat, Gorbachev undertook to develop an inter-republic treaty which would loosen the constraints of the Soviet Union and grant more rights to the republics—but this only fed Yeltsin's appetite and the effort became bogged down in concessions and behind-the-scene conspiracies.

Errors and Beginnings

Some early mistakes also created difficulties for Gorbachev. At the outset, the thinking had not been in terms of a socially mixed economy. It was a policy called acceleration, along lines proposed shortly before his death by General Secretary Yuri Andropov, who had sponsored Gorbachev's rise in the Politburo. It meant trying to solve problems simply by putting pressure on ministries and managers to intensify their operations, to improve the quality of their work. It turned out to not have much effect.

There had also been the campaign, beginning in May 1985, against alcoholism, a very serious problem, especially in the Slavic republics. Although a majority had approved the campaign in principle, its limitations on the production, sale, and distribution of vodka, a state monopoly, were apparently too repressive, with discontent, home-brewing, and crime growing rapidly. Two other members of the Politburo, Ligachev and Solomontsev, had been the prime movers in the campaign but it was Gorbachev, known to be only a very moderate drinker himself, who took the heat.

It put a dent in the high popularity his early political and diplomatic achievements had brought him but it put a more important dent in the national budget through a great loss in revenues. It was not a complete failure, having brought at least statistically some minor improvements in public health and work performance—but within less than three years the campaign was out of the picture.

Some small and hesitant steps toward a socially mixed economy began in November 1986 when a Law on Individual Labor Activity was passed which covered such things as taxi services, car and television repairs, and private tuition. Such operations and others of that kind could already be found on the black or gray market.

There was also a Law on the State Enterprise in 1987 but the most important of the early moves toward a market economy was the Law on Cooperatives adopted in May 1988. It allowed cooperatives to be set up independently, requiring a minimum of three members but setting no maximum. It did not allow hired labor but this was only a bow to socialist tradition as it did allow cooperatives to employ an unlimited number of non-members on a contract basis. Non-state economic activity was also promoted by a Law on Leaseholds in 1989 and a Law on Land in 1990. Written explicitly into all three laws was the principle that everything was permitted that was not specifically forbidden. This was a basic departure from the traditional principle that only such things may be done that are specifically permitted.

Fundamental in the development of a Russian socially mixed economy would be the question of land ownership. Disputes concerning it developed in the Gorbachev years, have continued into the present and appear likely to be waged in coming years. Radical reformers, always in the minority and sometimes admittedly pro-capitalist have kept on demanding fully private farming and the sale of land. As expected, Gorbachev stood with the majority and spoke against private ownership of land, although he was happy to accept leasing of land, even for a hundred years.

He felt the basic question was one for the people in each republic to decide by referendum. Most Russians consider it important to make a distinction between large-scale and lower-scale private ownership of land. Surveys have shown that large majorities favor private ownership of small plots of land but oppose the sale of large tracts of land. It betokens popular support for a true socially mixed economy.

The Gorbachev Market Plan

In the face of endless drag and decline, with the shining promises of the incentives and dynamism of the market economy, topped off with the prospect of Western finance, Gorbachev found himself "excited" by drastic reforms proposed by a team of economists jointly delegated by the USSR's central government and Russia. He approved of this Shatalin-Yavlinsky 500-Day Program at first but—besides running into a stone wall of vehement opposition by the party-state leaders and industrial managers—began to have second thoughts of his own. Convinced that he could work out a suitable compromise, as he had so often managed in the past, he fashioned one with the help of Abel Aganbegyan and got it approved by the Supreme Soviet of the USSR in October 1990 as the "President's Program."

Although it drew strong dissatisfaction from both sides of the issue and the dispute continued, it does present the only plan for a socially mixed economy that became official in the Gorbachev era and is worth study. The following is a rough summary as reported in the international press:

> **Prices:** State controls would gradually be phased out, beginning with some non-essential goods. By the end of 1992, only essential consumer goods such as bread, meat, dairy products, medicine and transport would remain controlled. Republics would be free to impose tighter controls, free prices, or rationing.
>
> **Property:** State-owned factories and farms, and other property such as housing, would be sold off to private entrepreneurs, collectives and stockholders.
>
> **Entrepreneurs:** "Freedom of economic activity" is established as a right, and protection of shopkeepers and businessmen from state meddling is to be established by presidential decree.
>
> **Farming:** Quotas and state management of farming would be abolished. Each state collective farm would decide for itself whether to dissolve or continue. Republics would have the right to go further, giving any member of a collective farm the right to claim a piece of land and farm on his own.
>
> **Foreign Business:** Foreign investors would have broader freedom, including the right to own companies in Soviet territory.

Ruble: The ruble would gradually be made a convertible currency, but the plan does not say when or how. Individual republics would be prohibited from printing their own currencies.

Power-Sharing: The central government would retain control of transport, communications, defense industries, energy, credit and monetary policy, customs, and regulation of prices on "key types of raw materials, production output, goods and services." All economic policies would be overseen by "an interregional economic committee" with representatives of the republics. Each level would have power to levy taxes.

Natural Resources: The export of oil, gas, gold, diamonds and other natural wealth would remain under central government control, although republics and local governments would get an unspecified share.

Budget: Sharp cuts in spending would begin in November, including unspecified reductions in the military and the K.G.B. Most uncompleted capital projects are to be halted. Foreign aid is to be cut, and dealings with allies are to be put on a commercial basis.

Wages: Pay would be indexed for inflation. Each family would have a guaranteed minimum income.

Banks: The central bank would be transformed to a federal reserve system, responsible for setting overall monetary policy. Other banks would be transformed into commercial enterprises.

Subsidies: State and republic funds would be created to bail out inefficient enterprises. Some "hopelessly inefficient enterprises" would be closed, but unlike more radical plans no number is given.

Consumers: Purchases of homes, cars and other items would be encouraged through several new measures, including cheap loans.[9]

The Defeat of Gorbachev

In his presentation of the "President's Program," Gorbachev had been brutally honest in describing the critical condition of the economy and the extreme urgency of remedial action. What he did not realize was the tragic fact that time had run out for him. He was the country's leader, the General Secretary of the CPSU, traditionally the "strong man" assumed as always to be virtually in total charge of the economy and of everything else. The brilliant statesman, the great humanist, the daring democratizer had in effect confessed that in five and a half years, he had been unable to turn the country around.

People could not be expected to understand that Gorbachev had not so much failed as been forcefully defeated by the obdurate, unprincipled, deceptive opposition which almost completely surrounded him—the well-spoken "collective" Party leadership who were themselves the subtly corrupt nabobs of the self-advantaged bureaucracy. Nor could people divine that he had become a victim of his own progressivism, the democratization that was gradually dismantling the power of the center and thereby willingly giving up the means of repressing his opposition, thus letting slip the traditional role of the big boss.

Worst of all there was a nemesis growing in power who was personally dedicated to bringing him down. Five months earlier, in May 1990, Boris Yeltsin had gotten himself elected Chairman of the Supreme Soviet of the Russian republic and had begun to stir up trouble both publicly and behind the scenes. The very same day the "President's Program" was presented, Yeltsin came out openly and denounced Gorbachev's "retreat" from the Shatalin 500-Day Plan which Yeltsin had gotten the Russian republic to adopt on its own. Demagogy became the order of the day for the Yeltsin cohort.

He offered an impossible "coalition" between the Russian republic and the USSR, claiming that Gorbachev was seriously considering it. Presenting himself as the true democrat, he accused Gorbachev of operating "by diktat." He pretended to favor and to cooperate with the new inter-republic treaty proposed by Gorbachev but then insisted he could not sign it unless the Russian republic was first granted full dominion over its natural resources, especially its oil, gold, and other precious metals, diamonds, etc. A skilled demagogue, he spread the word everywhere that his "reforms" could solve the people's problems if only the obstacles were removed, namely the restraints of the USSR's leadership whom the people found it easy to blame for all their troubles. It was only as he gained power that it became clear he would be making an all-out pro-capitalist attack on socialism itself.

The story is told that a former press secretary of his, when asked about an instance showing a lack of principles on Yeltsin's part, said, "He never had any." True or not, there is hardly any other way to explain how a man who had been not just a member of the Party but its strong public advocate, a leading Communist for twenty years, could so completely reverse himself when it suited his drive for personal power and the advantages of Western support.

Gorbachev's program of restructuring along the lines of a socially mixed economy was being stymied in a number of ways: by competing plans from left and right, by directly disruptive moves Yeltsin made, going even so far as to organize a mass demonstration to demand Gorbachev's resignation, and finally the reckless endangerment of the Soviet Union itself by the power drives of some republic leaders influenced by Yeltsin's example to make nationalist, secessionist moves.

Throughout the final year of his presidency, knowing he could not otherwise continue his economic reforms, Gorbachev fought tirelessly to preserve the USSR, reconstructed to provide more freedom of action for each republic. He made use of the obvious economic interdependence of the republics and managed a referendum in March 1991 in which three-quarters of the people approved a continuation of the Soviet Union in some renewed form. He had momentarily fended off the growing strength of Boris Yeltsin who, in April 1991, was given the right by his parliament to rule by decree and in June was elected President of Russia, giving his arbitrary use of power a democratic aura. Gorbachev had even persuaded the die-hards in the Communist Party to go along with holding a basic conference in November which would undertake to reform the Party itself. The day Gorbachev was to return from vacation, August 20, 1991, was the day the treaty was finally scheduled to be signed by the nine agreed republics. This was not to be.

The Catastrophic August 1991 Coup

The August Coup, a top-level conspiracy, took place on the 19th because the entrenched leaders of the Communist Party and the Soviet government knew that if they allowed the new inter-republic treaty to be signed the following day they would end up out of power. The tragi-farcical three-day putsch failed because neither the people nor the armed forces supported it, enabling Yeltsin to grandstand his defiance of it and to play the hero standing on a tank. He used the easy rescue of Gorbachev from house arrest in the Crimea to play up his own ascendancy, and in one display of crudeness virtually bullied him on television at the podium of the Russian Parliament.

So thoroughly discredited was the top party-state apparatus by the putsch that Gorbachev had to take drastic steps immediately. On August 24 he ordered the Cabinet of Ministers, the Soviet inner government council, to resign. He created a committee headed by a close Yeltsin aide, Premier of the Russian Republic Ivan Silayev, to take charge of the Soviet economy. He also ordered the Soviet parliament to take all Communist Party property into custody until its future was decided "in strict compliance with Soviet and republican law." He is reported to have had a final meeting for several hours with the CPSU's Central Committee. In view of the role played by the world's most influential political organization through most of the twentieth century, it is instructive to read the historically eloquent, terse appraisal of its culmination, the public statement on August 24, 1991, of its most progressive son, Mikhail Sergeyevich Gorbachev:

> The Secretariat, the Politburo and the Communist Party's Central Committee did not take a stand against the coup d'état. The Central Committee did not manage to take a firm position of condemnation and opposition. It did not inspire Communists to fight against the trampling of constitutional law.
>
> Among the conspirators were members of the party's leadership. A number of party committees and the mass media supported the action of the state criminals. This placed millions of Communists in a false position.

> Many members of the party refused to collaborate with the conspirators, condemned the coup and joined in the fight against it. No one has the right to blame all Communists and I, as President, consider it my duty to defend them as citizens from unfounded accusations.
>
> The Central Committee must take the difficult but honest decision to disband itself. The fate of republican and local party organizations should be decided by themselves.
>
> I consider it no longer possible to continue to carry out my duties as General Secretary of the Central Committee of the Soviet Union and I relinquish corresponding authority.
>
> I believe that democratically minded Communists, who remain faithful to constitutional law and to the course of renewal of society, will speak up for the creation of a new basis of a party capable, together with all progressive forces, of actively joining in the continuation of fundamental democratic reforms for the sake of working people.[10]

The Disruption of the Soviet Union

With epidemic speed in the one week of August 24-31, 1991, the four republics (Lithuania, Estonia, Latvia, and Georgia) which had previously declared their independence were joined in such declarations by Ukraine, Byelorussia (now Belarus), Moldavia, Azerbaijan, Uzbekistan, and Kirghizia, accompanied by expressions of awareness of their economic interdependence.

Almost as quickly, in a last-ditch attempt to halt the damaging fragmentation of the USSR, President Gorbachev and the heads of ten republics appeared at the September 2 opening of the USSR Congress and proposed to transfer all central authority to themselves and an appointed legislative council until a new union would be formed. The 1,780 deputies, who in 1989 had become the first and highest authoritative assembly elected by the entire Soviet Union, were in effect being asked to dissolve themselves. The discussion became heated.

Gorbachev and Yeltsin, their differing interests momentarily coinciding, acted as co-chairmen—and the statement for all the heads of republics was presented by Nursultan Nazarbayev of Kazakhstan. Gorbachev dominated the sessions and, after three days of bitter dispute, secured a vote of 1,606 for, 116 against, 83 abstaining and 37 not voting. Deputies were to keep their privileges and immunities for the remaining two and a half years of their tenure. There were to be no further assemblies. Instead, some deputies were to be involved in some small legislative bodies and an inter-republic economic body but the real power would be above them in a State Council consisting of Gorbachev and the heads of the ten republics.

Thus, power was passing from the Soviet central government to the republics, operating independently in a loose federation. For Yeltsin, however, if this became final it would not be a sufficient change for his unstated purposes. A few more pieces would have to fall in place for him but he acted as if he was going along. On November 14 he participated in an agreement worked out by Gorbachev and the leaders of seven republics to move toward a new confederated "Union of Sovereign States" with the central authorities exercising such rights as were delegated by the republics.

For the socially mixed economy that Gorbachev had been gradually developing, all these changes were not bringing it to an end but simply putting its implementation under each republic's control. It was a disarming expression of good will that the November 14 meeting was held in the suburb of Novo-Ogaryovo where republic leaders had first met in April to form a new association, the plan so rudely blocked by the August Coup and now resumed in a different way as projected at the September 3-6 Congress. Others were expected to join.

Washington now took a hand in the situation, reversing itself in just such a manner as Yeltsin could have asked for. On August 1, less than three weeks before the putsch in Moscow, President Bush made a speech in the Ukrainian capital, Kiev, against what he called "suicidal nationalism," saying the United States would not take sides between the Soviet government and the individual republics. Now, on November 28, 1991, it was reported that "President Bush has authorized a major shift in American policy away from the central Soviet government and toward the republics, deciding to recognize an independent Ukraine 'expeditiously' if the second-largest Soviet republic breaks with Moscow in a referendum on Sunday.[11]

As might have been expected, Gorbachev immediately issued a statement of "pained surprise" at this willful comment on the internal affairs of the Soviet Union but Yeltsin expressed no objection to Bush's about-face. Now things could move quickly.

Whereas previously the Russian republic had provided funds when the Soviet central bank could not meet a payment, now Russia refused to do so. Then Russia announced it was temporarily taking control of the Soviet Foreign Ministry building and embassies abroad because the Soviet Union did not have the money to keep them going. And then Yeltsin agreed to finance the Soviet payroll for the immediate future and to guarantee sufficient credits to meet the minimal needs of the Kremlin. Real control was shifting.

Finally, the most strategic piece needed in Yeltsin's unstated program fell into place. It was the two-fold Ukrainian election. The former CPSU official, Leonid M. Kravchuk, was elected president, topping five other candidates with 55 to 60 percent of the votes—and in the accompanying referendum 90 percent of the Ukrainians approved full independence, previously declared but subject to this ratification. The Russian republic immediately extended official recognition.

It was now possible for Yeltsin to pull off a grand coup of his own, one that undoubtedly required careful, secret preparation, well-timed to brush aside legal objections. On December 7 and 8, 1991, the heads of three Slavic republics: Boris Yeltsin of Russia, Leonid Kravchuk of Ukraine, and Stanislav Shushkevich of Byelorussia, met in a Byelorussian resort in the Belovezhskaya Forest near Brest and issued a series of pronunciamentos.

They declared that "the U.S.S.R., as a subject of international law and geopolitical reality, is ceasing its existence." They said they drew their authority to dissolve the Union from the fact (!) that they were its original cofounders. (They and the Trans-Caucasus Republic, later divided into Georgia, Armenia, and Azerbaijan, were co-signers of the original 1922 treaty that created the USSR.)

Declaring void all efforts to create a new union on the ruins of the old one, they called for the creation of new "coordinating bodies" for defense, foreign affairs, and the economy that would have their seat in Minsk, the capital of Byelorussia (Belarus)—and decided to maintain the ruble as the common currency. They proclaimed a new "Commonwealth of Independent States" open to all members of the former Soviet Union. They said that the "norms" and activities of the former Soviet Union ceased as of the moment of signing, and that the new Commonwealth assumed all international obligations of the USSR, as well as control over its nuclear arsenal.

The three leaders were scheduled to meet shortly with Mikhail Gorbachev and Nursultan Nazarbayev, President of Kazakhstan and unofficial spokesman of the muslim republics of central Asia. No one would be losing sight of the fact that the three Slavic republics accounted for 73 percent of the population and 80 percent of the territory of the Soviet Union.[12]

For the next three weeks Gorbachev fought a losing battle, arguing, as in a televised statement at the outset, that "The fate of our multinational country cannot be decided by the will of three republican leaders. This question can only be resolved through constitutional means with the participation of all sovereign states and taking into account the will of their peoples." The republics, however, voted with their feet and when the time came that the Commonwealth included eleven of them, resistance no longer made any sense. December 25, 1991, Gorbachev resigned the presidency, the last structural remnant of the sixty-nine-year-old Soviet Union.

The End of Ideology for Yeltsin

The victory of Boris Yeltsin would not be complete, nor his program durable, as long as he allowed Gorbachev's ideas to remain influential. As for the socially mixed economy, elements of which would persist despite his trashing, he would have to deny it could even exist. He tried in his typically crude, thoughtlessly pat manner to bury Gorbachev's ideology with a contrived epitaph: "He thought to unite the impossible: Communism with the market, public property with private property, political pluralism with the Communist Party. These are impossible couples, but he insisted on them, and therein lay his fundamental strategic mistake."[13]

Pure sophistry! "Communism with the market" had been considered possible in the socialist stage as far back as Marx—and Lenin. "Public property with private property" exists in every advanced capitalist country, let alone the socialist ones. And "political pluralism with the Communist Party" had been something even Lenin had favored and practiced at the time when it was possible. Yeltsin's empty judgment from on high has the ring of Western right-wing logic.

If there was a "fundamental strategic mistake" made by Mikhail Gorbachev it was not this, for some of his greatest achievements, like ending the Cold War, could be called efforts to "unite the impossible." One would rather have to say it was his excessively trustful good will, shown most deplorably in his incredibly poor judgment of the personal character of the colleagues he chose. One cannot forget, as a tragi-comic example, that when the Supreme Soviet had twice tried to deny him the appointment of Gennadi Yanayev as vice president—the same Yanayev who later headed the putsch and announced his takeover as president—Gorbachev had pushed through the appointment by saying, "I have to have someone I can trust!"

Gorbachev had not only brought his eventual nemesis Yeltsin into national prominence, he virtually surrounded himself with eventual traitors, opponents who in his over-confidence, he thought to win over by persuasion. Unfairly, but understandably in a people historically accustomed to belief in the need for "strong men" as leaders, this brought down upon his head their disrespect—and the pragmatic judgments to which dire circumstance committed them.

The New "Primitive Accumulation"

With the large presence of Gorbachev effectively out of the way, Yeltsin's drive for high power could proceed, provided he could cultivate sufficient material support. It was easy for him to take on the false persona of chief democrat and tribune of the people, posing as a fatherly figure above the battle. That came naturally to an experienced demagogue but it would not be enough when face to face with potential rivals and political enemies. As he no longer had a ruling party to lean upon, he had to create a new rulership.

As his chosen direction was pro-capitalist, this new class of political and financial supporters would have to be wheelers and dealers who would know how to gain pelf and privilege from the sledgehammer operations imported from the West as "shock therapy." These players would have to be welcomed by an unscrupulous government under the guise of so-called democratic reforms promising all manner of benefits to the people from a so-called free market.

There is no reason to believe that Yeltsin adopted his brash pro-capitalism as a result of some ideological conversion. It is more likely that a life-long experience with ways of maneuvering for power had taught him a new ruling class would fortify his overlordship, that making communism the everlasting villain would relieve him and his cohort from responsibility for all social ills, and that opening Russia to foreign capitalist exploitation would bring much-needed financial support for his program. The West had already indicated a coming benevolence to his side.

The problem was that a new capitalist ruling class could not be simply wished into existence, especially in a place where no system of private capital even existed and, therefore, there also did not exist any of the rules and regulations that had grown up in world capitalism. But there had to be capital. What was called for in this situation was the promotion by an unprincipled regime of some form of "primitive accumulation," the method of acquiring capital by wanton expropriation which had attended the brutal birth of world capitalism.

No time was lost. A free-for-all ensued in which favored people were allowed to treat Russia as a grab-bag of privatizations-on-the-cheap. This reached scandalous proportions. On March 13, 1992, only nine months after Yeltsin became President of the Russian Federation, First Deputy Premier Gennadi Burbulis had to admit that "Most residents of the Russian Federation believe the problem has become very acute, that corruption has reached unheard-of proportions."[14]

Bribery became systematized, so widespread and taken for granted that some bureaucrats felt free to put it on the books as "donations." The "anything goes" climate of deliberate misappropriation of state enterprises, including "insider-trading" practices considered criminal in the West, inevitably spawned an extraordinary growth of organized crime. This continued year after year with the government occasionally deploring it, never rising above a low level of prosecution, and when faced by popular rage or public exposure, appointing still another "committee against corruption."

Problems of the Yeltsin Regime

Under the guise of democratic reforms to establish a free market economy, whatever people could take that to mean, the administration's activity consisted mainly of measures to introduce and try to enforce capitalist practices and eliminate all socialized practices. But Russia's history made it a land in which this process was bound to be resisted. For example, an effort Yeltsin made December 28, 1991 to institute the buying and selling of land was cut back by the Russian parliament to a level that had been acceptable in Gorbachev's time—whereby collective farms could make limited arrangements for family farming and let non-farmers own small patches as country gardens.

That was about the time when, touting his free market program, Yeltsin freed the prices on most items, assuring the people that the resulting hardships would be short-lived, a matter of no more than six or eight months. This promise would remain empty for years to come. What did result in six months was a rise in the annual inflation rate to about 1,300 percent, with the ruble falling in value.

Also in 1992, the Cabinet, under Acting Prime Minister Yegor Gaidar, the economist who had been on the team favoring the 500-Day Program, was planning privatization of all trade and small industry by 1994, and of at least half of medium and large enterprises by 1995. This brought on such a battle with the tough-minded industrial managers of state-owned enterprises that the administration was forced into partial retreat and an alteration of plans.

In a typically promotional gesture a month later, in October 1992, Yeltsin presented the nation with his voucher plan for privatization. No one really benefited much, other than a few speculators who bought up vouchers and used them as stock options. Gorbachev called it a sham and in time the plan fizzled out. The conservative newspaper *Den* said: "The Government robbed the people with inflation and is now trying to tip them with a voucher worth a pair of shoes, while the country is sold to local and foreign capitalists.[15]

By the end of the year, after a two-week battle in the Russian Congress, Yeltsin had to reverse himself and demote Gaidar. Elected as the new prime minister and head of the Cabinet was Victor S. Chernomyrdin, the 54-year-old industrial manager of the giant Gazprom who had been deputy prime minister in charge of the state fuel-energy complex. This compromise choice, which turned out to be fairly durable, was a harbinger of Yeltsin's continuing trend toward the center of the dispute, indicated by his politic remark that "reforms must now acquire a somewhat different ring." That was December 14, 1992.

That was putting it all too mildly. Great damage had been done, having also multiplied the problems under Soviet rule. The dismantling of the old system of central planning (the abolition of Gosplan and Gossnab July 1, 1991) before developing a market system to replace it created a chaotic situation. This might have been corrected had not the Soviet Union itself been brought down not long afterward. Shock therapy hit the country January 2, 1992, causing an uncontrollable rise in prices with wages rising at a lower rate, so much so that most of the population was pushed below the poverty line. Industrial production collapsed because enterprises could not get credits to pay their workers and suppliers; by the end of 1992 Russia's gross domestic production had fallen by 22 percent, twice as much as in 1991. Consumer spending fell 38 percent in 1992, an astounding rate considering that in the entire first four years of the Great Depression in the United States, it had fallen only 21 percent!

It was already becoming clear that Russia could neither go back to the old way of doing things nor go forward to some simplistic imitation of Western capitalism.

Outlook and Questions for the Russian Mix

Many people were saying Russia would have to find "a third way." In the spring of 1993, Professor Stephen F. Cohen provided a profound insight into the situation, one that proved prophetic. Among other important observations, he noted:

> Marketization and the growth of private enterprises will almost certainly continue, however fitfully, if only because most Russian political factions, from left to right, now understand that the country cannot thrive without them. On the other hand, even that process is unlikely to conform to simplistic American expectations. Russia will probably 'walk on two legs,' moving toward what is being called a 'mixed economic system,' with a substantial state and private sector but with the state still dominant in large-scale industry, agriculture, transportation and finance, while private enterprise flourishes mainly in services, trade and small-scale production.
>
> Even so, many important economic questions will remain the subject of political dispute. What should be the relative proportions of state and private property? Which state-controlled industries and farms inherited from the Soviet past are essential and thus must be subsidized, and which can be abandoned to a market fate? Should private enterprise be actively encouraged or merely tolerated? And what should be the nature of the new market system: 'liberal and free' or 'social and regulated'? None of these problems can be

solved by American conceits or shock therapy, only by Russian consensus-building and gradual change.

As for political life, democratization has achieved a great deal since Mikhail Gorbachev began the process in the late 1980s, but despite many modernizing changes in Russian society in recent decades, centuries of authoritarianism cannot be overcome quickly, or in a leap, even with favorable conditions. And Russia's conditions today are not favorable. Indeed, many once-fervent democratizers now advocate suspending the process until stabilization and more marketization can be achieved. Various kinds of government are always possible that are neither fully democratic nor fully dictatorial, and Russia is likely to experience several of them in the years ahead.

But whatever the shape of Russia's political and economic future, it will not be a replica of America's present or the Soviet past. It will be, as is said increasingly in Moscow, some 'third way.' American cheerleaders for Yeltsin and shock therapy adamantly deny that there can be any kind of third way, and accuse its proponents of being 'enemies of reform.' But here is what the Russian president himself told the nation in October 1992: 'We are not leading Russia to any kind of capitalism. Russia is simply not suited for this. Russia is a unique country. It will not be socialist or capitalist.[16]

The Autocrat Posing as Democrat

The insincerity involved in making a statement inconsistent with his continued pro-capitalist initiatives is not as significant as the fact that Yeltsin felt constrained to say it. Recognizing that limits would be imposed on his program, perhaps even recognizing that what was beginning to prevail was the prospect of a socially mixed economy, it was evident that his actions were always designed to assure his personal dominance. Conveniently, he was not burdened by any scruples.

In April 1993, Yeltsin faced a financial crisis in government operations as well as unremitting Communist opposition in the Duma. He must have told President Clinton at a weekend summit meeting in Vancouver that he would leave no stone unturned to put the Communists down and would resolutely put through the reforms—for on April 4 Clinton announced full support for Yeltsin plus a larger than expected $1.6 billion aid package to provide "immediate and tangible" support for Russia's reforms. This showed the voters in the upcoming referendum on April 25 what Yeltsin could personally accomplish.

To assure success he proceeded immediately on his return to sweeten the pot for the voters, disregarding the effect on inflation and the government deficit. He raised wages, increased spending, issued low-cost credits for bankrupt industries, linked interest on savings to inflation, raised benefits for the military and maintained price controls. Surely voters would not want to lose such benefits by voting the wrong way.

Now the man who kept touting himself as the virtual founder of democracy, always quick to smear his opponents as totalitarian, put a process into motion to gain authoritarian power. To provide a legal basis, he carefully assembled and controlled a conference to prepare a new constitution containing provisions that would strengthen his hand, and which would be adopted by referendum at a manageable time.

Skirting legality and playing the strong man backed by the people, he made a series of daringly arbitrary moves. On September 1, 1993, at a time when numerous charges and countercharges of corruption in high places were being made, Yeltsin decreed the suspension of his Vice President and political opponent, Aleksandr V. Rutskoi. Based on the specious claim that Rutskoi's "accusations of corruption were seriously damaging to the authority of the Russian state," the suspension was asserted so that allegations of illegal financial dealing by Rutskoi could be investigated.

Two days later, by a vote of 141 to 10, Parliament voted to suspend the president's decree, said he had no right to remove a vice president who had been elected on the same ticket with him three years before, his automatic successor under the Constitution, and turned the matter over to the Constitutional Court for consideration.

Yeltsin ignored it. On September 16, he reasserted his stand on reforms by bringing Yegor Gaidar back into the government as first deputy prime minister in charge of all economic matters. Now he was ready for a fight to the finish. It would involve actions so incredibly arbitrary that were they not tragic, would belong in the theater of the absurd. He had no legal grounds for his actions but he had the ostensible neutrality and actual support of the armed forces for his executive power—and the open backing of the West.

On September 21 he appeared on television to announce the action he had repeatedly threatened to take in the nine months of his feud with the Communist-dominated legislature: its dissolution. His decree also called for new elections to a new bicameral legislature on December 11-12—a federal assembly with an upper Council of the Federation composed of leaders of the regions, and a lower State Duma of popularly elected deputies, for which even present deputies could run. Declaring that the present legislature had paralyzed his reforms and his ability to govern he said, "Power in the Supreme Soviet of Russia has been seized by a group of persons who have turned it into the headquarters of irreconcilable opposition. My duty as President is to state that the current corps of deputies has lost its right to be in control of a crucial lever of power." Of course, the legislature's opposition, surely a democratic prerogative, could not by itself justify his claim that it "has ceased to be an organ of rule by the people."[17]

After a telephone conversation with Yeltsin, President Clinton announced his full support, subsequently urging European leaders to do the same. To justify its unconscionable support of Yeltsin's illegal and authoritarian actions, Washington made the false (and irrelevant) claim that the Soviet Parliament had been elected under Communist Party voting rules and offered the lame excuse that Yeltsin was promising new balloting in the name of democracy.

Yeltsin's ministers of defense, security, and the interior declared their support and were shown on television in casual contact with him, while opposition legislators could only issue a series of defiant resolutions. Taking their anti-communist cue from Washington, Western governments quickly lined up behind Yeltsin, as did the governments of Ukraine, Belarus, and Kazakhstan.

The Shelling of the Parliament

Almost immediately after the dissolution decree, the Supreme Soviet voted by an overwhelming margin to depose Boris Yeltsin and ordered security forces not to obey him. With great enthusiasm, the deputies then swore in Vice President Aleksandr V. Rutskoi as acting president. Rutskoi, a hero general in the war in Afghanistan, had been an ally of Yeltsin but had become his most bitter foe and was also a champion of reconstituting the Soviet Union. As the Supreme Soviet was adjourning that day, the Constitutional Court, whose chairman, Valery D. Zorkin, had long been openly hostile to Yeltsin, upheld the decision to depose him, saying he should be impeached.

The formal basis for deposing Yeltsin was a constitutional amendment passed earlier in the year by the legislature, stating that if the president tried to dissolve parliament, he would automatically lose his powers. Force has its own logic, of course. A dissolved body may have a problem making an impeachment stick, especially when the intended target shrugs off the notion that he has "lost his powers."

Now the bullying began. Large numbers of police and some troops were deployed around the Parliament building, known as the White House, where inside many deputies had decided to remain while arming themselves. The night of September 24, they found their lights had been turned off and from then on they were without electricity, hot water, or telephone service. Yeltsin ordered the Interior Ministry to disarm them and Moscow's mayor, Yuri Luzhkov, obediently issued an order to confiscate their weapons.

The deputies offered a compromise, proposing simultaneous elections for parliament and president. This way out of the dispute, which was becoming distasteful in many regions of Russia, was actively promoted at a meeting of regional leaders on September 26 in St. Petersburg; but Yeltsin was adamant, saying a presidential election could be held only separately, six months after the new bicameral legislature was in place.

On September 29, the national and city governments issued a virtual ultimatum to the deputies to evacuate the building and surrender their arms by Monday, October 4. The two leaders, Rutskoi and Khasbulatov, were warned of "grave consequences" for failure to comply. Some parrying offers flew back and forth but got nowhere and the deputies began to fear the worst.

Becoming aware that Yeltsin was bringing the army into Moscow and fearing that he planned to storm the White House, Rutskoi appealed to the people to take up arms. Thousands responded, and with Rutskoi reportedly cheering them on, attacked the blockade, tried to storm the mayor's office, and attempted to seize the Ostankino television and radio facility. They were repelled with at least a score of deaths and hundreds wounded. Some 15,000 people are said to have taken to the streets in response to the Parliament's appeal. All this happened on Sunday, October 3, 1993.

On Monday, October 4, Yeltsin had the military combine the action of crack airborne troops routing the occupants of the White House floor by floor and tanks firing five-inch shells that blasted the building, leaving it battered and on fire. It made a horrifying picture on television that would be long remembered in Russia and abroad. A total of 160 people ended up being held in Lefortovo prison, including Khasbulatov and Rutskoi.

Yeltsin also banned a number of opposition parties and closed a number of opposition newspapers, but these blatantly anti-democratic actions were contested so hard and so broadly that in not too long a time he had to back off.

Hustling a Monarchical Constitution

Now Yeltsin dropped the pretense that he favored an early presidential election scheduled for June 1994. On November 6, 1993, he simply told a group of newspaper editors he wanted to stay in office until his term expired in 1996. The elections for the new parliament, however, had been set for December 12, 1993 and this had already set off a mad scramble among the twenty-one registered political blocs and parties to gather the 100,000 signatures each needed to enter the race.

A total of 628 deputies had to be elected: 450 for a new lower house, the State Duma, and 178 deputies for an upper house, the Federation Council. Half of the Duma members would be chosen directly by constituencies and the other half according to the vote for party lists. The Federation Council would be made up of two representatives from each region. The two chambers would form the Federal Assembly, Russia's seventh attempt at a Parliament.

The election was structured so that the complex process of electing deputies to Parliament would occur at the same time as the vote on a new Constitution. There was much criticism, all to no avail, ranging from the head of the Communist bloc, Gennadi A. Zyuganov, to the reform economist, Grigory A. Yavlinsky, claiming that the Yeltsin forces were rushing the elections, trying to assure a legislature they could dominate, as well as increase power for Yeltsin. Of truly greater importance than a cooperative legislature was the hidden calculation in publishing the final draft of the proposed constitution, designed to increase Yeltsin's power, only one month before the election. This would not allow enough time for critics to reach the widely spread electorate and convincingly explain their objections to this large and complex document.

As always with legal documents requiring studious examination, it was not to be expected that voters would do this. In addition to sorting out their selections among a welter of candidates for two separate chambers, plus a party or bloc choice for the Duma, the voters would have to answer the deceptively simple question: "Do you approve the new Constitution? Yes or no." Would it be reasonable to say no to such an important document when there was really no alternative? The existing Constitution had been amended three hundred times and was generally held in disdain.

Suppose it was true, as some were saying (and it was, of course) that it would greatly strengthen the president's hand. Wasn't this customary? Hadn't such a big and difficult country as Russia always required a "strong man" in charge? Besides, this document "guaranteed" an impressive range of people's rights, some held over from the past, some new ones. The result was predictable. Yeltsin received his monarchical charter.

The Constitution won by only a narrow margin, however, and in the Duma the Yeltsin forces took a beating. They were badly outnumbered by the bloc of Communists and Agrarians in first place and the Zhirinovsky jingo extremists in second. It led Prime Minister Chernomyrdin to make a candid analysis. He scathingly accused the Westernized reformers in his Cabinet of "poorly thought out experiments" and a failure "to think about the people, for the sake of whom the reforms were started."

As if to note the special need of Russia for a socially mixed economy, he said the government would focus more now on social protection and on state and private investment to create jobs. Speaking to the trade union newspaper *Trud* in an interview, he said

> We should face the truth that many people voted not so much for a particular platform or party as against the hardships and mistakes of the current reforms.

> As many as 35 million Russians live below the poverty line, which means that some 30 percent of the electorate were potentially 'against.' Naturally, any 'shock' methods must be precluded in the future.[18]

Durability of the Russian Mix

The year 1994 may very well have been the year in which, despite much uncertainty and continuing difficulty in the management of its productive capacity, Russia began to settle into its fourth effort to develop a socially mixed economy.

Not only did the results of the 1993 election shock the pro-capitalist administration into steering a middle course for its own survival, it was now obvious the people at large had begun to understand that the reforms would have to be restrained for self-protection. The reputable ARCSPO, the All-Russia Center for the Study of Public Opinion,stated:

> Sociological studies show that, beginning in 1994, support for market reforms began to weaken among the country's population. Whereas the percentage of people who believed it was necessary to continue market reforms grew in 1992-1993, the percentage of those supporting continued reforms fell in 1994-1995; conversely, the percentage of opponents of continuing the reforms increased. This trend is apparent from monitoring done by ARCSPO.[19]

Things became unnecessarily more difficult when Yeltsin, acting on the foolish advice of his defense minister, General Pavel S. Grachev, opened a large-scale military action against Chechnya on December 11, 1994. Grachev's mistaken belief that Chechnya's long-prepared rebellion could be put down in a matter of hours, sent Russia into a bloody quagmire that would go on for almost two years and end in a stalemate. Popular generals like Aleksandr I. Lebed and Deputy Defense Minister Boris Gromov said the invasion made no sense. Prominent leaders like Grigory Yavlinsky and even the former Prime Minister Yegor Gaidar denounced the action, but Yeltsin blundered on to the sorry end.

In late 1995 the country experienced one of the worst fall harvests in years due to a summer-long drought and previous poor management. Prime Minister Chernomyrdin was primarily in charge at this point due to Yeltsin's long hospitalization and convalescence from heart attacks that occurred in July and October of that year. An interesting factor in the subsequent management of the crisis—and one that bears on both the durability of the developing Russian mix and a certain uniqueness about it—was that the people had begun providing for themselves. More than a third of all meat and nearly half the vegetables in the country were already being produced privately in back yards or in communal garden plots. It is worth noting that communal activity in the countryside is an old Russian tradition dating back to the freeing of the serfs in 1861. Long before the Soviet collectives, a wide variety of village communes operated all through the latter part of the 19th century. Extended family operations and even ordinary mutual help were also traditional.

As for Yeltsin, facing a re-election campaign at a time when his personal popularity was at a very low point, a drastic change in policy was imperative. The election would be held in June 1996 after a year of unpopular and destructive war in Chechnya with tens of thousands dead, an upsurge of Communist power in the Duma, and the economy still in crisis.

On January 5, 1996 in an effort to show he was not, as often charged, a tool of Western capital, Yeltsin accepted the long-expected resignation of his Foreign Minister, Andrei V. Kozyrev, a known sycophant toward Washington, Bonn, and Paris. Apparently anticipating this eventuality, Kozyrev had run for the Duma and been elected a month before his ouster.

An impressive replacement was found in Yevgeny M. Primakov, director of the foreign intelligence service and a member of the powerful Security Council. A speaker of Arabic and English who had been active in the Middle East and a member of the prestigious Russian Academy of Sciences, he had maintained contact with Yeltsin's people while acting as foreign policy adviser to Gorbachev. Significantly, he had defied and denounced the August Coup. He was one who could be taken seriously by the West and be approved by the Duma Communists involved in confirming his appointment.

Eleven days later, on January 16, Yeltsin "accepted the resignation" of Anatoly B. Chubais, former head of the privatization program and one who had worked closely with Western bankers and the International Monetary Fund. To clearly show that he was veering away from the economic reforms of the free market crusaders, Yeltsin replaced Chubais with Vladimir V. Kadannikov, the director of Russia's largest automobile company and an advocate of protective tariffs. Named Deputy Prime Minister, Kadannikov became Russia's top economic official. After the virtuous purpose of the two big personnel changes was well established, Chubais became Yeltsin's campaign manager!

The campaign made history. It was an incredibly dishonorable and unscrupulous display of how a powerful incumbent could raise himself to victory from a very low level of acceptance by means of large-scale bribery, deception, and fanciful slander of his opponent. It was so blatant it drew exposés from many foreign newspapers—but the Russian people, of course, did not see these.

Breaking campaign rules, Yeltsin used state funds and I.M.F. loans to exceed limits on expenditures and essentially bribe large segments of the electorate. He spent hundreds of thousands of dollars buying pro-Yeltsin, anti-

Communist articles by journalists. His monopolistic control of the three major television networks, in a country where TV is the only means of national campaigning, assured that his Communist rival, Gennady Zyuganov, was virtually shut out of media access, while being targeted for a systematic disinformation barrage.

There were charges of falsification in reporting the returns. It was well documented that the Yeltsin government had threatened to fire governors if they didn't deliver their regions. Yeltsin campaigned against Yeltsinism, particularly shock therapy and free market policies "from the West."[20]

Yeltsin knew that his widely-touted "54-40 sweeping victory" was not really a majority mandate, that little more than a third of the eligible population had voted for him—and not so much in approval of his actions as in hope for fulfillment of his promises and in fear of the exaggerated evils his opponent was luridly pictured to represent. Of the 109 million registered voters, 40 million went for Yeltsin, 30 million for Zyuganov, 4 million voted against both and 35 million did not vote at all.

The fact that the Communists had gained strength in all three national elections since 1993—to the point where they gained control of Parliament in 1995—confirmed the need to move toward a middle course; a shift in policy declared, incidentally, by Chernomyrdin six months earlier. In view of his continued desire for closeness with the West, Yeltsin would surely not consider it politic to openly declare, as Zyuganov did repeatedly in favor of a mixed economy, but he would have to face the fact—and try to make the best of it—that the country was already moving in that direction.

It was definitely clear by then that in Russia, promoting capitalism would not get a politician very far. In the same ARCSPO survey previously cited, 2,000 residents were asked, "Are you pleased that Russia has embarked on the path of capitalism, and that businessmen, millionaires and bankers have emerged in the country?" In percent, on the average, 58 answered no, 20 yes and 22 didn't know. They were also asked, "If it were possible, would you want life in Russia to go back to the way it was in the USSR before 1985?" In average percent, 59 said yes, 26 no and 15 didn't know. The survey drew a "general conclusion" that "On the whole, the country's population is not hungering for capitalism, and the majority has a negative attitude toward it." Then it added: "A striking fact was discovered: The percentage of people preferring various structures connected with the state was almost 20 times as great as the percentage of those preferring any kind of private structures (59 percent and 3 percent respectively. On this question, the differences among people of different ages are not very great."

The Western media all too often makes the mistake of presenting Russian affairs in Western terms. For example, the simplistic notion that everything not public, i.e., state-owned or state-run, is private and therefore capitalistic. Thus, the frequent statement that eighty percent of Russian enterprises are no longer state-owned is taken to mean that privatization has been a great success for capitalism. Not so, says one of the more astute observers of the Russian scene, Jonathan Steele, writing in 1996:

> [T]he significance of Russia's privatization process is not the number of enterprises which have been denationalized—about which Chubais constantly boasts—but the method of privatization used. The reality is that Chubais suffered defeat after defeat. Pressure from Yeltsin's opponents in the Russian parliament ensured that most firms were not sold to the highest bidder, but were taken over by work-force buy-outs in which the existing management plus workers took a majority shareholding. A kind of Russian ESOP (Employee Share-Owning Partnership), this was known as Option Two in the legislation which went through the Duma in 1992. . . .Under Option Two they could decide to take a controlling share, set at 51 percent, under preferential terms. By December 1992, 60 percent of large firms with over a thousand employees and 70 percent of firms with more than two hundred employees had chosen Option Two.[21]

The truth will come out. The upshot was neatly stated in July 1997 by a leading Moscow correspondent: "Six years after the Soviet Union collapsed, Russia has emerged with an economy that is part free market and part socialist."[22]

The Primakov Consensus

The deeply felt convictions of the Russian people concerning the "economy that is part free market and part socialist" were well expressed by the country's famous historian, Roy Medvedev, in 1998:

> In Russia the working class and people at large are far from living in prosperity, but their historical experience makes them loathe both totalitarianism and rabid capitalism. This is the underlying reason for the mounting popularity of ideas associated with democratic and humane socialism based on a mixed economy and subscribing to many values cherished both in traditional and modern Western society.[23]

In September of that year, in an editorial in *The Nation* entitled "Twilight of the Czar," it had already become possible for Daniel Singer to write:

> President Clinton recently paid a visit to a fallen czar. The blundering Yeltsin may be clinging to his throne, but his effective reign came to a close on August

> 17 [1998], a date to remember. The collapse of the ruble and the defaulting on debt payments symbolically mark the end of a period of seven years of calamity leading to the ruin of the country's economy and the terrible impoverishment of the bulk of the population. It was good on this occasion that Clinton was in the limelight with Yeltsin because the Western powers in general, and the American presidency in particular, share the blame, having all along given their blessing to the policies that brought about the disaster.[24]

Yeltsin had been aware of the gathering crisis resulting from Chernomyrdin's five years of temporizing mismanagement, followed by Sergei Kiriyenko's brash and short-lived efforts to push through the right-wing reforms. But he was just as stunned as everyone else by the economic crash of August 17, 1998 in which the value of the ruble dropped from 15 cents to 4 cents and the default on debt payments scared off all Western lenders. He had no choice but to venture a workable compromise with the angry left and for this he needed the statesmanlike skills of Yevgeny M. Primakov, whom he made prime minister in September 1998.

Within two months, Primakov launched a program that strongly leaned toward more spending and government intervention, against the advice of its Western creditors. He had the government working on planned measures that would provide greater support for domestic industry, more vigorous tax collection, and a pledge to pay pensions and government salaries on time. Primakov insisted his program would not set off inflation or turn its back on Russia's free market reforms. "Without doubt, the market will remain," he said. He also told reporters that he still hoped to receive aid and support from abroad, adding that we will not get on our knees and beg. Russia will get on its feet anyway." He had also said that "the state must determine the parameters and trends in industrial restructuring," particularly in those enterprises where the government still has shares.[25]

Primakov was getting cooperation and achieving a gradual improvement of economic conditions by respecting the human needs that demanded attention while developing a socially mixed economy. If assuring the active cooperation of the left required the inclusion of Communist ministers in the government, so be it. In short, he was representing a consensus of public views of the national interest. This was making him popular and sufficiently respected to consider a run for the presidency. He was not a man to be relied upon for mimicry of Western economic views. More importantly, he was not the desired possible successor who would protect Yeltsin from the opprobrium Yeltsin knew he could expect.

On May 13, 1999, Yeltsin abruptly brought Primakov's eight months of service as prime minister to an end, substituting Interior Minister Sergei V. Stepashin, a Yeltsin loyalist and veteran of the security services whose views on the economy were unknown. In a televised statement, Yeltsin said he had made the "difficult decision" because Primakov had failed to pull Russia out of its economic crisis by putting too much emphasis on political consensus, claiming "The Premier's caution, his readiness to take only those measures that get maximum approval and support, are now beginning to cause damage."[26]

Vulnerability of the Yeltsin Family

The facts, as reported in the New York Times on October 7, 1999, read like a daytime soap opera:

> It is three hours by air from Moscow to Omsk. . . . Every month or two, a well-dressed, bespectacled young man arrives by commercial jet and is whisked away to a corporate apartment not far from the Omsk Oil Refinery, Russia's largest and most modern petroleum complex. After a day or two of unspecified business, he leaves as he came.
>
> Virtually nobody in this city of 1.2 million people would notice except for his name: Leonid Dyachenko, the husband of President Boris N. Yeltsin's daughter and right-hand strategist, Tatyana Dyachenko.
>
> Once so anonymous that even prying reporters were unsure of his first name, the 36-year-old Mr. Dyachenko turns out to have a colorful life.
>
> He popped into the headlines two weeks ago when it was disclosed that he had a bank account in the Cayman Islands with more than $2 million. His bank is the Bank of New York, which is at the center of an investigation into possible money laundering in the United States.
>
> Mr. Dyachenko is an oil trader. But he is more than that. He is a participant—if not a key figure—in a network of politically blessed companies that ship Siberian oil products to Ukraine and to Eastern Europe.
>
> His work is all the more colorful because, for many oil traders, oil is almost an afterthought. Virtually all of Russia's oil giants use creative financial transactions to ship billions of dollars offshore—beyond the reach of tax collectors and, for that matter, company shareholders.
>
> The officials of those companies, and Mr. Dyachenko's benefactors, include two Russian tycoons who are among Mr. Yeltsin's strongest supporters, Boris A. Berezovsky and Roman Abromovich, as well as the son of the autocratic pro-Yeltsin governor of the Omsk region.
>
> Mr. Dyachenko's operations stretch from Omsk to Moscow to Manhattan where he is allied with a frenetic Russian capitalist, Victor Y. Khrolenko.[27]

The Putin Ascendancy

Alarmed as Yeltsin may have become by the future dangers he could expect to arise from the exposé of Leonid Dyachenko, he had to confront the current and formidable political challenge in the campaign for the Duma in December 1999 and the Presidency in July 2000. The popular and powerful Mayor of Moscow, Yuri Luzhkov, had been organizing a strong center-left coalition involving a number of regional leaders, looking to win a large anti-Kremlin bloc in the Duma and the possible promotion of Yevgeny Primakov to the Presidency. Stepashin proved unable to handle either problem and so his turn at the wheel ended after only eighty-two days.

Yeltsin chose a far more competent man: Vladimir Vladimirovich Putin. Countering Putin's lack of public renown, right at the moment he named him prime minister, Yeltsin also declared him his preferred successor as president. An unassuming well-mannered Judo expert, he was vigorously active at forty-seven and quickly came to be known as a man in motion. Well educated, especially in economic law, his experience covered not only a fifteen-year stint in the KGB, mainly in East German intelligence where he became fluent in German, but also very capable work as a deputy mayor in St. Petersburg under the liberal Anatoly Sobchak.

Putin took to his responsibilities as prime minister as if already prepared for leadership in both domestic and foreign affairs. To appreciate his ability one need only read "Why We Must Act," an article he wrote for the *New York Times* Op-Ed page dated November 14, 1999. He had struck a chord with the Russian people for his strong military reaction to residential bombings by Chechen terrorists which had killed more than 300 people. He became and remained very popular.

What may have impressed Yeltsin most was the effective way he put together the new Unity party, a center-right coalition which surpassed the Luzhkov coalition in the Duma elections and came out second only to the leading Communist faction. He had also pulled off a surprise deal with Zyuganov whereby the two parties shared more committee chairmanships than they would otherwise normally have.

Now Yeltsin could undertake a stunt that might assure him of a successor who was independent enough to follow different policies, but who could also be expected not to denounce him and to be pragmatic enough to make a deal immunizing him from prosecution or loss of perks. On December 31, 1999, Boris Nikolayevich Yeltsin announced his resignation as president six months before the end of his term and handed over power to his favored successor, Prime Minister Vladimir V. Putin, who would remain prime minister during the three months preceding the election. The quick election required by the Constitution at this time would avert the danger of a loss of popularity even if the war in Chechnya were to drag on.

The transfer of power was done up in style at a private Kremlin ceremony with a personal blessing by Aleksy II, patriarch of the Russian Orthodox Church. One of Putin's first decrees as acting president, of course, was to grant Yeltsin immunity from criminal or administrative investigations, including protection of his papers, residence, and other possessions from search and seizure. Although the decree grants legal protection only to Yeltsin himself, and not to his relatives or aides, it does guarantee continued benefits, housing, salary, and staff for him and members of his family.

The Putin Program

Vladimir Putin, when still technically prime minister, wrote a remarkable 4,600-word programmatic statement, "Russia on the Threshold of a New Millenium," published December 29, 1999 on the Cabinet's Internet site and the next day in *Nezavisimaya Gazeta,* the day before Yeltsin's resignation.

Not since the example of Gorbachev had anyone in Russian leadership presented so candid and perceptive an analysis of the country's condition, its unique national interests, and the steps urgently required in the way forward. In the course of a comprehensively detailed review of the problems calling for hard work and a common effort, he states bluntly: "We shall need 15 years (with an annual 8 percent growth of GDP) to catch up with Portugal or Spain which are not among the world economic leaders. We shall need the same 15 years of 10 percent growth of GDP to catch up with per capita GDP of the UK or France."

Though Putin deals in this statement with the slowness of reforms and with social welfare, he never specifically refers to capitalism, socialism or any mixture of them. As if to explain why he omits such a reference, he says: "I am absolutely against any official state ideology in any form in Russia. There should be no enforced consensus in democratic Russia—it should be voluntary. It is very important to reach an agreement on such fundamental issues as the aim, values and development goals that would attract the majority of the nation." Referring specifically to "social solidarity," he says:

> It is a well-known fact that people in Russia always preferred collective forms of activity; it is a well-known fact that society has . . . always cherish[ed] paternalist sentiments. The majority has always looked up to the state and society for help and support and rarely relied on its own enterprising initiative. This habit is dying hard. Whether this is good or bad is irrelevant—such sen-

> timents are a fact, and an important fact. They are still dominating sentiments and have to be taken into account. They should not be ignored in our social policies either.

Confirmation of this view came six weeks later, published February 8, 2000, in a poll conducted by the independent Russian Public Opinion and Market Research Center. The report showed that 74.2 percent of Russians surveyed believe that the state is obligated to guarantee every family at least a minimally adequate standard of living. At the same time 22.6 percent of the respondents believe that every person should actively try to maintain a decent living standard for his or her family without relying on the state. All told, 75.8 percent of the survey respondents completely agree with the statement that the state should provide a job for everyone who needs one. Sixty-five percent of Russians also believe that the state should create equal opportunities for all its citizens to achieve success and prosperity.[28]

It is well established that a substantial number of the same respondents or people similarly situated also favor the gainful possibilities and conveniences in marketization, something on the order of capitalism without capitalist leadership. To call this best-of-both-worlds attitude a favoring of the socially mixed economy is a matter of nomenclature, of no decisive importance in itself. So far, wherever it exists in Russia, the socially mixed economy has been a result of economic programs, not a deliberate aim.

Putin may rather think of his government as social-democratic, in the sense of the modern German, French, or Italian state but it amounts to the same thing as a socially mixed economy, depending on the extent to which it meets the needs of the people. Putin is surely aware that the Russian Communist program favors a mixed economy, which Zyuganov has repeatedly expressed. It may well be that the existing commonality of views along this popular line is what has won Putin the necessary Duma support for his efforts to strengthen the state.

Indeed, Putin has been succeeding with that strengthening, without which his program would go nowhere. On May 13, 2000, he issued a presidential ten-page decree asserting control over Russia's far-flung and often headstrong provinces and organizing them into seven administrative districts, each overseen by a powerful Kremlin representative. On June 30, the lower house of Parliament voted solidly, 399 to 9, to give the Kremlin the right to fire any of Russia's eighty-nine regional governors for cause, subject to federal court approval. And on July 26, after two months of maneuvering, in a matter of hours the governors accepted almost without protest Putin's proposal to overhaul the federal tax code, a plan that breaks their control over billions of rubles in tax receipts. The council voted 119 to 18 to end the automatic right of governors and their legislative appointees to sit in the Parliament. The council members agreed to their own ouster after persuading the lower house and the Kremlin to accept a compromise that holds out the prospect of a new constitutional convention to set a final form for the Russian government. The council also allowed members to remain in the council until their terms expire and gave them then the right to appoint and remove their successors. Council members will now be elected by their peers.

In foreign affairs, Putin quickly drew respect abroad, showing a firmly independent, constructive grasp of relationships and priorities. On April 14, 2000, in his first legislative initiative as an elected president, he won parliamentary approval of Start II, the landmark agreement negotiated seven years earlier which calls for reducing by half the American and Russian nuclear arsenals.

He warned that Russia's willingness to carry out the treaty depended on Washington's continued adherence to the 1972 Anti-Ballistic Missile Treaty, which the United States had been trying to get Russia's approval to alter. Not only did the Russians refuse to budge on this but also made it clear they would not implement Start II until the U.S. Senate approved several protocols that had been proposed to extend the schedule for weapons reduction to 2007.[29]

Beginning on May 19 in Ashgabat, Turkmenistan, Putin moved to tighten Moscow's ties to Central Asia, promising to help Uzbekistan fight Islamic extremism—and striking a natural gas deal with Turkmenistan. On May 25, Russia and five other former Soviet nations agreed on new measures to jointly fight terrorism and drug and weapons smuggling, including rules governing the use of force, conduct of peacekeeping missions, and when they will collectively intervene in crises. It updated a 1992 pact among Russia, Belarus, Kazakhstan, Kyrgyszstan, Tajikistan, and Armenia.

On June 5, 2000, leaving President Clinton behind after their meeting in Moscow, Putin came to Rome to sell Europe—and the Vatican—on a Russian alternative to the U.S. missile defense proposal. After a meeting with the Pope, meetings in Milan with businessmen, and a two-hour session with the Italian Prime Minister Giuliano Amato, he told reporters: "Russia proposed working with Europe and NATO to create an anti-rocket defense system for Europe. On the one hand, it would avoid all the problems linked to the balance of force. On the other, it would permit in an absolute manner a 100 percent guarantee of the security of every European country." The offer, which Putin had made public just before Clinton's arrival in Moscow the week before, uses short and medium-range missiles to destroy rockets on their way up instead of intercepting warheads on their way down. It resembles what advocates in the United States call a "boost phase defense."[30]

The upshot of Putin's world tour, which began with a visit to Prime Minister Tony Blair in London shortly after the April election, was indicated in the headline of a *Business Week* article: "Putin Is Courting Everyone but the U.S." His visit to Italy produced agreements on trade credits worth up to $1.5 billion. In contrast, during Clinton's visit Putin made no pleas for economic assistance, a departure from past practice. His main interest seemed to be in three main blocs: selected Western European countries, the former Soviet republics such as the energy-rich Caspian Sea states—and Asian giants China and Japan. Russia's trade with Europe is seven times as much as its trade with the United States. In Milan, he visited ENI, which is building (with Gazprom) a $2 billion pipeline to carry Russian natural gas to Turkey via the Black Sea, aided by $1 billion in loans from Italian banks and $600 million from Japanese banks.[31]

This three month whirlwind of significant foreign visits was capped July 17, 2000 in Beijing where he signed six accords, including a joint statement condemning U.S. proposals for missile defense systems. Two days later he was in North Korea, the first visit there by a Russian leader since Soviet times. He then stopped in Blagoveshchenk in eastern Russia for a conference discussing increased immigration from China. This tour ended July 21 on the Japanese island of Okinawa where Putin attended the annual gathering of G8 leading industrial countries.[32]

No time was being lost in the cultivation of all possible foreign sources of support for the rehabilitation of Russia as a great nation. It is significant, that whether intentionally or not, none of the countries chosen for Putin's visits were those that might be hostile to that progress if it developed on the basis of a socially mixed economy.

Where he might come a cropper in the future would be to try to solve agricultural problems by opening up the sale of land to private ownership. Modernization as such would be just fine with the Russian people, but all through the years Yeltsin had tried to put over the sale of land, the great mass of people on the land had adamantly refused to let it happen. Opposition to outright purchase and sale, particularly of large parcels, while appearing to be a carryover of socialist thinking, was possibly even more deeply ingrained as discussed below.

Gorbachev had understood how the people felt about land, apparently feeling that way himself, and had favored leasing instead, even on a long-term basis. In the first year of Putin's tenure, the issue had not been raised—but problems in this decisively important economic field would have to be solved. Old forms, malnourished by the debilitated industry and commerce, have persisted because the only new forms so far have been ill-fitting Western-type "reforms." An *Izvestia* writer describes the subsurface reality this way in March, 2000:

> The term 'collective farm' may not disappear for at least another 50 years, although the term 'state farm' closely related in meaning, has already practically gone out of use. A collective farm is something more than a particular economic and legal way of organizing agricultural production. A collective farm is a way of life. At least three generations of Soviet people lived it, and most of today's rural generation still does.
>
> Only 13.6 percent of the country's 27,300 agricultural enterprises are officially called collective farms, but, with very rare exceptions, all the rest of the open-type joint stock companies, limited-liability partnerships, closed-type joint stock companies, agricultural cooperatives, associations and silent partnerships are actually collective farms.
>
> The collective farms are currently losing the economic race. Not to privately-owned farms, though, but to private plots. Agricultural enterprises—in other words, collective farms—produce about 45 percent of all agricultural output. Private farmers produce only about 2 percent. Meanwhile, private plots account for over 50 percent, but the reason they are in the lead is that they have a symbiotic relationship of sorts with the collective farms. This symbiosis in its best-known form would be the theft of a sack of grain from the farm.[33]

The complexity and difficulties being faced at this time in agriculture and industry were matched in other sectors. In the military, Putin mediated virtual mortal combat between the chief of the general staff and the defense minister over methods of downsizing; he tackled the vast spread of crime and both governmental and business corruption; he attempted to bring the oligarchs to heel in the economy as well as eliminate their influence in the government; and he set about rehabilitating education, medical care, housing, and other social services.

Through it all, the Russian people have generally shown a stubborn insistence on retaining the main features of a socially mixed economy.Throughout the first year of his tenure, Putin's conduct in all spheres indicates that he respects this. In turn, his continued high popularity shows that the Russian people generally consider that he may well be the long-awaited "democratic strong man" who can get the job done. The last word, appropriately, goes to Mikhail Gorbachev, in the following report by a Chinese Moscow correspondent on August 10, 2000:

> Former Soviet leader Mikhail Gorbachev praised Russian President Vladimir Putin Thursday, saying Putin 'is being guided by Russia's national interests, not by the interests of a clan.'
>
> Gorbachev, the last leader of the Soviet Union, now leads a Social-Democratic Party. During a two-hour meeting with Putin, Gorbachev assured the latter that he and his party would support the policy pursued by Putin, the Interfax news agency reported.

Gorbachev quoted Putin as saying 'Russia is in fact a social-democratic state which does not want to return to the past.'

He rejected as 'unfair' allegations that Putin is building a dictatorship. 'I support Putin's efforts to strengthen order and responsibility,' Gorbachev said, noting that 'regionalism is threatening to lead to the country's disintegration.'[34]

Notes

1. Stephen F. Cohen, *Bukharin and the Bolshevik Revolution* (New York: Oxford University Press, 1980), 70.
2. ———, *Rethinking the Soviet Experience* (New York: Oxford University Press, 1985), 75-6.
3. Roy A. Medvedev, *Let History Judge: The Origins and Consequences of Stalinism* (New York: Columbia University Press, 1989), passim.
4. Georgi Arbatov, *The System* (New York: Times Books, Random House, 1992), 211-212.
5. Tatiana Zaslavskaya, *The Second Socialist Revolution* (Bloomington: Indiana University Press, 1991), 2-3.
6. Mikhail S. Gorbachev, *Perestroika: New Thinking for Our Country and the World* (New York: Harper & Row, 1987), 85.
7. ———, "Report to the CPSU Central Committee plenum" as recounted in *Pravda* and *Izvestia* (July 26, 1991), translated in *Current Digest of the Soviet Press,* 43, no. 30 (28 August 1991).
8. Roy A. Medvedev and Giulietto Chiesa, *Time of Change* (New York: Pantheon Books, Random House, 1989), 202-203.
9. Summary of "The Gorbachev Market Plan," *New York Times,* 17 October 1990.
10. Mikhail S. Gorbachev, public statement made Aug. 24, 1991, *New York Times,* 25 August 1991.
11. Andrew Rosenthal, "U.S., Turning from Moscow, Would Grant Recognition to an Independent Ukraine," *New York Times,* 28 November 1991.
12. Serge Schmemann, "Declaring Death of Soviet Union, Russia and Two Republics Form New Commonwealth," *New York Times,* 9 December 1991.
13. ———, "The Future Is Now, with Russia Unready," *New York Times,* 22 December 1991.
14. Celestine Bohien, "Corruption Grows Greedy in Russia," *New York Times,* 14 March 1992.
15. ———, "Citizens of Russia to be Given Share of State's Wealth," *New York Times,* 1 October 1992.
16. Stephen F. Cohen, "American Policy & Russia's Future," *Nation* 256, no. 14 (12 April 1993): 476-485.
17. Serge Schmemann, "Yeltsin and Legislature Act to Oust Each Other, Clinton Backs President," *New York Times,* 22 September 1993.
18. Steven Erlanger, "Russian Premier Assails Reformers in Cabinet for Poorly Thought-Out Experiments," *New York Times,* 19 December 1993.

19. Rozalina Ryvkina, Leonid Kosals and Yuri Simagin, "Experts re Russia's Future: A Conflict Between Fathers and Sons—the Possible Alternatives," *Sevodnya,* (7 June 1996): 5, excerpted and translated in *Current Digest of the Post-Soviet Press,* 48, no. 24 (10 July 1996): 11-13.

20. Katrina van den Heuvel, editorial, "Tomorrow in Russia," *Nation* 263, no. 4 (29 July–5 August 1996): 3-4.

21. Jonathan Steele, "Why Gorbachev Failed," *New Left Review* 216, (March–April 1996): 3.

22. Michael R. Gordon, "Yeltsin Attacks Soviet-Era Housing Benefits," *New York Times,* 13 July 1997.

23. Roy Medvedev, "People and Power," *Svobodnaya Mysl (Freedom Thought)* no.4 (1998), translated reprint from *Social Sciences Quarterly of the Russian Academy of Sciences* 30, no. 1 (1999): (English) 80.

24. Daniel Singer, "Twilight of the Czar," editorial, *Nation* 267, no. 8 (21 September 1998): 4-5.

25. Celestine Bohlen, "Russia Approves Plan for Tighter State Control of Economy," *New York Times,* 1 November 1998.

26. ———, "Yeltsin Dismisses His Prime Minister in a New Shake-Up," *New York Times,* 13 May 1999.

27. Michael Wines, "Yeltsin Son-in-Law at Center of Rich Network of Influence," *New York Times,* 7 October 1999.

28. *Rossuskaya Gazeta,* "Rely on the State, but Keep Your Powder Dry," condensed and translated in *Current Digest of the Post-Soviet Press,* 52, no.6 (8 March 2000): 10.

29. Michael R. Gordon, "Putin Wins Vote in Parliament on Treaty to Cut Nuclear Arms," *New York Times,* 15 April 2000.

30. Alessandra Stanley, "Putin Travels to Promote Russian Arms Control Alternative," *New York Times,* 18 July 2000.

31. Paul Starobin and Kate Carlisle, "Russia: Putin is Courting Everyone but the U.S.," *Business Week* (10 June 2000).

32. Craig S. Smith, "Putin Visits China in Hope of Strengthening A Strategic Axis," *New York Times,* 18 July 2000.

33. Yelena Yakovleva, "Limited Liability Collective Farm," *Izvestia* (15 March 2000): 2, condensed and translated in *Current Digest of the Post-Soviet Press* 52, no. 12 (19 April 2000): 16.

34. Xinhua News Service, http://www.xinhuanet.com/english/htm/0810203621l.htm, [accessed 10 August 2000].

Chapter 19

The Arena of Future Third Ways

A Zigzag in the Trend

In the much-changed world of the early twenty-first century, the durable trend toward the socially mixed economy appears to be, if not everywhere stronger, at least as strong as when it was scrutinized by John Kenneth Gaibraith and Stanislav Menshikov in their 1988 discussion-book, *Capitalism Communism and Coexistence* (see chapter 11).

In light of Mikhail Gorbachev's initiatives for disarmament, reforms, democracy, and "new thinking," these two world-class economists, friends from opposed systems, saw that the order of the day was the peaceful coexistence of the capitalist United States and the communist Soviet Union. It was to be a bipolar world.

Galbraith had said: "I would guess that we would have a mixture. There would be a move to the market in what is now the socialist world. . . . There will be a commitment in the capitalist world to greater social concern." And Menshikov concurred, with an amendment: "I generally agree with you that the future will be a mixture of the existing forms, with perhaps some new forms putting in an appearance."

They could not foresee the disaster that would befall the Soviet Union only three years later in the coup d'état in Belovezh where Boris Yeltsin and his co-conspirators, the heads of Ukraine and Belarus, would arbitrarily dissolve the Soviet Union, with Russia taking over its power, followed by Yeltsin's ruinous eight-year regime of gangster capitalism. Nor did they take into account the economic movement underway in world politics from bipolarity to tripolarity.

Change was taking place with startling rapidity. A year after the Belovezh coup, Lester Thurow's 1992 book *Head to Head* could already describe "the coming economic battle among Japan, Europe, and America." No longer could the United States and Japan benefit from the limitations of their individual European competitors. Now they had to contend with powerful alliances among fifteen or more countries within the European Union all sharing a common currency, the euro. Assuring a durable future for the socially mixed economy, the EU had adopted regulations requiring all members, new or old, to respect civil rights and other social welfare standards already practiced by leading members, who are the most advanced in this respect in the capitalist world.

Again, it was only a year later that world financial circles had to take a major change into account, the prospect of a tripolar world becoming quadripolar. Noting in 1993 that the prodigious growth of China's economy had already made it the third largest, the World Bank estimated that if this continued, the combined economies of mainland China, Hong Kong, and Taiwan would become larger than the United States economy in less than a decade. At the turn of the century, that growth was continuing at a high rate.

Significantly, in the very years when the old status of Russia as a communist-led power with the program of a socially mixed economy was being severely degraded, the new status of China, which could also be described as a communist-led power with the program of a socially mixed economy, was very much on the rise. The old balance between opposed social systems on a world scale, the coexistence between capitalist and socialist powers, has changed its personnel, so to speak, but it endures systemically.

Some Effects of Multipolarity

With respect to the rebound in Russia, with its gradual economic recovery under President Putin's leadership, there is a special value in his characterization of it as a social-democratic country like the leading European countries, knowing full well the proclivity of the Russian people for the social mixture of those economies. This is consistent with his strongly nationalist but friendly assertion of international relations with both China and the United States. On the one hand, as China's military supplier and a close observer of its remarkable progress, and on the other hand with the United States, now that the United States has recognized the miserable failure of both its authorship of shock therapy and its financial support of Yeltsin's reckless anti-communist, pro-capitalist program.

The failure of U.S. policy toward Post-Soviet Russia was publicized at the end of October 2000 in a study released by the non-partisan General Accounting Office of the U.S. Congress. The report detailed how $66 billion in misapplied aid over the years, together with criminal misuse of privatization, had resulted in severe economic decline.

The United States was displaying a markedly different policy in its joint leadership with Russia on a most significant project: the building of the International Space Station along with fourteen other nations. On November 2, 2000, Russia and the United States presented the world with a historic symbol of scientific cooperation 240 miles above the earth. A Soyuz spacecraft docked with the station and three astronauts who had long trained as a team, one American and two Russians, entered and began the station's first human habitation, to be followed after a four-month stint by other teams working to complete the great facility by 2006.

Contrast this with President Ronald Reagan's braying against "the Evil Empire!" And how easily the United States embraced communist China during this same period. Have the communist leaders of China been any less obdurate in the statement of their ultimate aims than were the communist leaders of the Soviet Union in its latter years? Yet note how the United States has bent over backwards to facilitate China's entry into the World Trade Organization and has made other friendly gestures to gain investment opportunities there at least comparable to those of Europe and Japan.

The old and long-standing practice of establishment ideologues beating those of other countries on the head for the menace of their alleged ultimate aims appears to be facing obsolescence. In the new atmosphere, a developing multipolarity is forcing sharper, more equalized economic competition to be conducted more reasonably and less war-like than in the past.

It is not as if believers in socialism or capitalism are giving up their respective dedication to systemic principles or even their dogmatic proselytizing for them. It rather recalls the time before their reunification when the West Germans, facing the Eastern communists, tried to characterize their advanced social welfare not as socialistic but as "the capitalist civilization"—but the French, not having the problem, were satisfied to refer to their similar social welfare as simply "la civilisation."

A mutual respect for diversity and for the socially mixed economy will be heightened in the quadripolar period and will also influence other big countries who may hope one day to rise to that level, such as Russia, India, and Brazil.

The Power of the People

The social gains shown in these pages to have been won by one means or another, depending on what political system was involved, were always the result of arduous popular effort under the banners of various political or social concepts. For example, Mao Zedong set down this exhortation: "Every Communist must grasp the truth, 'political power grows out of the barrel of a gun.'"

Styled as a truism, it may have been persuasive in building a voluntary, revolutionary army and was widely accepted as a fact of life, but as an unmodified generalization when presented as a "teaching" in 1938, it was not a reliable truism. His own experience eventually proved this. Mao and his talented associates defeated Chiang Kai-shek notwithstanding Chiang's far greater access to firepower because Mao had far greater access to people. Power comes from the people, not from a gun. Given circumstantial possibilities, history has demonstrated this, even in cases of passive resistance.

Britain, for example, even after the rack and ruin of World War II, was bristling with firepower but India won its independence because millions of people were willing, at the risk of their lives, to march unarmed behind Gandhi and Nehru. Consider also the revolution in civil rights in the United States, which in the face of deadly brutality, made enormous gains by the movement of passive resistance led by Martin Luther King Jr.

And unarmed mass protest against the war in Vietnam grew strong enough in the United States to bring down a president and force acceptance of defeat. Vietnam provides the most dramatic and longest-term demonstration that power comes from the people rather than its firepower. Vietnam is a hero country. Bitter as the fact may be, it can be said that victory in its war of liberation from France and then the U.S. was won by its millions of dead. No country has fought for its nationhood more bravely, over a longer time, under a more ruinously punishing experience. In its own decade of direct involvement, the United States used twice the volume of munitions it had used in all of World War II.

Social gains marking the development of socially mixed economies vary qualitatively and quantitatively, whether resulting from contention between opposed classes or from joint ventures between entities in opposed systems. A sense of constructive power naturally develops in people who are involved in such gains, confidence grows, and the hope spreads that further improvements in life can be brought about. Even the knowledge drawn from history that there can be no guarantees, and that reverses can occur, cannot destroy the ever-present desire to move forward. However the ways in which the causes and results of these gains may vary, it appears generally true as indicated in the countries studied, that they have one very important thing in common: when willingly agreed upon, such change makes for a better life.

Index

abortion rights, 40–41, 42
Adams, John: and Bill of Rights opposition, 4, 6; and women's rights, 31–32
Adams, Samuel, and class distinctions, 2–3
African Americans: discrimination against, 53–55, 66, 67; education for, 54, 66; and suffrage, 53–55
Alien and Sedition Acts of 1798, 5, 6
Allotment Act of 1887, 28–29
American Federation of Labor, and women's rights, 38–39
American Revolution: and class distinctions, 2–3; and economic depression, 5–6; and suffrage, 3
Australia, health care in, 60–62

Bill of Rights (U.S.): capitalism and, 3, 4; and concessions to social reform, 7–8, 65–68; Economic, 50–52; opposition to, 4, 6; suffrage and, 4; support for, 4; and violation of first amendment, 5
Black Reconstruction, 21–24
Bulgaria: move toward *socially mixed economy* in, 93–94; as *socially mixed economy* model, 89–99. *See also* Eastern Europe
Bush, George, and discrimination legislation, 55

Cable Act, 39
Canada, health care in, 59, 60–62
capitalism: and appeal to Eastern Europe, 89–91; and Bill of Rights, 3, 4; with influences of socialism, 47–48, 47–48, 49–50; precursors to American, 1–2; versus socialism in France and Italy, 81–83; and Yeltsin, 162–63, 164–65, 166–68. *See also socially mixed economy(ies)*
Chapman Catt, Carrie, and women's movement, 33
child labor, 34, 66
China: agricultural development in, 140–44; anticorruption war in, 139–40; communications problems in, 136; economic expansion and stimulation in, 131–35; energy problems in, 135–36; pollution problems in, 135–36; reform toward market economy in, 132–33; as *socially mixed economy* model, 131–44; *socially mixed economy* of, 138–39, 186–87;

technological advancements in, 137; two separate economies in, 131–32
civil rights. *See* discrimination, social reform, *specific right*, women's rights
Civil Rights Act, 54–55, 67
Civil Rights Restoration Act of 1987, 54–55
Clinton, William, and universal health care, 58–60, 62
Colonial America: labor conditions in, 11–14; rulership problem in, 8–9; women's rights in, 31–44
Committee on Civil Rights, 53–55
Committees of Correspondence, and class distinctions, 2–3
Communism: among original Native Americans, 26–29; influences in India, 125–26; Stalin and, 150–51; and U.S. protests during Depression, 46–47; and women, 32–33. *See also specific country*
Communist Manifesto, 2
Constitution (U.S.): and class distinctions, 3. *See also* Bill of Rights (U.S.)
Constitutional Convention, and class distinctions, 3
Cuba: maintaining socialist control in, 101–02; move toward *socially mixed economy* in, 102, 106–12, 113–14; as *socially mixed economy* model, 101–14; U.S. policy toward, 113
Czech Republic: move toward *socially mixed economy* in, 93–94, 97–99; NATO membership for, 93–94; as *socially mixed economy* model, 89–99. *See also* Eastern Europe

Dawes Act. *See* Allotment Act of 1887
Declaration and Platform for Action (UN), 43
Depression (U.S.): and labor conditions, 46–48; and National Recovery Act, 46, 47–48; and New Deal, 45–47; protests and strikes during, 46–47; reasons for duration of, 46
discrimination: against African Americans, 53–55, 66, 67. *See also* women's rights
Du Bois, W. E. B., and Black Reconstruction, 21, 23–24

Eastern Europe: appeal of capitalism in, 89–91; move toward market economy in, 91–93; move toward *socially mixed economy* in, 93–99; as *socially mixed economy* model, 89–99. *See also specific country*
Economic Bill of Rights (U.S.), 50–52
economic incentives in American Revolution, 3
education: for African Americans, 54, 66; for children, 23–24, 34–35; for freedmen, 23–24, 34–35; for women, 34–35
Emancipation Proclamation, 15–16, 21–24
Engels, Frederick, and class distinctions, 1–2, 5
England, health care in, 61
Equal Rights Amendment, 41
Europe: Germany's role in, 77–78; health care in, 60–62. *See also* Eastern Europe and *specific country*
European Economic Community: as a cooperative, 83–85; as *socially mixed economy* model, 81–87; statism in, 81

Fair Labor Standards Act, 34, 48, 67
Federal Deposit Insurance Corporation, and protection of savings, 67
foreclosures, following American Revolution, 5–6
France: capitalism versus socialism in, 81–83; health care in, 61, 86–87; labor conditions in, 81; as *socially mixed economy* model, 81–87; statism in, 81–83
Franklin, Benjamin: and Bill of Rights support, 4; and labor theory of value, 2; and property rights, 6; and suffrage support, 4; and support of working class, 13–14

Galbraith, John Kenneth, and prediction of *socially mixed economies*, 67–72, 185–86
Germany: health care in, 60–62, 75, 78; its role in Europe, 77–78; labor conditions in, 75–79; as socialism model, 75–79; as *socially mixed economy* model, 75–79; as *welfare state*, 79
Gorbachev Market Plan, 155–56
Gorbachev, Mikhail: and conflicts with Yeltsin, 157–63; and efforts toward socialism, 151–59; fall from power, 162–63; and Soviet Union disruption, 159–61
government, and private interests, 2

Hamilton, Alexander, and Bill of Rights opposition, 4, 6
Harris Jones, "Mother" Mary, and child labor, 34
health care: in Australia, 60–62; in Canada, 59, 60–62; in England, 61; in Europe, 60–62; in France, 61, 86–87; in Germany, 60–62, 75, 78; in Italy, 86–87; in Japan, 61; managed, 59–60, 62–63; and Medicaid, 57–58; and Medicare, 57–58; national insurance program for, 57–63; countries as models for, 60–62; universal (U.S.), 57–63; and World Health Organization, 86–87. *See also specific country*
Health Maintenance Organizations (HMOs), 59–60, 62–63
Hungary: move toward *socially mixed economy* in, 93–94, 95–97, 99; NATO membership for, 93–94; as *socially mixed economy* model, 89–99. *See also* Eastern Europe

income and property distribution: and class distinctions, 2; during Depression (U.S.), 46; following American Revolution, 5–6
India: communist influences in, 125–26; fiscal developments in, 124–25; influence of Soviet Union and China in, 120–21; leadership problems in, 126–29; move from statism toward socialism in, 119–20, 121–24, 129–30; religious influences in, 118–19; as *socially mixed economy* model, 117–30; statism in, 117–19
Indians. *See* Native Americans
Italy: capitalism versus socialism in, 81; health care in, 86–87; as *socially mixed economy* model, 81–87; statism in, 85–86

Jackson, Andrew: and genocide of Native Americans, 25–26; and support of working class, 13–14
Japan, health care in, 61
Jay, John, and Bill of Rights opposition, 4
Jefferson, Thomas: and Bill of Rights support, 4; and suffrage support, 4; and support of working class, 13–14; and women's rights, 31–32
Johnson, Lyndon: and discrimination reform, 54–55; and universal health care, 57

Keating-Owen Act, 34

labor conditions: in Colonial America, 11–14; during Depression, 46–48; and Fair Labor Standards Act, 48, 67; in France, 81; in Germany, 75–79; and health insurance, 47; and overtime pay, 11–14; and pensions, 47; and protests during Depression, 46–47; and retirement funds, 47–48; and social security benefits, 47–48, 66–67; and unemployment insurance, 46–48; and wages, 46–47, 48, 67; for women and children, 37–40, 66; and workday length, 11–14, 16–17, 48, 66, 67.
labor organizations: and abolition of slavery, 15–18; and child labor, 34, 66; development of, 5, 11–14; and National Labor Relations Act, 47–48, 66; and overtime pay, 11–14; and shortened workdays, 11–14; and women's rights, 38–39; *See*

also *specific subject area*
Lenin, Vladimir, and efforts toward socialism, 148–50
Lincoln, Abraham, and support of working class, 13–14, 18
Luther, Seth, and labor organizations, 12–13

Madison, James: and Bill of Rights support, 4; and class distinctions, 1–2
managed health care, 59–60, 62–63
market economy: China's move toward, 132–33; Eastern Europe's move toward, 91–93. *See also* capitalism
Marx, Karl: and abolition of slavery, 16–17; and class distinctions, 1–2; and labor theory of value, 2
Medicaid, 67; and *socially mixed economies*, 57–58
Medicare, 67; and *socially mixed economies*, 57–58
Menshikov, Stanislav, and prediction of *socially mixed economies*, 67–72, 185–86

National Labor Relations Act, labor organizations and, 47–48, 66
National Organization for Women, and sexual discrimination, 41, 42
National Recovery Act, 46, 47–48
Native Americans: genocide of, 25–26; and primitive communism, 26–29; U.S. government treaties and concessions with, 26, 29–30
New Deal, 45–47
Northwest Ordinance of 1767, 26

overtime pay, and labor organizations. *See* labor conditions

Paine, Thomas: and Bill of Rights support, 4; and suffrage support, 4
Perkins, Frances, and child labor, 34
Poland: move toward *socially mixed economy* in, 93–95, 99; NATO membership for, 93–94; as *socially mixed economy* model, 89–99. *See also* Eastern Europe
Primakov, Yevgeny, as prime minister, 175–76
property distribution. *See* income and property distribution
Putin, Vladimir, and social-democratic government, 177–83, 186–87

racism: following abolition, 21–22. *See also* discrimination
Revolutionary War. *See* American Revolution
Romania: move toward *socially mixed economy* in, 93–94; as *socially mixed economy* model, 89–99. *See also* Eastern Europe
Roosevelt, Franklin: and Economic Bill of Rights, 50–52; and National Labor Relations Act, 47–48; and National Recovery Act, 46, 47–48; and New Deal, 45–47; social reform and, 47–49, 50–52; and stock market regulation, 48; and support of working class, 13–14; and universal health care, 57
rulership in Colonial America, basic problem of, 8–9
Russia: development of *socially mixed economy* in, 171–76; and Gorbachev Market Plan, 155–56; Gorbachev's efforts towards socialism, 151–59; Lenin's efforts towards socialism, 148–50; outlook for *socially mixed economy* in, 165–66; under Putin government, 177–83, 186–87; as *socially mixed economy* model, 147–82; *socially mixed economy* of, 186–87; Stalin and Communism in, 150–51; War Communism in, 149; under Yeltsin rule, 162–83.

Sedition Act of 1798, enforcement of, 6
Sexual discrimination. *See* women's rights
Shay's Rebellion, 5–6
slavery: abolition of, 15–18; racism following abolition of, 21–24. *See*

also Black Reconstruction, Emancipation Proclamation
Slovakia: move toward *socially mixed economy* in, 93–94; as *socially mixed economy* model, 89–99. *See also* Eastern Europe
Smith, Adam: and labor theory of value, 2; and *The Wealth of Nations*, 2
social reform: and Bill of Rights, 7–8, 65–68; health care programs and, 57–63; Franklin Roosevelt and, 47–49, 50–52; Harry Truman and, 53–55; and universal health care, 57–63.
social reform in U.S., and abolition of slavery, 15–18
Social Security Act, 47–48, 66–67. *See also* Medicaid; Medicare
socialism: capitalism with influences of, 47–48, 49–50; and Fair Labor Standards Act, 48; Germany as a model for, 75–79; Gorbachev and efforts toward, 151–59; India's move from statism toward, 119–20, 121–24, 129–30; Lenin and efforts toward, 148–50; and National Labor Relations Act, 47–48; precursors to American, 15–17; *socially mixed economies* under, 70–72, 75–79; Sweden as a model for, 70–72; and Tennessee Valley Authority, 47; Vietnam's maintenance of, 101–02
socially mixed economy models: Bulgaria, 89–99; China, 131–44; Cuba, 101–14; Czech Republic, 89–99; Eastern Europe, 89–99; European Economic Community, 81–87; France, 81–87; Germany, 75–79; Hungary, 89–99; India, 117–30; Italy, 81–87; Poland, 89–99; Romania, 89–99; Russia, 147–82; Slovakia, 89–99; Sweden, 70–72; Vietnam, 101–14.
socially mixed economy(ies): in Bulgaria, 93–94; in China, 138–39, 186–87; in Cuba, 102, 106–12, 113–14; in Czech Republic, 93–94, 97–99; in Eastern Europe, 93–99; in Hungary, 93–94, 95–97, 99; Medicare and Medicaid and, 57–58; outlook for, 185–88; in Poland, 93–95, 99; in Romania, 93–94; in Russia, 165–66, 171–76, 186–87; in Slovakia, 93–94; in Vietnam, 102, 103–06, 113–14
Sons of Liberty, and class distinctions, 2–3
Soviet Union: coup d'état and disruption in, 158–61; and influence on India, 120–21.
Stalin, Joseph, and communism in Russia, 150–51
statism: in European Economic Community, 81; in France, 81–83, 81–83, 81–83; in India, 117–19; India's move toward socialism from, 119–20, 121–24, 129–30; in Italy, 85–86
stock market regulation, Franklin Roosevelt and, 48
suffrage: for African Americans, 53–55; Bill of Rights (U.S.) and, 4; and class distinctions, 3, 4; supporters of, 4; and Voting Rights Act, 54–55, 67; for women, 31–32, 33, 39, 66
Sweden: and socialism, 70–72; as *socially mixed economy* model, 70–72

taxation, following American Revolution, 5–6
Ten-Hour Movement and Laws, 11, 14
Tennessee Valley Authority, and socialism, 47
The Wealth of Nations, and labor theory of value, 2
Truman, Harry: and civil rights, 53–55; and universal health care, 57

United Nations, women's rights and, 43–44

Van Buren, Martin, and support of working class, 13–14
Vietnam: maintaining socialist control

in, 101–02; move toward *socially mixed economy* in, 102, 103–06, 113–14; as *socially mixed economy* model, 101–14
voting rights. *See* suffrage
Voting Rights Act, 54–55, 67

welfare state, 47–48. *See also* socialism
welfare state, Germany as, 79
Whiskey Tax, resistance to, 6
Wilson, Woodrow: and child labor, 34; and suffrage, 34
women's rights: and child labor, 34, 66; in Colonial America, 31–44; and control of one's own body, 40–41, 42; and education, 34–35; international movement for, 43–44; and labor conditions, 37–40, 66; and labor organizations, 38–39; and National Organization for Women, 41; and political positions, 39–40; and property, 35–37; and suffrage, 31–32, 33, 39, 66; United Nations and, 43–44
workday, shortening of. *See* labor conditions
working conditions. *See* labor conditions
World Health Organization, and health care, 86–87

Yeltsin, Boris: and conflicts with Gorbachev, 157–63; and coup d'état and disruption of Soviet Union, 158–61; deposing of, 168; and end of Gorbachev ideology, 162; procapitalism of, 162–63, 164–65, 166–68; reform problems under, 164–65; reforms under, 162–63, 164–83; and restructuring of Parliament and Constitution, 168–83; rise to power of, 157–62

About the Author

1910-2001

John Weber's lifelong interest in the study of world politics was always accompanied by personal activism in the labor movement and related efforts at social and cultural progress. His first career was a fourteen-year climb in Hollywood from the bottom as a script reader, to the top as a motion picture producer. It was characteristic that he began by organizing a union, the Screen Story Analysts Guild. It also appears that it was such social activism that finally ended that career, placing him among the well-known Hollywood Blacklistees. That era also raised inevitable barriers to public teaching and related educational activities in his main area of interest.

During the years when such activity was limited to work on a part-time basis, he published more than a dozen magazine articles of a theoretical nature on a range of specific topics in his field. When it became possible to work on these issues full-time, he was able to fully develop his original analyses of the turbulent events of the twentieth century and the trends developing from them in the twenty-first. The result is the development of a time-tested basis for a series of significant books on world politics and economic systems, of which the present volume is the first.

Editor's Note:

John Weber (1910-2001) passed away shortly before publication, after completing the final draft. The second book in this series was in progress at the time of his death.

www.ingramcontent.com/pod-product-compliance
Ingram Content Group UK Ltd.
Pitfield, Milton Keynes, MK11 3LW, UK
UKHW021907150926
475560UK00003B/231

9 780739 102701